Peace Love Yoga

Peace Love Yoga

The Politics of Global Spirituality

ANDREA R. JAIN

OXFORD
UNIVERSITY PRESS

OXFORD
UNIVERSITY PRESS

Oxford University Press is a department of the University of Oxford. It furthers
the University's objective of excellence in research, scholarship, and education
by publishing worldwide. Oxford is a registered trade mark of Oxford University
Press in the UK and certain other countries.

Published in the United States of America by Oxford University Press
198 Madison Avenue, New York, NY 10016, United States of America.

Library of Congress Cataloging-in-Publication Data
Names: Jain, Andrea R., author.
Title: Peace love yoga : the politics of global spirituality / Andrea R. Jain.
Description: New York, NY, United States of America : Oxford University Press, 2020. |
Includes bibliographical references and index.
Identifiers: LCCN 2020008381 (print) | LCCN 2020008382 (ebook) |
ISBN 9780190888626 (hardback) | ISBN 9780190888633 (paperback) |
ISBN 9780190888657 (epub)
Subjects: LCSH: Spirituality. Classification: LCC BL624 .J55 2020 (print) |
LCC BL624 (ebook) | DDC 204.09/051—dc23
LC record available at https://lccn.loc.gov/2020008381
LC ebook record available at https://lccn.loc.gov/2020008382

3 5 7 9 8 6 4 2

Paperback printed by LSC Communications, United States of America
Hardback printed by Bridgeport National Bindery, Inc., United States of America

For my dear friends. Connections are everything.

If solutions within the system are so impossible to find, maybe we should change the system itself.
—Greta Thunberg, addressing the COP24 climate talks in Katowice, Poland, December 12, 2018

Contents

Peace Love Yoga

NO BAD VIBES

An Introduction

When I participated in the Indianapolis Women's March on January 21, 2017, I held a sign that read, "I didn't come from your rib. You came from my vagina." I did not come up with that; I borrowed it from a sign I saw at a protest long before. Nonetheless, the sign felt especially personal, not only because I feared the threats the election of Donald Trump posed to women's access to healthcare and other basic human rights, but also because my identity as a scholar pivots around a commitment to historicizing religion and unveiling its social contingencies and ramifications. All of those dimensions of my identity infuriate those right-wing adherents committed to heteropatriarchal visions of divinity, creation, and God's intentions for humankind. The sign was also personal because I have birthed and breastfed two sons who I hope will become committed and vocal feminists.

But the sign, with its attention on my body and my desire for power over it, also signified something else about the culture I am embedded in. It reflected an envisioning of the body that infuses our global consumer culture and that denies a fundamental difference between the body and the self (Featherstone 1991, 171). In that same context, enhancing the body, controlling and perfecting it, is a soteriological achievement, and it is only possible through the careful orchestration of "free" choice, from the government officials we elect to the products we buy.

My sign was also about loneliness. My body, as if isolated from space and time. My "leave my body to me" doctrine, in other words, was not entirely disconnected from what scholars frequently refer to as the Protestant work ethic. In *The Protestant Ethic,* Max Weber suggests that the "unprecedented inner loneliness" (1992, 104) caused by the question of salvation incites an externalized, rationalized ethic that social institutions systematize, resulting in the force behind early capitalism. The loneliness in the drive for salvation remains the force, I think, behind neoliberal capitalism, exhibited through the constant demand to display one's perfection and the promises of

Peace Love Yoga. Andrea R. Jain, Oxford University Press (2020). © Oxford University Press.
DOI: 10.1093/oso/9780190888626.001.0001

perfection made through consumer branding. It fits, in other words, within the long-established tradition of Protestant-capitalist self-improvement, a staple in numerous religious and capitalist texts. This occurs, in large part, through acts of cultural appropriation, resulting in what I describe in later chapters as an orientalist fantasy of enlightenment-ethics. There is truth in Slavoj Žižek's joke that, if Max Weber were alive today, he would "definitely write a second, supplementary, volume to his Protestant Ethic, entitled *The Taoist Ethic and the Spirit of Global Capitalism*" (2001, 13).

The consumer must responsibly select from commodities ranging from dietary and fitness regimens to medications and medical procedures, all constitutive of what we often refer to as "self-care."[1] This type of consumption is considered a part of the transformative and salvific process of personal growth. Other people's attempts to oppress or violate one's body or to limit choices with regard to managing one's body, in turn, are not only physical and ethical violations, but also religious ones. This particular envisioning of the body is detectable throughout global popular culture, but especially serves as a cornerstone of that infamous and growing "alternative" to religious orthodoxies: spirituality. The excesses of spirituality—retreats, yogaware, workshops, health foods—signify the reversal of ordinary life and conduct, a life in which we are largely not in control, for the sake of rebirth back into that life a person who has undergone transformation, personal growth, and even salvation, liberation, or "freedom."

There have been scholarly attempts to identify what *spirituality* means in the popular imagination. Perhaps most known among them, the 2012 Pew Forum on Religion & Public Life provided a snapshot of what twenty-first-century Americans often imagine when they hear the term. The Pew study, which exclusively covers religion in the United States, suggested the *nones* or the *religiously unaffiliated* were "on the rise" and were "less religious than the public at large." According to the survey, about 18 percent of the US population identifies as *spiritual, not religious*, including 37 percent of the nones and only 15 percent of the affiliated. Beyond its attempts to capture just how many Americans are nones or invoke that seemingly innocuous term *spiritual* or *spiritual but not religious* to characterize themselves, the report also tried to capture their political leanings. The study indicated that the nones are more likely to identify as Democrats than as Republicans, and, more

---

[1] I use *commodification* to refer to any action or process of treating something as a commodity, that is, as a product that can be bought and sold.

significantly, that they are more liberal on social and political issues (Pew Research Center 2012).

In North America and Western Europe, when it comes to those who frequently describe themselves as *spiritual*, this is not really all that surprising. Although self-identifying spiritual communities are not monolithic, are fraught with divergence and debate, and, as I will show in this book, in many ways uphold certain conservative, moralizing, and nationalist agendas, there are a number of progressive commitments that many of them claim to embrace. These can include commitments to the following: religious and cultural pluralism, gender equity, racial, gender, and sexual diversity, environmental sustainability, scientific inquiry and historical-critical analysis, and a public space that guarantees both freedom of and from religion.

Given all of that, I was certain the number of self-proclaimed spiritual people at the marches on that day in January 2017 was significant. But, more importantly, I wondered if those same people would resist the oppressive policies and efforts of the Trump administration or, on the contrary, if they would choose political impotence in favor of self-care. It struck me as not enough to raise signs at marches—full stop. What about the various daily, monthly, or annual activities through which many spiritual consumers create and condition their bodies and construct identities and communities? Could those be politically subversive? Could they constitute forms of political dissent?

At the time of Trump's election, I was in the preliminary stages of writing a book on "prison yoga" in the United States, Africa, and India, that is, on the uses of yoga as a mode of rehabilitation and transformation among prisoners. Now, I paused; I asked whether yoga consumers' concerns with self-care, adjustment, and perfection, the training of expert teachers to observe and assess, technologies of physical, mental, and emotional labor, and individualized approaches to rehabilitation and transformation were more akin to those aims of discipline whereby violence is replaced by interventions meant to "improve" and "correct" problematic individuals. Over time, I came to see them as that.

Modern discipline, according to Foucault, is corrective (1977, 19, 20–21, 251–255). It relies on diagnostic and prognostic assessments as well as prescriptions to produce "normalized" individuals. The distinction between rehabilitation and reform on the one hand and control and surveillance on the other is a problematic one; rehabilitative practices and policies, rather, have long been strategies of control (see Garland 2012 and Harcourt 2010).

Now I asked: are spiritual modes of discipline, like rehabilitative ones, strategies through which resistance to dominant power structures is contained? Where are these disciplinary strategies put to use in global spirituality? The scope of my project broadened.

I started thinking about the mass gatherings of spiritual consumers. Since 2015, for example, the masses have gathered in urban spaces all over the world to celebrate the International Day of Yoga (see chapter 5), but such gatherings had even started before then. Beginning in 2012, tens of thousands of participants have contorted their bodies into various yoga postures at Lolë "peace" events as a part of their "White Tour." At locations across Europe, the United States, and Canada, yoga practitioners dress in white and gather at high-profile locations, such as New York's Central Park. Clutching their "swag bags," they sit down on their uniform yellow Lolë mats and do yoga. Lolë is a Canadian-based high-end yoga apparel brand. The Lolë website states, "White: a symbol of purity, elegance and peace." These events have promised to be a place where "hearts create a continuous flow of peace and harmony that has the ability to transform a community." Lolë markets its "white kits," providing everything you need to "look and feel amazing all in white" for "spreading inner peace and wellness all around the world" (Lolë 2018). One of the yoga teachers, Elena Brower, once stated, "We're part of an intentional gathering of minds and hearts dedicated in practice together, and the symbolism of wearing all white only adds to the sweetness. It's a way to bring us together in peace and purity, and with potency—to engage with an ancient primordial call to be together, to rise together, to get strong together, to rest together, and to listen together." "Together," according to Brower, "we are far more potent and powerful" (Brower 2015). The Lolë company also promotes "intelligent consumption," which "empowers you to give a second life to gently worn outerwear while funding food banks in North America" (Lolë 2018).

I came to refer to the type of spirituality such behavior and consumption represented as *neoliberal spirituality*. In what sense and when can we describe spirituality as *neoliberal*? Neoliberalism relies on the selective deployment of key ideological assumptions, such as the importance of self-governance and individual responsibility. Commodities and other areas of culture confront us with consumer choices that direct the blame for social problems onto the ostensible poor decision-making, the "free choices," of individuals. Neoliberalism, in other words, delegitimates political protest in advance of it by claiming that the current state of affairs, including socioeconomic circumstances, is what we have all chosen. By privatizing social and political concerns, neoliberalism protects entrenched social structures.[2]

The types of spirituality I turned my attention to are rooted in neoliberal meritocracy—it revolves around its adherents' ability to discern and certify the merit that leads to the envied lifestyle of balance, wellness, success, freedom, and self-care. At the same time, spiritual spaces have suffered the fate of other areas of culture under the global dominance of neoliberal capitalism. Adherents must "do more with less," cutting costs while meeting ever-greater demands. Yoga teachers, for example, most of whom in much of the world are women, face shrinking wages, and this workforce is increasingly precarious, even as yoga teachers are called on to teach more students than ever before and with an attitude of "positive acceptance" (Bell 2012), to do more unpaid *seva*, or "service," and to demonstrate that they are doing it better than ever.[3] In short, spiritual industries betray the contradictions of neoliberal capitalism.

Hence I came to write this book in which I set out to provide a feminist socialist perspective, a perspective, however, that does not see spiritual consumers as merely passive victims of dominant cultural formations and their mass manipulation and deception, as merely the products of the forces and relations of capitalist production. Yes, spirituality is located in neoliberal capitalist social structures. Its forms are commercialized, produced as a means to profit. It also, however, embodies forms of liberation and salvation, resistance and discontent; in fact, I think that the latter characteristics are what makes it so appealing to spiritual consumers.

Spirituality cannot be reduced to products of the forces and relations of capitalist production, not in the sense that capital is a social relation of economic or commodity value, and that capitalism, the dominant economic system today, is a system of capital accumulation based in class exploitation and that runs by the laws of market competition. I insist, rather, on analyzing spirituality as an area of global popular culture in the sense of that which consists of relations "in continuing tension" (Hall [1981] 2002, 189). Since I rely on Stuart Hall here, I will quote him at length:

---

[2] When I refer to *social structures* throughout this book, I use the term in a way that is theoretically situated within Marxist theory, more specifically to refer to products of the "forces and relations of production."

[3] *Seva* is a Sanskrit term referring to a devotional practice, often considered an offering to a guru or god. The term has been widely appropriated by spiritual consumers to refer to any kind of charitable giving or volunteerism.

What is essential to the definition of popular culture is the relations which define "popular culture" in a continuing tension (relationship, influence and antagonism) to the dominant culture. It is a conception of culture which is polarized around this cultural dialectic. It treats the domain of cultural forms and activities as a constantly changing field. Then it looks at the relations which constantly structure this field into dominant and subordinate formations. It looks at the *process* by which these relations of dominance and subordination are articulated. It treats them as a process: the process by means of which some things are actively preferred so that others can be dethroned. It has at its centre the changing and uneven relations of force which define the field of culture—that is, the question of cultural struggle and its many forms. Its main focus of attention is the relation between culture and questions of hegemony. ([1981] 2002, 189)

I am in agreement with Hall, who famously described popular culture as the "struggle for and against a culture of the powerful," an "arena of consent and resistance." Popular culture, according to Hall, is a site of cultural struggle, "partly where hegemony arises, and where it is secured. It is not a sphere where socialism, a socialist culture—already fully formed—might be simply 'expressed.' But it is one of the places where socialism might be constituted." Hall continues with these famous lines: "That is why 'popular culture' matters. Otherwise, to tell you the truth, I don't give a damn about it" ([1981] 2002, 192).

This is also why neoliberal spirituality is worthy of our attention. Even though the most popularized forms of spirituality are also commercial, and their commodities are produced and sold as means to the end of profit, they also serve transformative and liberatory ends and reflect discontents with and subversions of the dominant culture. And if it were not for the ways spirituality struggles against entrenched power structures, I would not write about it and neither should you care to read this book.

This study explores how spiritual industries, corporations, entrepreneurs, and consumers embody and transmit a neoliberal mode of governance; hence I use the category *neoliberal spirituality*, which I argue epitomizes a crucial node in global neoliberal capitalism. Spiritual industries, corporations, entrepreneurs, and consumers relate spiritual practices to ethical values through marketing and purchasing activities. However, in addition to leaning on Hall's work on popular culture, I draw on Mark Fisher's (2009) work on capitalist realism to develop the argument that *gestural subversion*, subverting dominant power structures through gestures, is a key area of spirituality's valuation (see chapter 1). The subversive expressions appliquéd across yogaware and the industry's "do good" discourses, for example, signal to the consumer that the products are characterized by values antagonistic to or at least in tension with the forces and relations of capitalist production. They provide the language for spiritual consumers' discontent.

From the high-end yoga apparel company Spiritual Gangster to the much more affordable Target brand yogaware, the consumer can purchase T-shirts with the common expression PEACE LOVE YOGA appliquéd across the front. Spiritual Gangster is also known for its leggings with GOOD KARMA appliquéd across the butt.[4] According to the Spiritual Gangster website, "We exercise love as the most powerful form of activism" (2018b). The company also donates an unspecified percentage of every sale to provide food for those living in poverty.

Some spiritual consumers might greenwash the products they buy, from yoga apparel to tableware. Everywhere in the developed world, plastic has taken over our households, our accessories, and even our clothes. And there is growing concern over the images broadcast across the mainstream media of plastic waste filling oceans and washing up on beaches. Most middle- and upper-class consumers are unmoved by the violence that takes place in the dairy and meat industries (not to mention the impact these industries have on the environment), but they shudder at the image of a sea turtle suffocating on a plastic straw that is lodged in its mouth. Spiritual consumers might respond to such discomforting images or the larger threat of climate change by opting for the high-end apparel of the global corporation Satva Living, which offers "mindfully designed organic fashion" (Satva 2018b). The company claims to improve the health and wellness of "conscious consumers" as well as the lives of Indian organic farmers by partnering with Suminter India Organics and working under the model of "creative capitalism," an approach that ensures that a portion of profits are invested back into the communities and agricultural programs of the farmers who grow the cotton used in Satva

---

[4] Throughout this book, examples of text printed across yoga apparel and other spiritual commodities, such as T-shirts, pants, or food and wellness products, will be indicated with SMALL CAPS. In my attention to spiritual discourses as appliquéd across yogaware or printed on the packaging of other products, I am conscious of the fact that I am dealing principally with the representation of ideas, practices, and prohibitions within a textual tradition and that one cannot simply assume an isomorphism between the textual material and the real social world. That said, I give the text its due, insisting that it reflects and is reflected in the social reality of the majority of those who display the text across their bodies or put into their bodies the products printed with the text.

Living products. These products are sold across India as well as the United States and are available, for example, at Whole Foods Market, where spiritual consumers might also shop for "eco-friendly" biodegradable paper plates. The multimillionaire entrepreneur John Mackey, founder and co-CEO of megacorporation Whole Foods Market, uses the pithy phrase "conscious capitalism" as the title of his 2014 book, in which he argues that capitalism's "heroic spirit" is the key to creating "a world in which all people live lives full of prosperity, love, and creativity—a world of compassion, freedom, and prosperity" (Mackey and Rajendra 2014, 9).

That there are ethical and social problems with neoliberal capitalism, given its dire consequences for individuals, communities, and the natural environment, is indisputable. In other words, if one's ethical agenda includes maintaining a stable global community of equal persons and a sustainable natural environment, the dominance of neoliberal capitalist culture is rightfully perceived as an obstacle. Yet, despite the countless ways spiritual entrepreneurs and consumers embrace values like environmental sustainability and world peace, there is a difference between gesturing toward such alternative values and collective dissent through concrete actions and platforms. Here lies the thesis of this book: the texts of neoliberal spirituality embody a tension between the values of the dominant neoliberal capitalist order and values antagonistic to it through, for example, *intelligent consumption, creative capitalism,* or *conscious capitalism.* Although they gesture toward wanting to resolve the real devastating social and environmental conditions that neoliberal capitalist structures create and perpetuate, they put the burden for resolving those conditions on individual consumers, as opposed to supporting collective dissent and radical policy changes. In other words, spiritual consumers, entrepreneurs, corporations, and industries struggle against the dominant culture, yet their modes of resistance are gestural.

The gestural subversions of neoliberal spirituality illustrate the need for social structures with different (noncapitalist, nondominant, non-white supremacist, nonpatriarchal) capacities, because whatever spiritual consumers choose (in terms of commodities), their decisions emerge out of brutal capitalist conditions that they did not in fact choose. Put simply, the contexts in which consumers are located contain them as surely as do the commodity "choices" they make.

Spirituality is not only linked to the rise of global neoliberal capitalism; it is also complicit in and perpetuates certain forms of conservatism, legitimating and depoliticizing social inequities by attributing them to individual moral failures and emphasizing the need for disciplinary obedience and purity. In fact, neoliberal spiritual disciplines and products provide paternal guidance, authoritarian dictates, and the logics of control meant to transform and reshape conduct toward entrepreneurship and self-optimization. We will see this, for example, in what is printed across yogaware, from GOOD VIBES. ALL DAY. EVERY DAY and BREATHE. PRACTICE. REPEAT to simply NO BAD VIBES. Even as spiritual consumers create self-identities through "free choice" and gestural subversions, the commodities they choose in many ways uphold class hierarchies, racism, misogyny, and trans- and homophobia. The spiritual logic, which is only possible because of the space a colonialist, capitalist context instituted, prescribes a rigid path to purification and eventual salvation. Yet, as with the presences and absences that haunt spiritual advertising, the indirect discourses of spiritual consumers, entrepreneurs, corporations, and industries fuel contradictions, tensions, and conflicts. Their discourses, in other words, perpetuate the dominant valuations that equate salvation and liberation with capitalist class structures, whiteness, patriarchy, and heteronormativity.

They evoke and capitalize off discourses of purity alongside greenwashing and charitable activities, none of which are substitutes for political dissent since they do not entail efforts to actually transform the policies and systems (ideological, economic, behavioral, or political) that produce the environmental degradation, poverty, hunger, and other inequities they gesture against. Spiritual adherents, instead, resist the system and its consequences for living beings and the environment by consciously choosing certain commodities as an act of resistance. In this way, they make "good choices" without actually doing anything to prevent inequality, oppression, environmental devastation, or violence.

The reigning order of neoliberal capitalism that gave birth to the Trump administration was also characterized by the growth of neoliberal spirituality. Its discourses reflect capitalist-individualist understandings of "freedom" and "progress." This largely stands in place of radical antihierarchical, egalitarian, and socialist understandings of liberation. Alternatively, political subversion on the part of spiritual communities would require them to combine their individual privileges, skills, or knowledge with collective dissent, disruptive action or a refusal to cooperate with the systems and structures that create and oppress vulnerable outgroups.

As alternatives to the most common gestures toward equity, justice, peace, and love in the commodities of neoliberal spirituality, consider the political dissenter Aldous Huxley's dystopian novel *Brave New World* (1931), the feminist Betty Friedan's call to arms in *The Feminine Mystique* (1963), or the feminist scholar and political activist Angela Davis's analysis of the American women's movement and its weddedness to racist and classist biases in *Women, Race and Class* (1981) and what these texts represented to many participants in 1960s, 1970s, and 1980s countercultural movements that subverted the social status quo.

Examples of contemporary political resistance include the efforts of groups like the antiwar Code Pink that resorts to reason, empirical evidence, and visibility to challenge US development policies, the Platform for the Movement for Black Lives, which is one of the most advanced and inclusive political visions ever articulated, or the Fight for $15 movement that successfully campaigned to raise the minimum wage in many parts of the United States. Consider disruptive feminist solidarity movements, inspired, not by neoliberal modes of discourse or conduct, but by a vocabulary of rights and modes of protest similarly used by the Occupy Wall Street and the Arab Spring movements (Kurian 2017). Examples from twenty-first-century millennial Indian women's movements, which used social media campaigns against cultures of sexual violence to launch a radically new kind of feminist politics, include the 2003 Blank Noise Project against eve-teasing, the 2009 Pink Chaddi (underwear) movement against moral policing, the 2011 SlutWalk protest against victim blaming, the 2011 Why Loiter project on women's right to public spaces, the 2015 Pinjra Tod (Break the Cage) movement against sexist curfew rules in student halls, and the 2017 Bekhauf Azadi (Freedom without Fear) March. Examples also include the protesters of the Dakota Access Pipeline who called for a boycott of its investors, including Chase Bank (see "Boycott the Banks" 2017 and Garfield 2017), and the government scientists who went "rogue" by using Twitter as a way to defy Trump's attempts to quiet spokespeople for climate change research (Schlanger 2017).

As a final example, consider the climate activist from Sweden, Greta Thunberg. Thunberg demands action in the form of concrete policy changes to reverse and prevent further catastrophic climate change. She addresses world leaders, attending UN climate summits around the world, and the general population. Thunberg is a leading figure in the climate justice movement, inspiring millions across the globe since she launched a school strike in 2018.

As rain poured down on Trump's inauguration (Chan 2017), I looked at the friends, family, colleagues, and strangers who surrounded me and wondered, would the self-describing "spiritual" people, moved by compassion and troubled by the imminent threats to vulnerable communities and to our ecosystem, subvert the white supremacist, neoliberal-capitalist-exploitative heteropatriarchy Trump represents through collective action and a call for systemic change, or would they merely gesture toward their discontent, resorting to T-shirts and biodegradable paper plates that contain resistance and commitments to justice and sustainability, putting the burden of transformation on individuals?

Those who self-describe or market their products as "spiritual" pride themselves on giving individuals the tools they need to heal and be well, and there is an abundance of evidence suggesting many of those tools are physically and psychologically effective. But that is not enough. They must also use their resources—strong bodies, communities, and commitments to evidence-based knowledge and reason—as tools for achieving the common good and therefore to resist the structural violence that causes so much of the trauma that necessitates healing to begin with, to demand social justice, and, as Angela Davis speaking at the Women's March on Washington put it so well, to recognize "that we are collective agents of history and that history cannot be deleted like web pages." Davis insisted, "The next 1,459 days of the Trump administration will be 1,459 days of resistance: Resistance on the ground, resistance in the classrooms, resistance on the job, and resistance in our art and in our music" (Davis 2017). But would there be resistance among spiritual adherents?

* * *

I want to bring into the foreground the fact that this book is moored in concrete political and personal realities. This project arose from my devastation at the success of various right-wing movements, not only the 2016 election of Donald Trump to president of the United States, but also the 2014 election of Narendra Modi to prime minister of India and the 2016 Brexit vote in the United Kingdom. I simultaneously confronted the extent of the climate crisis and came to adopt a rather apocalyptic outlook on the bleak future of life on this planet. With these developments, what was left of the veil was lifted and the deceit behind myths of progress exposed. I am fully aware that all thought emerges at particular times and places, as discourses are established, get resisted, and so on, in response to both political and personal realities as well as academic fashion, but I also hope that throughout this book I remain acutely aware of my particular embeddedness in a situation that is dire, in which bodies suffer and the environment is destroyed, and so resist analytic abstraction.

This investigation is fueled by a confrontation with the dire social and environmental situation we are in, but intellectually, it also builds on concepts and arguments from my previous scholarship, especially *Selling Yoga: From Counterculture to Pop Culture* (2014). There, I explored the global yoga boom and argued that commercial yoga is a body of religious practice, critiquing competing studies that bemoan the consumer branding, commodification, and popularization of yoga as the loss of an imagined purer, authentic Hindu religious tradition. Crucial to that endeavor was the notion that commercial yoga represents a religion of consumer culture. I used *consumer culture* there but not *neoliberal capitalism* as, prior to recent political and cultural developments, *neoliberalism* had not emerged in mainstream usage, and I wanted the book to be accessible to academic and nonacademic audiences. Whereas in *Selling Yoga* I sought to understand how yoga became a part of popular culture and to theorize religion in the context of consumer culture, in the present book I offer a critique of global spirituality and the mode of governance, namely, neoliberalism, on which it firmly stands today.

My project is ultimately driven by the question of how the study of neoliberal spirituality, and especially yoga, can help us better understand religion's role in contemporary society. At the time that I began developing the core argument of this book in the middle of 2016, the neoliberal consensus seemed nearly unassailable. As I tried to come to terms with the increasingly surreal political and environmental events that kept unfolding, the concepts I had been working with in my previous scholarship on yoga proved helpful. At the same time, I felt compelled to adjust my set of tools of critique to shed a different kind of light on the order of things, to offer an analysis of spirituality that illuminates the politics that shape the present, the devices invented to give effect to rule and to subvert it, and the ways that these impact many contemporary consumers, the adherents of spiritual practices.

Neoliberal capitalism shapes social realities worldwide, yet theoretical work analyzing it draws disproportionately on North Atlantic contexts and Christian or Christian-secular cultures and traditions. Scholars of religion examine the ways Christian cultures and traditions produce and respond to capitalist structures (e.g., Bowler 2013; Porterfield 2018). Work on religion in

American culture illustrates how consumer behaviors can uphold Christian theological categories and can even constitute domains of religion in themselves (e.g., Moreton 2010; Lofton 2017; and Vaca 2019). Focusing largely on North American commodifications of yoga, I argued in *Selling Yoga* (2014) that yoga constitutes a body of religious practice; in other words, it is a religion of consumer culture. There are, of course, important exceptions, studies that address religion in other social and cultural contexts while analyzing its relationship to capitalism, class, and economic structures (e.g., Ahmad 2004; Birla 2009; Rudnyckyj 2018). This book seeks to identify global correspondences, differences, and resemblances in the ways that urban spiritual consumers respond to or mirror the idioms, practices, and infrastructure of the neoliberal capitalist order.

I have organized this book thematically into five chapters, each of which covers a particular area of neoliberal spirituality through attention to cases primarily drawn from the global yoga industry, including specific gurus and teachers, discourses, styles, brands, and trends. The chapters also situate spiritual discourses, practices, and institutions concretely in the shifting social, political, and economic contexts of neoliberal capitalism, examining the ways in which spiritual adherents at once respond to, create, and resist the changing dynamics of global consumer culture.

In chapter 1, I suggest we can better understand the apparent conflicts and contradictions of the practices and commitments of neoliberal spirituality by approaching it as both a body of religious practice and a neoliberal ethical complex. I understand that it will be difficult to convince many readers that neoliberal spirituality is religious, given its entanglement in processes of appropriation, commodification, and commercialization, and I take the scholarly task of convincing them otherwise seriously, devoting a large part of this chapter to definitions and theory. I especially hope to make a case for the ways neoliberal spirituality reflects and affects adherents' values. I also argue that spirituality can betray ritual, mythological, and other religious qualities even as it is made up of industries that operate by the logic of multinational corporations, so consideration of its religious qualities generally need not (and should not) avoid a critique of neoliberalism itself. This chapter suggests we can consider some of the religious qualities of neoliberal spirituality while not slipping into nostalgia about the past nor a kind of relativism that renders it immune from serious criticism. The chapter also explains what is meant by *neoliberalism* and *neoliberal governmentality* and the ways they are embodied by the neoliberal subject who dissents against neoliberal capitalism but through gestural subversions, ultimately conceding to its domination.

In chapter 2, I evaluate the ways much of the scholarship on commercialized forms of spirituality represents and analyzes it, arguing against the common trope that bemoans the commodification of spirituality as the loss of an authentic, pure expression or as a numbing device that blinds consumers to the problems of neoliberal capitalism. This chapter, therefore, is a response to studies that reduce neoliberal spirituality to mere consumer sellouts and spiritual consumers to dupes. I suggest such critiques depend on the assumption that there is an original, static tradition to be preserved (e.g., Indian yoga), one that preexisted the profanation of religion through commodification, and consequently they produce nostalgic representations, mirroring the essentialisms of consumers themselves. As Courtney Bender notes, spiritual narratives are often sites for "staking out claims and possibilities for a certain kind of authentic and authoritative experience" (2010, 59). Much of the scholarship on spirituality falls prey to this too. This chapter also points out how previous studies fail to account for the ways spiritual consumers and entrepreneurs do resist (even if through mere gestures) the dominant culture.

In chapter 3, I look at the appropriating and commodifying practices of spirituality industries and ask how corporations, entrepreneurs, and consumers relate spiritual practices to ethical values through marketing and consumer activities. I aim to demonstrate how the powerful and subversive expressions appliquéd across yogaware, the packaging of spiritual goods, and the industry's "do good" discourses are tied to a commitment to particular "yogic" or "spiritual" values. Yet, for all of the self-actualization it offers through PEACE LOVE YOGA, these industries also play a capitalist game that thrives on nostalgia about lost cultural norms, as well as neoliberal narratives about the capitalist market, self-care, and personal improvement.

In chapter 4, I evaluate the relationship between gender, sexuality, and neoliberal spirituality, arguing that the ascent of spiritual industries is no doubt in part about some women's reclamation of control over their bodies; yet, it is also a site of rampant and various manifestations of sexual violence. On the one hand, the Indian mega-yoga guru and wellness industry leader Baba Ramdev was instrumental in recriminalizing same-sex sex in India, which exacerbated the social and physical vulnerability of LGBTQ Indians. On the other hand, there have been countless revelations, especially since #MeToo, that influential gurus and teachers, for example, Pattabhi Jois and

Bikram Choudhury, have sexually assaulted female students. Attempts to diagnose the problem range from blaming the "guru model," pointing to the
flawed attribution of infallibility and insistence on submission to gurus, to
blaming the conservative sexist and heterosexist ideals certain teachers and
gurus represent. The relationship between spiritual industries and sexual
violence, however, is more systemic than these diagnoses suggest. None of
them sufficiently explains how so many industry leaders and gurus get away
with violence against women and sexual minorities, especially when, in the
popular imagination, doing yoga and consuming other spiritual goods are
often associated with health and wellness, women's empowerment, self-care,
peaceful coexistence, and universalism. I argue that attention to different
and conflicting narratives of sexual violence in spiritual industries sheds
light on larger systemic issues, particularly by illuminating the following: a
globally pervasive neoliberal logic whereby control over one's body is valued,
but is defined as an individual achievement; policing of deviant bodies or
bodies that resist the wellness ideal; and capitalist strategies of commodification that contain dissent against neoliberal individualism through gestural
subversions. Together, these brew spiritual industries that neither challenge
dominant heteropatriarchal ideologies nor holds the superwealthy and otherwise powerful industry leaders accountable for sexual violence.

Chapter 5 examines how neoliberal spirituality's reliance on discourses
of purity and moral policing by examining its relationship to public space
and dominant political values in India, especially by focusing on prime minister of India Narendra Modi's 2015 inauguration of the International Day
of Yoga with a vast public ritual. Drawing on Steven Lukes's argument that
political rituals manipulate an agenda in order to make it appear that community power is at play when in fact they empower a select few, I argue that
Modi's Yoga Day demonstration demarcated out-groups and empowered
a heteropatriarchal Hindu elite. Yoga was an instrument of domination
through which Modi mainstreamed Hindutva, the position that the strength
and unity of India depends on its "Hindu-ness," and therefore that unorthodox or foreign social practices and religions should be resisted.

In the conclusion, I pose the question of whether the adherents of spirituality put it to work in ways that organize the world so as to counter neoliberal capitalism. In other words, I ask whether spirituality takes forms that
resist the neoliberal demand to produce, consume, and police. The tendency
to self-describe as "spiritual but not religious" or simply "spiritual" is increasingly entangled with neoliberal capitalism, which has mobilized many

entrepreneurs to enhance the market value of various wellness and spiritual commodities. Yet, at the same time, spirituality is not one thing, and various forms have emerged and gained popularity. I examine prison yoga and meditation as a way of exploring the question of whether a form of spiritual militancy could attempt to go beyond simply self-describing as "alternative" or "spiritual" and gesturing toward resistance to facilitating actual structural change. In other words, I ask whether these forms of rehabilitation serve as a counter to or a part of the rise of invocations of spirituality as gestural subversions. Do they build political power through the unity of those most disenfranchised by neoliberal capitalism in an effort to center the spiritual ethical framework on the imprisoned and dispossessed, or do they, like their commodified counterparts, offer defanged subversions of the neoliberal order? I conclude that they do the latter, embodying one more modern disciplinary regimen meant to produce good neoliberal subjects.

1

BREATHE PRACTICE REPEAT

Theorizing Neoliberal Spirituality, or, Religion under Neoliberal Capitalism

BREATHE PRACTICE REPEAT, NAMASTE ALL DAY, GOOD KARMA, SELF LOVE CLUB, ZEN AF (that is, "Zen as Fuck"), PEACE LOVE YOGA, and my personal favorite: YOUR EGO IS NOT YOUR AMIGO. These are just a few of the pithy expressions found on Spiritual Gangster yogaware. The website for Spiritual Gangster (2019) displays beautiful, slim, young, (usually) white bodies clad in remarkable combinations of cotton and spandex and forever in a state of leisure at varying locations, ranging from an urban basketball court to a bed of white linens in what appears to be a high-end resort, but nearly always with an exotic backdrop.

This is the person you should be. Lounging in your yoga pants, you would feel beautiful, relaxed, and spiritual, but in a fleeting moment, you might also slip into a painfully reflexive state as you realize you are also a cog in the economic and social machinations of neoliberal capitalism. You might marvel—and then recoil—at the neoliberal project's magical abilities to cultivate perpetual anxiety about, not only your productivity, but also your responsibility for every dimension of life; to make you work more even when doing so brings less in return; and to create a void and then to fill it, for those who can afford to do so.

Spiritual Gangster yogaware is one articulation of a peculiar variant of spirituality that has come to the forefront of global culture in the past few decades, one that incessantly incites its adherents to accept full responsibility for not only their own health, beauty, and fitness, but also their own wellness, self-care, success, and happiness. Many consumers spend their money on yoga, health foods, and mindfulness because they believe there is something wrong with them—they are sick, in pain, sad, anxious, tired, unsuccessful, aging, dying—and it is their responsibility to resolve these problems or at least improve their situations. The reasons consumers give for buying spiritual products, however, are often also broader. Although many outsiders

Peace Love Yoga. Andrea R. Jain, Oxford University Press (2020). © Oxford University Press.
DOI: 10.1093/oso/9780190888626.001.0001

assume yoga practitioners practice primarily for health, beauty, and fitness, according to a *Yoga Journal* survey, "wellness" is the number one reason people practice yoga, with "sense of peace/calm" and "health" coming in second and third (Yoga Journal Editors 2015). It is difficult to discount the reported transformative effects of spiritual commodities. This is a pop culture phenomenon in which the path to salvation from suffering, sickness, pain, and brokenness is paved with the spiritual goods consumers keep buying.

There is a rich archive of this type of spirituality, which combines an exhortation for individuals to take responsibility for their conditions with effective commodifying and purchasing strategies and usually some kind of nostalgic attachment to the past, pursuit of purity, and cultural appropriation. These can take form in a range of consumer goods, from yoga classes and mindfulness apps to health foods and crystals.

In response to the question of how to change your attitude when you cannot change your circumstances, Jewish American health coach, mindful weight-loss entrepreneur, and "foremost expert" on Maimonides and ancient health David Zulberg advises, "Change your perception, belief or opinion of the situation—and that will help you change your attitude." Some other tidbits of advice include "Admit to yourself that you're not happy"; "Realize optimism is a choice"; "Use positive words"; "Hang out with friends who have a happy vibe"; and "Say a daily affirmation" (Zulberg 2015). Hindu yoga guru, activist, entrepreneur, and television celebrity Baba Ramdev similarly espouses a message of "positive thinking" and self-care, which he disseminates across India through speeches, interviews, advertisements, and other media platforms. This is precisely the kind of spirituality that informs bestselling manifestos, such as Whole Foods Market CEO John Mackey's *Conscious Capitalism* (2014), in which the ideal person is construed as atomized, self-optimizing, and entrepreneurial.

I call this phenomenon *neoliberal spirituality* for its deep elective affinity with the dynamics of neoliberal capitalism and tendency to wed the goal of material success to the quest for spiritual liberation, rooted in some form of ancient wisdom. "Personal growth," "self-care," and "transformation" are just some of the generative tropes in the narrative of this spiritual identity. In Spiritual Gangster's, Zulberg's, Mackey's, and Ramdev's discourses, we find a metanarrative that frames things in terms of market value, but it also reflects certain assumptions about human existence, value, and purpose, and works hard to control morality, condition the body, and regulate authority. Huge swathes of consumers in urban spaces all over the world spend their money on the commodities spiritual entrepreneurs sell, hence the emergence of large transnational corporations, indeed entire industries, producing neoliberal spirituality's products.

As in other areas of urban globalized culture, spiritual consumers pick and choose from a variety of practices and worldviews to construct individualized *lifestyles*.[1] Effective marketing depends on the perpetual production of novel images—late capitalism is dominated by the reproduction of images or *simulations* (Baudrillard 1983). Consumers of neoliberal spirituality have a tendency to appropriate freely from different cultures and religious traditions, resulting in products meant to help them meet their personal goals.[2]

The increasing importance of symbolic goods has accelerated the demand for cultural specialists who draw from other cultures and traditions in order to produce desirable commodities (Bourdieu 1984 and 1991). And, in many parts of the world, representations of the exotic Other are particularly profitable (Baudrillard 1983). Spiritual commodities feature evocative objects, images, or ideas appropriated from other, oftentimes ancient, cultures, resulting in a wide range of products, from Ganesha T-shirts to Ayurvedic face cream.[3] Unsurprisingly then, the *Yoga Journal* survey previously mentioned asked American yoga practitioners how many of them had given their children or pets Sanskrit names. The answer: 5 percent (*Yoga Journal* Editors 2015).

The fact that cultural appropriation is at the heart of many industries' successes among middle- and upper-class white consumers is not historically surprising given the relationship between capitalism and settler colonialism. Furthermore, the ascent of neoliberal spirituality is one (and the most dominant) development of historically white-dominated countercultural currents, including the 1960s hippies' turn to Hindu, Buddhist, and other spiritual wares and women's reclamation of their bodies in the 1970s, those

---

[1] Mike Featherstone explains the use of the term *lifestyle* in consumer culture: "It connotes individuality, self-expression, and a stylistic self-consciousness. One's body, clothes, speech, leisure pastimes, eating and drinking preferences, home, car, choice of holidays, etc. are to be regarded as indicators of the individuality of taste and sense of style of the owner/consumer" (2007, 81).

[2] *Appropriation* is derived from the Latin *appropriare*, meaning "to make one's own," which is derived from the Latin root *proprius*, meaning "own," also the root of *property*. This parallels the use of the term in legal contexts, strengthening the connotation of an unfair or unauthorized taking, that is, theft (Rogers 2006, 475).

[3] See, for example, Shanti Om products or the books and services by self-proclaimed "medical anthropologist, psychologist and practicing shaman" Alberto Villoldo at http://onespiritmedicine.com.

same currents that quickly took a turn as they largely retreated from public welfare concerns in favor of capitalist commodification and neoliberal individualism.[4] Spiritual commodities became status symbols, forms of conspicuous consumption, especially for a capitalist class far removed from the production of those very commodities.

Analyzing spiritual consumption under neoliberal capitalism requires attention to conspicuous consumption, a term Thorstein Veblen introduced in *The Theory of the Leisure Class* ([1899] 1994). In Veblen's model, *conspicuous consumption* refers to spending money on and acquiring luxury goods and services in order to publicly display economic power rather than to cover utilitarian needs. Veblen suggests that the consumer behaviors of members of the "leisure class" conform to certain "schemes of life" (84), "changing styles" (174), or "branches of knowledge" (45). In other words, they reflect what is in vogue at the time. Veblen's model looks at these schemes of life vertically, according to different points on the socioeconomic hierarchy. In much of contemporary society and especially in global cities, however, consumers' behaviors are not exclusively determined by their positions on that hierarchy, but also by lifestyle choices that cut across social classes (Featherstone 1991; McIntyre 1992). Given that, using the concept of *habitus* and distinguishing between the cultural and economic capital individuals hold, Bourdieu develops a model in which lifestyles can vary horizontally, cutting across social classes, such that the social structure both determines and is determined by individual behaviors, and different types of lifestyles are associated with particular combinations of cultural and economic capital (Trigg 2001, 109–112).

Cutting across social classes in global cities around the world, consuming the commodities of neoliberal spirituality signals cultural capital as well as economic capital. Spiritual consumers occupy the neoliberal spiritual habitus, which is not only about buying expensive products—though spiritual commodities are often expensive—but also about a certain type of conspicuous consumption, that is, consumption for the sake of signifying a spiritual lifestyle of responsible self-care. In this sense, a primary school teacher

---

[4] Commenting on the rise of fitness culture, Barbara Ehrenreich notes the attitude that the industry reflects: "I may not be able to do much about grievous injustice in the world, at least not by myself or in very short order, but I can decide to increase the weight on the leg press machine by twenty pounds and achieve that within a few weeks." She continues, "The gym, which once looked so alien and forbidding to me, became one of the few sites where I could reliably exert control" (2018, 56–57).

who does not earn nearly as much money as a CEO of a large corporation could, like that CEO, tirelessly attend yoga classes and study mindfulness. Consumer choices, in both cases, signal cultural capital, though economic capital remains significantly variable. The specific brands and luxuries one can afford will obviously differ depending on one's income, and some people are so low on the socioeconomic hierarchy that they simply have no consumer "choice" to begin with. Furthermore, the ways the neoliberal spiritual lifestyle privileges self-care consumption as the route to some form of achievement, be it "freedom," "balance," or "liberation," further relies on vertical schemes of life insofar as the same logic says those who smoke, eat unhealthy foods, or do not exercise fail as individuals and deserve their health problems and low life expectancy. Those lowest on the socioeconomic hierarchy, in this framework, are far more likely to be "failures." Interestingly, it also relies on vertical schemes of gender, since, for example, working mothers are also doomed to fail at achieving that envied "work-life balance," even though they are endlessly reminded to keep striving for it.

Although spiritual consumers often imagine their spiritual lifestyle as representing a unified, universal, and coherent system, their commodities in fact represent a remarkable bricolage, a combination of heterogeneous ideas and practices (Jameson 1991, 96) appropriated from a tremendous array of sources, for example, yoga, tantra, Native American cultures, Taoism, and Buddhism as well as Western metaphysical traditions. Consider Karma Keepers, a successful online retail website for ritual accoutrement that bundles different cultures and traditions, packaging them as eclectic technologies for spiritual development. Among the many products appropriated from Wicca, Native American traditions, Hindu, and Buddhist ones, the Karma Keepers' retail site features a "White Sage Smudge Kit" that includes an "authentic sinew wrapped wild turkey feather," an "abalone shell," and an "organic white sage smudge stick," all for $9.99. In an eclectic move, the retailer offers the "White Sage Smudge Kit 02 with 3 Tibetan Silver Charms" for just four dollars more (Karma Keepers 2018). The Spiritual Gangster website similarly bundles spiritual products appropriated from different cultures. Although the products primarily fit in the yogaware category, the text of yogaware sometimes appeals to the authority of other traditions (e.g., ZEN AF T-shirts), and the corporation's blog frequently features discussions of nonyogic spiritual practices (e.g., smudging) (Spiritual Gangster 2018a). Through products like these, retailers make it possible for consumers to feel as if they can experience a Japanese meditation or Native American ritual without actually encountering Japanese or Native American people.[5]

All of this explains the rise to prominence of entrepreneurial gurus and other spiritual teachers who make products attractive to large target audiences of consumers even when they do not necessarily want to go to Hindu ashrams or Buddhist temples in order to embrace the evocative ideas, symbols, and practices associated with these traditions. Spiritual transmission takes new forms under global neoliberal capitalism. Instead of relying on transmission through traditional teacher-disciple relationships, most consumers of spirituality prefer the easily accessible wares and brand-name forms of self-actualization or enlightenment-ethics offered by entrepreneurs or corporations and available on television, through cheap paperbacks, or at their local grocery store, shopping mall, or gym.[6]

This kind of spiritual consumption also embodies all sorts of contradictions, giving rise to social and political controversies, including that which arose around the closure of the Burrard St. Bridge for the 2015 International Day of Yoga (see Bramadat 2019). In 2015 in Vancouver, home to yoga apparel giant Lululemon, a scheduled Yoga Day event threatened to "divide the city and the local yoga community" due to the $150,000 price tag, corporate sponsors (including Lululemon), and the planned seven-hour "Om the Bridge" closure. The added irony was that the event was largely sponsored by an affluent white Canadian demographic and threatened to eclipse National Aboriginal Day, all while its organizers claimed to celebrate an ancient system of knowledge indigenous to India, that is, yoga. The event was canceled following a week of protest. Events for Yoga Day have also sparked controversy in India itself (discussed at length in chapter 5), where some citizens, including many Muslim leaders and journalists, vocally protest Yoga Day events, arguing they serve right-wing prime minister Narendra Modi's "saffron agenda," that is, his brand of Hindu nationalism.

Although this book will illuminate many of the contradictions of neoliberal spirituality, it is not meant to be just one more study bemoaning spiritual commodification and appropriation as numbing devices through which marketers and consumers ignore the problems of our dominant social and economic structures or as the corruption or loss of "authentic" religious forms (on "authenticity debates," see chapter 2). Many scholars have already

---

[5] On metaphysical religion as a mode of spiritual appropriation without contact with another culture, see Viswanathan 2000.

[6] I previously discussed this process as it pertains to the yoga industry in *Selling Yoga* (2014a).

offered referenda on spiritual commodities, suggesting they merely serve as palliatives or coping mechanisms.[7] These commodities, in their view, function as a mere fetish that helps consumers feel as if they have escaped the "impact of reality" (Žižek 2001a). In other words, they offer consumers an escape into an experience (of the present moment, of a romanticized or orientalized Other, or of an idealized ancient past) that allows them to imagine themselves as separate from the busyness of everyday life, and by extension disconnected from the social and economic relations of neoliberal capitalism. Most famously, Slavoj Žižek critiques western commodifications of Buddhism, arguing that they serve as the remedy for the "stressful tension of the capitalist dynamics" in ways that facilitate consumers' complicity in capitalist systems (2001b, 12).

I agree that spiritual commodities offer solutions to consumers' problems that do not defy or undermine the structural and economic undergirding of the earth's population's greatest threats, namely, pervasive inequalities, the threat of nuclear warfare, and environmental destruction. The consequences of neoliberal capitalism in the light of modern ethical commitments to the individual (or human rights), the social world (or social justice), and the natural environment (or sustainability) are dire. If our ethical agenda includes maintaining a stable global community of equal persons and a sustainable natural environment, capitalist structures and their effects are rightfully perceived as obstacles. In fact, the obstacles capitalism poses are the very

---

[7] Many such approaches to commercial spirituality are indebted to Slavoj Žižek's critique of western Buddhism as the paragon of a late capitalist ideology. One well-known study by Jeremy Carrette and Richard King, *Selling Spirituality: The Silent Takeover of Religion*, critiques commercial spirituality more broadly, targeting the co-optation of spirituality by market forces and arguing that spirituality is a "vacuous cultural trope" and represents the "silent [capitalist] takeover of religion" (2005, 46). *Selling Spirituality* serves as the paragon of the tendency to reduce spiritualities to mere consumer sellouts. See also Roof 1999; Lau 2000. The authors target the "big business" of spirituality. Though the authors claim that their concern is with the sociopolitical consequences of the spiritual marketplace and not with the truth, authenticity, or the question of "what counts as real spirituality," their analysis of the spiritual marketplace is framed as the capitalist "takeover," "commercialization," and "replacement" of religion. This opposition between capitalist commodification and religion amounts to an assessment of what counts as real religion. For example, we see in their study the reduction of spiritual products to the mere commodification of what were traditional religious wares: "What is being sold to us as radical, trendy and transformative spirituality in fact produces little in the way of a significant change in one's lifestyle or fundamental behaviour patterns" (Carrette and King 2005, 5). This approach frames spiritualities as distinct from religion and presumes, therefore, that practices identified by insiders as *spiritual* are not religious. In short, there is no religious substance to self-proclaimed spiritualities. Some recent work on spirituality and religion in consumer culture avoids the dichotomy between spirituality and religion. See, for example, Lofton 2011; Aschoff 2015; Goodchild 2002; and Lofton 2017. For my critique of the position that spirituality is a *replacement* of religion, see Jain 2014a, 95–129.

challenges of the Anthropocene.[8] The main force behind the Anthropocene is capitalism's global exponential growth, particularly since the mid-twentieth century (Foster, Holleman, and Clark 2019). "Capitalism," as Fred Magdoff and John Bellamy Foster explain, "recognizes no limits to its own self-expansion—there is no amount of profit, no amount of wealth, and no amount of consumption that is either 'enough' or 'too much'" (Magdoff and Foster 2011, 43). Governments embedded in the neoliberal capitalist economy, rather than design universal social programs with the aim of reducing inequality and establish market regulations in order to serve the common good and protect the environment, usually delegate the task of managing markets to corporations under the guise of "free markets" and scale back social programs in order to minimize government spending.

As a consequence of capitalism's exponential growth, as I write, the world suffers from increased global warmth and the natural catastrophes to which it contributes, more specifically: carbon dioxide emissions, ocean acidification, fossil fuel combustion, mass species extinctions and other losses in biological diversity, nitrogen and phosphorus cycle disruptions, freshwater depletion, forest loss, and chemical pollution, resulting in a planetary ecological emergency or Earth system crisis (Foster, Holleman, and Clark 2019; Foster, Holleman, and Clark cite Angus 2016; McNeill 2016).

There are climate refugees here in the United States where I write (see Davenport and Robertson 2016). Devastating natural events, from flooding and hurricanes to tornadoes and forest fires, are becoming the norm. The vast number of studies on environmental politics continues to grow. Those making the most impact include Aldo Leopold's *Sand County Almanac* (1949), Rachel Carson's *Silent Spring* (1962), and more recently Naomi Klein's *This Changes Everything* (2014), which call for government regulations of the gasses that threaten life on earth. Even Greta Thunberg, the leader of a climate justice movement that has led millions of people to protest with the hope of putting pressure on world leaders to implement concrete policy changes in favor of sustainability, has not been enough to cultivate dramatic

---

[8] The term *Anthropocene,* often said to have been coined by Paul Crutzen and Eugene Stoermer (2000), first appeared in English in "The Anthropogenic System (Period)" in *The Great Soviet Encyclopedia* (1973). An international consensus is emerging about the designation of the Anthropocene as a new geological epoch, the one in which we are currently located. Scientists attribute the advent of this epoch to mid-twentieth-century capitalist growth, as a consequence of which "changes on a scale that can be seen as dividing major geological epochs, previously occurring over millions of years, are now taking place over decades or at most centuries due to human action" (Foster, Holleman, and Clark 2019).

shifts in popular attitudes or policy changes. At the 2019 UN Climate Action Summit in New York, Thunberg responded to the inaction:

> My message is that we'll be watching you. This is all wrong. I shouldn't be up here. I should be back in school on the other side of the ocean. Yet you all come to us young people for hope. How dare you! You have stolen my dreams and my childhood with your empty words. And yet I'm one of the lucky ones. People are suffering. People are dying. Entire ecosystems are collapsing. We are in the beginning of a mass extinction, and all you can talk about is money and fairy tales of eternal economic growth. How dare you! (Thunberg 2019)

As Thunberg incites world leaders to adopt radical policy changes, spiritual marketing campaigns incessantly incite consumers to accept full responsibility for their individual (as opposed to collective) well-being. The types of spirituality evaluated in this book are not actively challenging the socioeconomic and cultural structures that shape our lives (and are literally killing us off). In other words, they enable conformity to the dominant ideology of neoliberalism and the reigning socioeconomic system of capitalism, which not only uphold the threats of major conflict and environmental destruction, but are also largely responsible for conditions of exploitation and a dehumanizing workplace, assaults against democracy, and vast social inequalities.

Many critical contributions to the study of spirituality examine the material and social operations of spiritual commodities, pursued with a sensitivity to subtle—and sometimes not-so-subtle—power dynamics, complicating any straightforward progress narrative about religious democratization, increased choice, or individual autonomy among spiritual consumers. With the aim of bottom-line profit, industry leaders call on consumers to choose the right commodities, ultimately directing their address to the middle and upper classes, effectively erasing from view the problems faced by the vast majority of the population. As much as individual consumers are not in control of their physical living conditions or places on the socioeconomic hierarchy, spiritual shopping gives consumers a sense of control over their lives. In other words, adherents use the notion of *consumer choice* to convince themselves they are in control of their well-being, success, self-care, health, and happiness. A wide range of commodities—yoga mats, smoothies, mindfulness meditations, malas, crystals, hemp clothing, anything with "Zen" printed or appliquéd across it—are celebrated as good consumer choices, products that lead to better living outcomes or personal growth.

While acknowledging the accuracy of these insights, which other studies on commercial spirituality have already offered, in four ways I aspire to put forth a more nuanced analysis in the present book.

Neoliberal Spirituality Is Religious

First, following my primary argument in *Selling Yoga*, I challenge analyses that pit commodification against religion. All contemporary human institutions are enmeshed in neoliberal capitalism, in most cases as complicit with and in some cases as reactions against. So the idea that what neoliberal spirituality has done is given religion to consumerism and made religion consumable is too simple; spiritual commodities do not *replace* religion. Rather, new religious forms—within and beyond religious institutions—have emerged in the context of neoliberal capitalism. In other words, in contrast to dichotomous approaches to spirituality and religion in contemporary society, I approach the study of neoliberal spirituality, not as a *takeover* or *replacement* of religion or as an *alternative* to religion, but as a modern *manifestation* of religion. We can therefore better understand the conflicts and contradictions of neoliberal spirituality's practices and ideological commitments as well as the power dynamics at play in its institutions by approaching it as both a body of religious practice and a neoliberal ethical complex.[9]

Furthermore, this book is not a polemic against all forms of spirituality or the increasing number of people, institutions, and communities around the world that self-describe or are labeled as "spiritual" or "spiritual but not religious." Nor is it an attempt to trace in detail the history of neoliberalism as an ideological force or to identify all of the incredibly damaging

---

[9] I use *body of religious practice* here to refer to a set of behaviors characterized by the following: they are treated as sacred, set apart from the ordinary or mundane; they are grounded in a shared ontology or worldview (though that ontology may not be all-encompassing); they are grounded in a shared axiology or set of values or goals concerned with resolving weakness, suffering, or death; and the preceding qualities are reinforced through narrative and ritual. Religion concerns things that are shared. It is therefore *social*; religious behaviors demarcate social structures and organize social interactions. They are therefore also political insofar as they demarcate authority and frequently organize people and other living beings into hierarchies. I first discussed my use of *body of religious practice* in *Selling Yoga* (2014a, 95–129).

consequences that have come about from its ideological dominance around the world. It is, however, an attempt to understand neoliberal spirituality through attention to its religious discourses, institutional practices, and ethical values as well as to analyze the networks of power and knowledge within which they are situated. I ask how corporations, governments, and consumers embody relations of religious ideas and practices to ethical values and processes of valuation through marketing, promotional, and consumer activities.

An attempt to identify the intersections of religion and neoliberalism solicits reflection on value. For a long time now, scholars of religion have reiterated that the subject of their work is not rooted in a set of essential qualities. Yet my current use of religion is rooted in how I previously defined it in part in terms of a set of behaviors grounded in "a shared axiology or set of values or goals" (Jain 2014a, 98). Furthermore, I follow Gail Hamner's suggestion that

> What distinguishes each approach particularly as *religion* (and not *not* religion) has to do with modalities of valuation, that is, with how persons demarcate (acceptingly or not) an element of life as part of a larger structure of valuation and against other, competing valuations. . . . Not everything humans value gets marked or described as religion, yet whatever is claimed for religion is always marked or described in terms of values and in terms of the lived structures within which these values are embraced or rejected. Values thus refract larger social valuations, the sense, orientation, and depth of which are infinitely variable. (Hamner 2019, 1032)

As Hamner also reminds us, "the term 'value' here indicates regard, importance, worth, or usefulness, whereas the term 'valuation' indicates a process of assessment of value" (2019, 1033). Because religion concerns shared values and because social structures precede the assessment or determination of the value of things, religion is *social*; social structures demarcate religious behaviors and organize religious interactions. Religion is also political insofar as processes of valuation, the determination of the value of things, also entail organizing them into hierarchies and demarcating authority. "Even so," as Hamner points out, "transvaluation, in the sense of resistance to structures of valuation and the production of counter-values or new values, is also an ongoing and important social process" (2019, 1033).

One of the things I am trying to point out by means of this excursion into the definition of religion is that popular and scholarly assumptions often miss the many things global spirituality shares with traditional religious complexes. Social and cultural critiques that exclusively acknowledge profit, status, or power as the goals of spiritual corporations, industry leaders, and consumers remove narrated experiences from their embedded socioeconomic contexts and settings, therefore reducing spirituality to market dynamics and commodity exchange. In other words, they divest religious ways of organizing, approaching, and interacting with the social world, especially in terms of value and valuation, from their view of spiritual commodity production and consumption. Neoliberal spirituality, however, is not immune from the religiosity of consumer culture at large. As Kathryn Lofton argues, how we organize our consumer life and how consumer practices organize us are religious issues; the religion of corporate culture, for example, "is in the consumer interests they protect, the social possibilities they promote, the hierarchies they reiterate, and the commodities they sell" (2014, xii). Religion is in everything corporations do. It is also in what consumers do.[10] In other words, the relationship between religious and consumer behaviors is a dynamic and mutually constitutive one.

The juxtaposition of neoliberal spirituality against religion, I think, is a framework based on the faulty commitment to the demarcation of authenticity (see chapter 2). The dichotomy between authentic and inauthentic often lets certain religious complexes, and their complicity in neoliberal capitalism, off the hook too easily, while demarcating other religious complexes, such as commercial yoga or mindfulness, as false religions or capitalist corruptions of *real* religion. In other words, we should offer up strong critiques of neoliberal spirituality without slipping into the reduction of it to mere commodifying practices or marketing discourses.

I do not see commercial spiritualities as stripped of ethical and religious values, as consumed by a robotic workforce numbed into acceptance of neoliberal society based on private gain. Rather than ask simply whether spirituality is a product of neoliberal capitalism, I aspire to shed light on more complex issues by asking generative questions like these: How is neoliberal spirituality deployed toward economic, political, and ethical ends? What do neoliberal spiritual discourses tell us about entrepreneurs' and consumers'

---

[10] I made a related argument regarding the religious practices of yoga consumers in *Selling Yoga* (2014a, 95–129).

attitudes toward living beings vis-à-vis each other or the natural world? What are the values and processes of valuation at play in neoliberal spirituality, and how are they connected to the power dynamics at play? In what ways do religious idioms become intertwined with ideas about economic value and class status? How are religious idioms deployed to challenge or reproduce certain social structures and economic conditions?

Neoliberal Spirituality as "Arena of Consent and Resistance"

The second way I aspire to put forth a more nuanced analysis is by asking what we should make of the subversive discourses of spiritual commodities, consumers, and corporations, ones that do call on adherents to think beyond the individual and even out into society and the natural environment. My analysis builds on Slavoj Žižek's observation that anti-capitalism is widely disseminated in capitalism, yet the overvaluation of belief means that consumers continue to participate in capitalist exchange (because as long as they *believe* capitalism is bad, it is acceptable for them to *behave* otherwise) (n.d.; 2010), Stuart Hall's suggestion that the dominant culture and counter-culture exist in continuing tension in popular culture, an "arena of consent and resistance," ([1981] 2002), and Mark Fisher's theory of capitalist realism and the ways consumer commodities perform our anti-capitalism for us, allowing us to consume with impunity (2009).

Neoliberal spirituality offers all kinds of calls for consumers to resist unreflective consumption and instead think about their interconnectedness with others and with the environment. One of the most famous global advocates of mindfulness, Thich Nhat Hanh, for example, calls on his readers to be mindful of interconnected systems of production, exchange, and consumption that implicate people living in places all over the world, describing mindfulness as a tool for contemplating the interconnections between seemingly disparate phenomena—what he calls "interbeing" (Nhat Hanh 2009a, 28–33). In fact, in several of the books he wrote for a popular audience, Nhat Hanh advocates for mindfulness as a practice for thinking about political and economic reality (e.g., see *The Miracle of Mindfulness* [(1975) 1987a] and *The Heart of Understanding* [2009a]).

Good Place

What about the many corporations profiting off spiritual commodities that claim to counter the problems of unbridled capitalism with charitable giving or various forms of *conscious capitalism*? What should we make of the Indian state's efforts to challenge the imperialism behind Western commodifications of yoga, especially the North American multi-billion-dollar yoga industry, by reclaiming yoga for India? What should we make of the feminist discourses—the calls for women's empowerment—that are nearly ubiquitous in neoliberal spirituality?

This book attends to these subversive elements of neoliberal spirituality, suggesting that, rather than a mode through which consumers ignore the problems of our dominant neoliberal capitalist global culture, neoliberal spirituality does actually acknowledge those problems and, in fact, struggles against them. But it does so through *gestural subversions*, subversions that largely function as superficial points of resistance already contained within the totalizing framework of neoliberal rationality.

Fisher describes this kind of anti-capitalism as a by-product of *capitalist realism*, the idea that there are no viable alternatives to capitalism (Fisher 2009, 16–19). These subversions, therefore, do not in fact hinder the structures of neoliberal capitalism. In the context of neoliberal spirituality, from provocative taglines printed across T-shirts or packaging to various forms of charitable giving, commodification serves as a strategy through which subversion is itself colonized. In other words, spiritual consumers, entrepreneurs, corporations, and industries participate in a popular religious complex through which protest against the dominant socioeconomic and cultural order is simultaneously expressed and contained. The protester subverts neoliberal capitalism by buying (the right) stuff.

I find it helpful to consider the gestural subversions of spirituality as they compare to diversity work. Sara Ahmed writes about the contradictions of such work. When a person is hired to do diversity work, an institution hires that person to transform it. Sometimes, this is evidence that the institution has a commitment to transformation. Other times, this is merely a sign that the institution knows it ought to transform, but it uses its hiring of a diversity person as a signal that it has already transformed, and then it carries on without implementing actual structural changes (Ahmed 2017). In this book, I explore how something similar is going on in neoliberal spirituality as countless products and services are being bought and sold around the world in part based on the appeal of their subversive qualities, in other words, the anti-capitalist values they embrace, without actually hindering the functions of capitalism.

Neoliberal Spirituality Is Decentralized, Multifocal, and Multidirectional

Third, I hope this study of the workings of neoliberal spirituality contributes to the literature on religion and globalization. Neoliberal capitalism shapes what is possible socially, economically, and politically around the world, yet much of the scholarship on this dominant global cultural complex and religion draws disproportionately on North Atlantic contexts and Christian or secular traditions. Much of the religious studies scholarship on these topics address how Christian ideas and practices produce and respond to capitalism. Studies of religion in non–North Atlantic, Christian, or secular contexts rarely attend to neoliberal capitalism and the ways it constitutes religion across the boundaries of specific nation states.

This book addresses the skewed understanding of religion and neoliberal capitalism by bringing together case studies that examine the multitude of ways that spiritual corporations, entrepreneurs, and consumers around the world respond to the idioms, practices, and infrastructure of the dominant global capitalist order. Studies on the commodification of spirituality, largely focused on North Atlantic and Christian or secular contexts, fail to account for the reality that we now live in a globalized world in which people, movements, and commodities are not isolated by geographic boundaries.

Furthermore, much of the scholarship on religion and globalization focuses on religious violence (especially in Islamic contexts) and global Christianity (Tulasi Srinivas [2010]; Hugh Urban [2015]).[11] There is little work, comparatively, on spiritual ideas, practices, or commodities coming out of India or other parts of Asia, yet Indian-based movements or those that locate their products within myths of ancient Indian origins offer alternative narratives to the usual ones on religion and globalization.[12] Globalization is by no means simply a Western phenomenon and not a matter of the "East" responding reactively to ideas and goods flowing from the "West." It is overly simplistic, in my view, to speak about the westernization of Eastern practices, invoking terms like "American Yoga" or "McMindfulness" (see, e.g., Syman 2010; Purser 2019). These approaches tend to ignore that globalization is a far more decentralized, multifocal, and multidirectional process emerging from

---

[11] See, for example, Juergensmeyer 2003, 2008; Lincoln 2006; Thomas 2005; Miller 2007; Miller, Sargeant, and Flory 2004; Brown 2011; Linden 2009; Jenkins 2011; Lechner and Boli 2011.

[12] See, for example, Lucia 2014; Jain 2014a; Tulasi Srinivas 2010; Smriti Srinivas 2008; McKean 1996.

countless points across a shifting, interconnected network. Cultural ideologies, Tulasi Srinivas suggests, flow not simply from "the West to the rest" but also from India and other parts of Asia, revealing a far more dynamic and multidirectional global flow of religious forms (Tulasi Srinivas 2010, 7). Borrowing terms from Arjun Appadurai (1996), spirituality is better understood as a crucial *node* in a far more complex, fluid, and shifting transnational network of people, ideas, and capital now emanating from multiple sites across the globe. It is a *postnational movement* uniquely adapted to the increasingly *deterritorialized* nature of contemporary global capitalism.

In this book, I imagine neoliberal spirituality as taking many forms, which categories such as "American yoga" or "Indian yoga" do not capture, at various intersections of global networks of people, ideas, and capital, playing critical roles in the circulation of resources and information that go beyond the boundaries of the nation state. With its wildly eclectic practices and its following drawn from every global city of the planet, neoliberal spirituality is not simply *transnational* but *postnational* in Appadurai's sense of the term. As Appadurai suggests, we are increasingly living in a postnational world in which new forms of sodality and new forms of community are emerging that "frequently operate beyond the boundaries of the nation" (Appadurai 1996, 8). With its corporate models and its embrace of capitalism, neoliberal spirituality is uniquely adapted to the current global system.

Neoliberal Spirituality Is Conservative

My fourth intervention concerns spirituality as an "arena of consent," and more specifically, a conservative draw toward purity and moral policing. I analyze the relationship between the dominance of neoliberal capitalist ideology, conservative and right-wing agendas, and spiritual industries. Although many have seen spirituality as deeply neoliberal, they have theorized the rise of spiritual industries, from yoga to mindfulness, as an isolated and unrepresentative happening within the broader historical arc of global neoliberal capitalism rather than a phenomenon closely linked to the twenty-first-century successes of right-wing movements around the world. In other words, the rise of spiritual industries and the rise of conservative movements are usually studied as different ends of the neoliberal arc; they have largely not been thought about as related neoliberal developments. For reasons that I hope will become clear as my argument unfolds, I think the two go hand in hand; these are a part of a single, if complex, phenomenon whereby neoliberalism leans on discourses of purity and moral policing.

Accordingly, I seek to provide a fuller account of the neoliberal era that renders the devastating successes of right-wing movements and the rise of neoliberal spirituality as integral and related features of the dominant global order. Privileged spiritual consumers largely fail to see and critique themselves from a distance, either historical or from the vantage of another race, gender, sexual orientation or identity, ability, or class, and their consumer choices often signal a profound, sometimes violent, draw toward purity. In all of these ways, neoliberal spirituality reifies forms of racial, gender, class, and other forms of privilege as well as heteropatriarchy, lending itself not only to neoliberal, but in some cases conservative, social and political agendas.

Neoliberal Rationality

Scholars love arguing over the meaning of words, and it is fair to say that *neoliberalism* is one of the most contested terms in our contemporary lexicon. I use the term to refer to a particular modern paradigm and mode of governance. Neoliberalism, as opposed to classical liberalism, depends on state policy as a means to actively cultivate and maintain the conditions necessary for vigorous market competition, but it is more than simply policy. It is best understood, following Wendy Brown, "not simply as economic policy, but as a governing rationality that disseminates market values and metrics to every sphere of life. . . . It formulates everything, everywhere, in terms of capital investment and appreciation, including and especially humans themselves" (2015, 176). Signs of the rising dominance of neoliberal capitalism are everywhere around the world in the increasing monetization of all public space and the commercialization of everything. Human relations, therefore, become transactional, navigated through monetary exchange. A hallmark of the neoliberal age, in other words, is the casting of every human endeavor and activity in entrepreneurial terms (Brown 2005, 40).

This mode of governmentality "produces subjects, forms of citizenship and behavior, and a new organization of the social" (Brown 2005, 37). In other words, neoliberalism moves to and from the management of the state to the inner workings of the subject, normatively constructing individuals as entrepreneurial actors, resulting in new political and social subjectivities (e.g., the *neoliberal spiritual subject* discussed throughout this book, or, as discussed in chapter 4, the *neoliberal feminist subject*).

Neoliberalism is the governing rationality upon which the economic policies of late capitalism stand, an economic system in which the means of production and distribution are owned by individuals or corporations, and profits fund their operations. Capitalism works by producing a capitalist class of people who own the means of production but do not produce anything themselves, and a working class made up of the overwhelming majority, those who actually produce everything and only have their labor power to sell for a wage or salary. We see the consequences of this economic system in the ability of multinational corporations to avoid taxation, the increasing wealth of the capitalist classes at the expense of the working classes, and the decreasing availability of public services for the non-capitalist classes.

Neoliberal discourses of self-sufficiency, which reify the individual, construed as an automaton, ideally self-optimizing, self-sustaining, and entrepreneurial, uphold the system. According to Will Davies, "Political-economic systems typically need to offer certain limited forms of hope, excitement, and fairness in order to survive, and cannot operate via domination and exploitation alone"; given that, neoliberalism "rests on claims to legitimacy, which it is possible to imagine as valid, even for critics of this system" (2017, xxii).

Legitimacy, under neoliberal capitalism, resides in the market. Capitalism is defined by the imperative that the capitalist classes and working classes alike access what they need through the market alone. For the political theologian Adam Kotsko, under neoliberal capitalism, the only way in which so-called freedoms can be legitimately curtailed is through the seemingly neutral demands of the market. Neoliberalism relies on "an account of human nature wherein freedom is best expressed through economic exchange and competition and is continually menaced by extra-economic forces such as the state" (Kostko 2018, 36). Kotsko elaborates: "The key concept in neoliberalism's attempt at self-legitimation is freedom, which neoliberalism defines in deeply individualistic terms that render market competition the highest actualization of human liberty" (2018, 10).

Most significantly for the argument I make concerning the interrelatedness of the rise of neoliberal spirituality and the robust health of right-wing movements, neoliberalism is "a political theological paradigm that governs every sphere of social life—not just the state and the economy, but religion, family structure, sexual practice, gender relations, and racialization—by means of a logic of demonization," and "the reactionary populist wave" we are currently facing "is a kind of 'heretical' variant on the neoliberal para-digm, which accepts its core principles and pushes them to almost parodic extremes" (Kotsko 2018, 10). Neoliberalism, according to Kotsko, "aspires to be a complete way of life and a holistic worldview," a "combination of policy agenda and moral ethos," with a "world-ordering ambition," a "form of po-litical theology" (2018, 6, 7) that depends heavily on processes of demoniza-tion. Spirituality, in turn, is an instrument of legitimation for neoliberalism; It, too, depends on the creation of "demons," of inadequate and deviant outsiders who have failed to exercise their freedom correctly by consuming the right goods.

Since the late 1980s, neoliberalism has increasingly functioned as the "hegemonic mode of discourse" (Harvey 2005, 3), a discourse that deploys state power "to reshape society in accordance with market models":

> In some cases this meant creating markets where none had previously existed, as in the privatization of education and other public services. In others it took the form of a more general spread of a competitive market ethos into ever more areas of life—so that we are encouraged to think of our reputation as a "brand," for instance, or our social contacts as fodder for "networking." Whereas classical liberalism insisted that capitalism had to be allowed free rein within its sphere, under neoliberalism capitalism no longer has a set sphere. We are always "on the clock," always accruing (or squandering) various forms of financial and social capital. (Kotsko 2018, 5–6)

As the dominant governing rationality, neoliberalism colonizes more and more domains of contemporary life, spreading its ideological norms into public and private spaces, discourses, and relations, from our workplaces, prisons, doctors' offices, gyms, and classrooms to our church pews, dinner tables, sex lives, and yoga classes. In other words, it frames the way we in-terpret, live in, and understand the world around us. Hence, we are "always accruing (or squandering) various forms of financial and social capital," in-cluding that of the spiritual and self-care kind.

Under neoliberalism, emotional regulation is an obligation to both the individual and society; it is not just a personal project, but a civic duty. As Barbara Cruikshank argues, within the neoliberal paradigm, high self-esteem vaccinates against sources of social instability, such as gender ine-quality and violent crime (1996, 232). In other words, it is up to individuals to develop the emotional proficiency necessary to overcome structural barriers and their consequences. Subjects are increasingly expected to not only manage, but also to prosper in the context of ongoing volatility (see Berlant 2011). The popularity of relaxation, self-improvement, self-care, and stress management technologies, therefore, reflects the salience of models of subjectivity that prioritize the subject's ability to respond to and exercise control over their feelings in response to precariousness.

Consumers go so far as to wear devices that will help them monitor their productivity and self-care endeavors, optimizing their resources through incessant calculation. Are you making time for self-care? Do you take time to breath? Perhaps you need the Breathe app for your Apple watch, which "reminds you to take time to breathe every day." Your breathing is carefully monitored, tracked, and the data recorded. "You can track your [breathing] sessions with the Health app," and therefore monitor your self-care by holding yourself accountable for breathing every day, simply "tap Mindfulness, then tap the graph to see more" (Apple 2019).

Neoliberalism, then, is not just a set of economic policies or an economic system that facilitates intensified privatization, deregulation, and corporate profits, but also itself one form of governmentality in the Foucauldian sense of regulating the "conduct of conduct" (Foucault [1977] 1991, 100), that is, "a way to comprehend all *rationalised and calculated regimes of government, which conduct the conduct of (at least partially) free and multiple subjectivities through specific techniques and technologies, within particular fields of visibility*" (Death 2013, 764; italics original). *Governmentality* shapes human conduct among the population at large by calculated means in the name of securing the "welfare of the population, the improvement of its condition, the increase of its wealth, longevity, health, et cetera" (Foucault 1991, 100). Since power operates at a distance through governmentality, individuals are "not necessarily aware of how their conduct is being conducted or why, so the question of consent does not arise" (Li 2007, 275).

Discourses and discursive assemblages extend neoliberal governance and responsibilization, putting the burden on the individual for their position in society, by problematizing prevailing social practices and rendering certain modes of self-governing the "appropriate" responses (Burchell, Gordon, and Miller 1991; Miller and Rose 2008; Shamir 2008; and Hamann 2009). In other words, neoliberal discourses are accompanied by practices and technologies, such as programs or tools for "self-care," for individuals to work on themselves. As Kotsko puts it, "Neoliberalism makes demons of us all, confronting us with forced choices that serve to redirect the blame for social problems onto the ostensible poor decision making of individuals" (2018, 2–3). These neoliberal discourses provide "frames" that diagnose a problem situation, including an attribution of blame or causality, and a prognosis or intervention that suggests a solution (Lemke 2001). Hence, neoliberal discourses would diagnose as problematic any societal conditions that prevent individual agents from effectively assuming responsibility for their living outcomes. As to the prognosis, neoliberal discourses set out to reframe and reconfigure the conditions so that the fate of the neoliberal subject depend predominantly on their own choices, actions, and abilities. The consequences of the actions, therefore, are borne by the subject alone, who is also solely responsible for them (Lemke 2001, 201).

Wendy Larner argues that, in addition to a set of practices that facilitate the governing of individuals, neoliberalism is also a political discourse about the nature of rule. This form of governance transforms the logic by which institutions such as schools, workplaces, health and welfare agencies operate, while creating a new form of subjectivity, which "encourages people to see themselves as individualized and active subjects responsible for enhancing their own well-being" (Larner 2000, 13). Collective forms of action or well-being are eroded, and a new regime of morality comes into being, one that is linked to notions of self-reliance and efficiency, as well as to the individual's capacity to exercise autonomous choices. Harvey explains,

> A contradiction arises between a seductive but alienating possessive individualism on the one hand and the desire for a meaningful collective life on the other. While individuals are supposedly free to choose, they are not supposed to choose to construct strong collective institutions (such as trade unions) as opposed to weak voluntary associations (like charitable organizations). They most certainly should not choose to associate to create political parties with the aim of forcing the state to intervene in or eliminate the market. (Harvey 2005, 69)

This kind of neoliberal governmentality undoes notions of social justice, undermining efforts to resist the capitalist market, and pushing instead for privatization and the rights of the wealthy to be free of democratic government controls or limitations.

Finally, neoliberalism conflates "individualism and liberation," along with "consumption and activism" through its consumer-driven logic (Butler 2013,

46). A person is a good citizen when they engage in appropriate consumption. In other words, the shift to neoliberal governance, according to Jess Butler, entails "the development of discourses that emphasize consumer citizenship, personal responsibility, and individual empowerment" (2013, 41).

But liberation is only for the few. "The construction of a natural economy according to capitalist relations, and its appropriation for purposes of reproducing domination, is deep," as Donna Haraway puts it. "It is at the level of fundamental theory and practice, not at the level of good guys and bad guys" (Haraway 1991, 68). Neoliberal capitalism relies on the very differences it sows: it needs patriarchy, for example, to help keep the assembly lines running; women's work, which reproduces the labor market, is itself one of the most important but invisible forms of labor. It needs racial, religious, sexual, and ethnic conflict to fuel competition and create new markets, and it needs a global division of labor in order to maximize the output from the working classes.

The Neoliberal Spiritual Subject

At a conference on the "spiritual but not religious," one of my colleagues shared about how he had sat down with his young adult daughter so she could tell him about the dating app she and her friends were using. His daughter walked him through the long questionnaire she filled out in order to find "matches." They came across a ticked box indicating "spiritual but not religious." "What does that mean?" my colleague asked, pointing to the ticked box. "It means you want a lot of dates," his daughter replied.

The media of communication contemporary consumers use produce neoliberal spiritual subjectivities rather than simply reflect them, and they restructure social interactions rather than merely express them. Furthermore, neoliberal spirituality is not on the periphery of public life, but at its center. Self-describing as *spiritual* or *spiritual but not religious* is pervasive in contemporary urban society. Spiritual subjectivity not only has become a way of building industries and forging romantic partnerships, friendships, and communities, but also serves as cultural capital, so much so that commercial spirituality in the form of yoga, mindfulness, and sundry spiritual accoutrement has inundated mainstream and social media. It comes as little surprise that yoga is now a multi-billion-dollar industry. It is popular among high-profile celebrities and politicians; think of Oprah or the close-knit collaboration of Prime Minister of India Narendra Modi and celebrity yoga guru Baba Ramdev to promote yoga as a daily practice across India. Corporate figureheads are regularly celebrated for their spirituality; think of Apple's Steve Jobs, who is said to have had only one book on his iPad, that is, *Autobiography of a Yogi*. Everywhere, people are buying and selling spirituality as well as selling themselves and their companies under the rubric *spiritual*. The overlapping global wellness industry is currently a USD 4.3 trillion one. Wellness tourism is the fastest-growing sector, and Asia is the region where growth is happening most rapidly (Global Wellness Institute 2018).

We can examine the language and shifting discursive registers in mindfulness, yoga, and other spiritual commodities as symptomatic of a larger cultural phenomenon in which neoliberal spirituality serves as one mode of neoliberalism and neoliberalism as one mode of governmentality. Meeting the market's demand for spiritual accoutrement is big business from New York to Kyoto, London to Zurich, and Toronto to Delhi. From thousands of bodies spread across rubber mats in annual mass yoga demonstrations to countless individuals imbibing daily "detox" smoothies, spiritual subjectivity is frequently about consumer choices.

Those choices often revolve around self-care ritual management. Neoliberal spiritual subjects must decide, for example, how they exercise their bodies, enrobe their bodies, and feed their bodies. For that reason, this book is largely concerned with commodity consumption's entanglement with bodies. Is the body of the neoliberal spiritual subject merely a site of society's anxieties? Can it achieve transformative agency? Or is it merely reinscribing? Through delineating neoliberal spirituality and the ways it acts upon and produces social relations and subjects, I argue that agency is located in a number of areas, from spiritual consumers' bodies to their rituals and even their texts.

Bodies are not the only places where the dynamic agency of spirituality's performance is located. Agency is also located in texts. Catherine Bell asks about the agency of texts: "How does writing a text or depicting ritual in a text act upon the social relations involved in textual and ritual activities? Ultimately, how are the media of communication *creating* a situation rather than simply reflecting it; how are they restructuring social interactions rather than merely expressing them?" (1988, 369). In these questions, Bell encourages a shift in focus beyond understanding "texts-in-contexts" and toward analyses of texts as "dynamic *agents of change*" (Bell 1988, 369). A text's agency is most salient when it is analyzed as a physical object whose medium is integral to its message. In other words, agency derives from form, which is both performative and generative.

Neoliberal spirituality is an instance where neoliberal responsibilization is brought forth by discursive reframings in and through commodification, appropriation, and purchasing activities. A solid body of literature documents a range of areas where neoliberal responsibilization brings forth discursive reframings along these lines, including public sector management (du Gay et al. 1996, governing the unemployed (Dean 1995), education (Olssen and Peters 2001), healthcare (Doolin 2002), and consumer culture generally (du Gay 1996).

From transnational corporations selling yogaware to the attempts of states to mark dysfunctional citizens and make them undergo self-improvement for the sake of contributing to the system as efficiently and as quickly as possible, neoliberal spirituality is everywhere under the banners of self-care, personal growth, and liberation. The multivalence of its aims and values makes it easy to produce and sell, but it is not only meant to speed up adherents' efficient and cost-effective work; the objective is also to heal and liberate the individual. Spiritual products are considered cures for every ill, and, as a side effect, to make us better capitalists, better consumers, and overall, more effective and functional in the capitalist system.

Although insiders to neoliberal spirituality would debate what it means to experience radically liberated subjective experiences, and invoke concepts such as freedom, awakening, liberation, and so on, such ideas only find value within the shared, social space. With the rise of neoliberal spirituality, the adherents of which largely encourage individuals to focus on themselves and their own aspirations, spiritual commodities can be more easily popularized, circulated, and sold in the market because they dovetail, often seamlessly, with neoliberal capitalism.

The normative ethical framework for spirituality is another iteration—rather, various iterations—of neoliberal governmentality. Many studies (mentioned previously) take up the ways neoliberal forms of spirituality construct their appeal to (predominantly middle- and upper-class) consumers and the ways they represent new modes of governmentality that are increasingly commodified and reflect the interpellation of subjects as entrepreneurial agents in every area of life. These studies argue that spirituality has been marshaled to figure out ways to make us all work more so we can buy more commodities that are, effectively, meant to make us complacent.

Spirituality is undoubtedly increasingly entangled with neoliberalism, which mobilizes entrepreneurs to enhance the market value of spiritual products. The intervention I offer with regard to the neoliberal spiritual subject, however, complicates the view that spiritual neoliberal subjects are wantonly instrumentalist capitalists. I suggest that, from the entanglements of neoliberalism and spirituality, there emerges a new subject who acknowledges and even draws attention to the contradictions of neoliberalism and capitalism and the rampant problems they produce, yet, ultimately contains protest against it. Neoliberal spirituality, in other words, is a powerhouse for discourses that colonize and contain various counterdiscourses and forms of dissent in and through its commodities. Neoliberal spiritual subjects bring attention to the problems of neoliberal capitalism only to prevent protest against them by putting the onus for their resolution on themselves and their consumer choices.

Concentrating on the shifting discursive registers in yoga, mindfulness, or health foods industries gives us insight into the ways in which liberalism is mobilized to spawn a neoliberal spirituality as well as a new neoliberal spiritual subject. In an era of heightened anxiety and self-governance, the emphasis is increasingly placed on individuals to manage contemporary risks generated by economic deregulation, increased unemployment, environmental degradation, and so on. The neoliberal spiritual subject accepts full responsibility for their own wellness and self-care, which is increasingly predicated on crafting a felicitous balance of demands by means of spiritual and self-care commodities.

But why has neoliberal capitalism spawned a form of spirituality that gestures toward its own problems and contradictions, drawing, in other words, attention to the global crises to which it contributes? This new form of spirituality is yet another domain neoliberalism has colonized by producing its own variant. However, it simultaneously serves a particular cultural purpose: it hollows out the potential of mainstream liberalism to underscore the constitutive contradictions of liberal democracy, and in this way further entrenches neoliberal governmentality and an imperialist logic. Neoliberal spirituality, in fact, is a discursive modality that reproduces capitalism as the bastion of progressive liberal democracy. This discursive formation generates its own internal critique of contemporary society, yet inscribes and circumscribes the permissible parameters of that same critique.

Within this discursive formation, becoming a spiritual person is seen as the result of good consumer choices made by morally autonomous and efficacious citizens. Spirituality, then, is a central site of moral transformation and civic participation. Moreover, appropriate self-care management and the consumption of spiritual commodities are ways in which citizens both abate and ultimately reinforce anxiety. Spiritual industries require the strict ordering of the body and the mind, subjecting both to stringent routines and modes of discipline, hence all those yoga consumers co-opting the symbol of the "warrior." In other words, spiritual commodities are often disciplinary devices, part of a global culture that inflicts steep penalties for not being sufficiently "balanced." Ironically, the price of "work-life balance" is endless toil and self-monitoring. Teachers, gurus, entrepreneurs, and marketing teams begin from the assumption that there is something wrong with our bodily and mental capacities and that, through discipline and practice, a person can gain everything from self-control and inner peace to increased productivity and pleasure. Of course, these spiritual disciplines are available at conveniently located shopping malls or retail websites, can be managed through an app on your phone, or might be offered through and even incentivized by your employer. Google, for example, keeps on staff a "chief motivator," who specializes in "fitness of the mind," and Adobe's "Project Breathe" program allocates fifteen minutes per day for employees to "recharge their batteries." These amazing combinations of discipline and self-care compels adherents to exert effort in order to become better citizens, consumers, and employees.

Although associated with such pursuits as self-actualization, freedom, and empowerment, spiritual practices are also a form of labor: measured, timed, purchased, sold, and even financially incentivized. As Barbara Ehrenreich explains concerning wellness culture at large, "Whichever prevails in the mind-body duality, the hope, the goal—the cherished assumption—is that by working together, the mind and the body can act as a perfectly self-regulating machine" (2018, 89). This all requires an enormous amount of self-control and even pain. As a friend of mine reported following his first ever yoga class, "On the positive side of the ledger, I didn't black out. There was a moment when she asked us to bring attention to our inner thoughts, and all I could think was, 'Fucking pigeon! Fucking pigeon!' I swear that pose is a standing contradiction to the principle of ahimsa."[13]

---

[13] Personal communication with Brett Malcolm Grainger, June 22, 2018.

Neoliberal Spirituality and Religious Affiliation

Leaving affiliated religion for spirituality—and not all spiritual consumers abandon institutionalized religion or their religious affiliations—means leaving one neoliberal habitus for another. Institutions across all areas of life are increasingly informed by a market rationality and neoliberal governmentality. The rise of global spirituality is telling, not because it is distinct from religious institutions or other forms of institutional governance, but rather because it is consistent with them in spite of frameworks that assume spirituality serves as an "alternative" to or negation of mainstream religion or religion that happens in secular institutions (see also Jain 2014a and Lofton 2017).

Nevertheless, adherents of spirituality, by distinguishing themselves from religion, attempt to escape a common critique. One of the central premises underlying the idea that social critique is a "secular" exercise is the assumption of a break between reason and religion. The former is assumed to "unveil error," whereas the latter is its irrational opposite (Brown 2013, 2). This reflects an Enlightenment discourse in which the "rational, material, real, scientific and human" supplant religion (Brown 2013, 6–7). Adherents of spirituality seek to escape this critique by including the secular or making itself present in secular space. Employers' wellness, yoga, or mindfulness programs, for example, and neoliberal spiritual industries in general are not about empowering individuals in any democratic sense, but imposing new modes of governance and maintaining social hierarchies in which those who attain perfection through these modes are and remain at the top.

Under capitalism, however, this is precisely what is not supposed to happen. Instead, market competition is supposed to fix the problems of despotism and authoritarian abuse. Sure, in the old authoritarian churches and ashrams, where it was both a right and a duty for priests and gurus to exercise their authority, power structures were systematically upheld. Yet an analysis of neoliberal spirituality helps illuminate the fact that the capitalist classes, whether the kind sitting in "secular" yoga studios or "religious" churches, do not want a productive population with free time on their hands. The lesson that productivity is a moral value in itself, and that those who are not willing to submit to an intense routine of professional work, spiritual work, and self-care for most of their waking hours deserve nothing, is pervasive across neoliberal spaces, including spiritual ones.

Conclusion

In this book, I use the concept of neoliberal governmentality to provide a framework for analyzing spiritual entrepreneurs, consumers, corporations, and industries. I should, at the start, identify the limitations of this approach. First, it is broadly diagnostic and critical; it does not provide solutions to the problems of neoliberal capitalism. This is a project in cultural diagnostics without a prescribed cure or path forward. Second, it approaches subjectivity as constituted through particular power relations and forms of governance; given that, it does not help us understand consumers' motivations or intentions. Despite these limitations, I maintain that approaching the rise of spirituality through the lens of neoliberal governance provides a coherent and illuminating framework for analyzing the manner in which spirituality is constituted through rationalized and calculated practices, transcends public-private and domestic-international boundaries, and is made up of products and services that simultaneously rely on coercion and calls for freedom.

I argue that neoliberal spiritual commodities—for example, a T-shirt with PEACE LOVE YOGA appliquéd across the front—enact an often orientalist fantasy of enlightenment-ethics that demands individuals take responsibility for their conditions, make good consumer choices, and, consequently, achieve personal growth, wellness, liberation or "freedom," and even counter global crises, from poverty to climate change.

This religion of consumer culture is especially seductive in a world of ever-expanding global precarity and increased obligations and needs. Spiritual consumers are not unaware of or numbed to ecological destruction, injustice, and inequality; in fact, they are deeply troubled by them. But their real dissent and discomfort is expressed and then contained through spiritual consumption. This is a form of gestural protest against the devastating effects of neoliberal capitalist structures, a protest that stands in place of active protest, which would not cooperate with dominant social structures but would attempt to dismantle them. In and through its creative usage of neoliberal-orientalist tropes, the text of spiritual commodities contains subversion, privileging a theoretical model and ideological justification for a neoliberal ethic. The text of spiritual commodities provides the impetus, language, and justification for the bloody and fiery outcomes of neoliberal capitalism. Subversion is colonized through commodification.

For all of the peace and love it offers through yoga, health foods, mind-fulness, and countless other commodities, neoliberal spirituality plays a divisive, capitalist, and sometimes right-wing game that thrives on nostalgia about lost cultural norms, demarcating outsiders, questing after purity and policing morality, as well as on narratives about self-care, personal improvement, and the pursuit of freedom.

2

GOOD KARMA

Debating Authenticity in the Study of Neoliberal Spirituality

In 2012, the director of religion research at the Pew Research Center, Alan Cooperman, reported on the rise of the "nones," or the religiously unaffiliated, a group of Americans who are "less religious than the public at large."[1] "The rise of the nones" was one of the biggest stories coming out of the 2012 Pew research on religion and public life. According to the survey, about 18 percent of the US population identifies as spiritual, but not religious (SBNR), including 37 percent of the "nones," or unaffiliated, and only 15 percent of the affiliated. According to the Pew Forum, the nones think that religious institutions and organizations are too concerned with money, politics, rules, and power (Pew Research Center 2012).

There is every reason to believe that not only is the Pew Forum right about the rise of the unaffiliated among Americans, but also that this rise is happening globally. In India, for example, sociologists and anthropologists have noted that, as India has undergone economic liberalization over the past quarter-century, there has been an explosion in the market for spiritual products and resources, leading to increased detachment to traditional religious identities and practices. Studies among employees of the information technology sector, which has long been seen as the success story of India's economic liberalization measures, suggest possible reasons for an unprecedented growth of spirituality industries. For example, Carol Upadhya conducted research among IT professionals in Bengaluru in the early 2000s and found that they believed that "the price of their new-found wealth is the inability to maintain social and family relationships or even to have a meaningful existence outside of work" (2008, 66). In her reading "This lack of a

---

[1] In survey studies, the term "nones" is often used to describe people who indicate that they have no religion or do not affiliate with a particular religious institution. See, for example, Kosmin and Keysar 2009. See also Smith 2007.

Peace Love Yoga. Andrea R. Jain, Oxford University Press (2020). © Oxford University Press.
DOI: 10.1093/oso/9780190888626.001.0001

sense of social connection or community may account for the fact that a large number of IT professionals attend courses offering 'fast food' packaged spirituality, such as 'Art of Living'" (Upadhya 2008, n. 15). The research C. J. Fuller and John Harriss conducted among IT professionals in Chennai around the same time yielded similar insights, suggesting that nonresident Indians and resident middle-class Indians both seek to fill their "cultural vacuum" by turning to spiritual "godmen" and teachers (Fuller and Harriss 2005, 219).

A quick survey of the use of *spiritual* or *spirituality* in the global media attests to the increased demand for products branded this way, for example, *Spiritual* Gangster, or otherwise associated with "spiritual" lifestyles, values, or communities. Aside from the Pew research, there have been several studies over the last quarter-century that offer insight into what constitutes contemporary spirituality in the United States and Western Europe. To summarize some of their points, those who identify as SBNR do see wisdom in traditional religious ideas and practices. However, they contest claims to absolute authority and point to traditional religions' complicity in unfair power structures or hierarchies (e.g., patriarchy). They tend to valorize individualism, the freedom to exercise creative choice and expression, egalitarianism, a psychological or therapeutic approach to spiritual growth, and a seeker, quester, or consumer mentality. SBNRs are more educated than not, lean liberal politically, and, befitting a pluralistic culture, are eclectic. They see humans as basically good, reject a traditional community in favor of multiple and entangled forms, are on the whole pantheistic or monistic in outlook, and are likely to believe in reincarnation (see, for example, Zinnbauer and Pargament 1997; Bender 2010; Mercadante 2014; Heelas 2012; Pew Research Center 2012; Lopez 2012; McMahan 2008). Many scholars, as discussed in chapter 1, also equate the rise of spirituality with the desire for a distraction or escape from the dreadful social and environmental realities of neoliberal capitalism (see, e.g., Carrette and King 2005. See also Roof 1999; Lau 2000). All that said, as I will argue, neoliberal spiritualities constitute a wider spectrum of diversity, depth, and nuance than past research has claimed.

Returning to the Pew Forum, its research concludes that the nones are less religious than the public at large, but this bifurcation misses much about how people *do* what we often call *religion*. Problems with the Pew report include, for example, measuring how religious a person is based on their beliefs about God, heaven, and hell and whether they pray daily or attend religious services regularly. A Protestant notion of what it means to be religious, religion in terms of belief in God, prayer, and attendance at religious services, suggests that these efforts to quantify religion and spirituality distract from more nuanced understandings. Like much of the scholarship on spirituality, this buttresses popular representations, which are often based on the assumption that you are either religious, spiritual, or neither, but cannot be religious and spiritual. In other words, you are inside religion (and therefore outside spirituality), you are inside spirituality (and therefore outside religion), or you reject both.

Respondents to the Pew research were asked, not whether they believe that "optimism is a choice" or whether they "do yoga" and, if so, to what effect, but rather whether they "believe" in yoga "not just as exercise, but as a spiritual practice" (Pew Research Center 2012). In other words, the research did not attempt to capture religious beliefs the nones might hold even if they do not believe in God or heaven. Yoga practitioners, for example, often share beliefs, such as the idea that self-perfection entails a certain kind of optimization of the body (Jain 2014a, 104).[2] They ritually act on this belief in yoga studios and retreats across the world (Jain 2014a). Kathryn Lofton (2017), furthermore, has explained how people exercise their religion in many areas of consumer culture, basically wherever they articulate their desires and values, from the corporate culture of Goldman Sachs to the shows they watch on television. People can be religious in the consumer choices they make. As Mike Featherstone suggests, "If we focus on the actual use of commodities it is clear that in certain settings they can become de-commodified and receive a symbolic charge (over and above that intended by the advertisers) which makes them sacred to their users" (2007, 119).

These studies on religion in consumer culture testify to something the Pew Forum misses, that is, the ways neoliberal capitalism colonizes areas in which people exercise their religious lives, namely, through consumer choices. It is not the other way around, that religion is some timeless, placeless entity that exists outside of the socioeconomic context of neoliberal capitalism. As soon as we dismiss the assumption that religion exists separately from processes of commodification, it becomes readily apparent that self-identifying Christians, Hindus, and other religiously affiliated and nonaffiliated consumers embrace spiritual commodities, that it is not helpful, in other words, to think in terms of "spirituality" as separate from "religion."

[2] Several others have noted this nondualist worldview in other areas of metaphysical religion and consumer culture, including Turner 1997; Urban 2000, 2003; and Albanese 2007.

In this chapter, I challenge the debates over religious authenticity that pit the rise of commercial spiritualities against the fall or decline of religion. If capitalism could colonize feminism (see my discussion of neoliberal feminism in chapter 4), why not religions? No single ideology, culture, or tradition is immune. We have witnessed the creation of an endless variety of new jobs and industries in the past one hundred years, including the production and distribution of religious and spiritual goods. Entire spiritual industries and the corporations selling their goods have emerged and thrived. Rather than a decrease in religiosity among the public, we have seen the ballooning of religious areas of consumption.

What is often called *spirituality* is yet another form that religion assumes under certain historical, social, political, cultural, and economic conditions. This argument will likely make sense to readers already situated within my own academic discipline, that is, religious studies, but I recognize that to religious insiders, especially to adherents of a given tradition, questions of the true or authentic version of their tradition are quite salient. Often critiques of spirituality stem from those religious commitments, commitments to what is understood as religious orthodoxy or orthopraxy.

Nevertheless, the juxtaposition of spirituality against traditional religion is a framework that has a lot to do with the faulty tendency to make authenticity arguments, which end up letting certain religious complexes off the hook too easily, all while demarcating certain institutions and leaders as false religions or capitalist corruptions of "real religion." These forms of reductionism, that is, seeking causal explanations at the lowest level of complexity, do not accurately account for the ways neoliberal spirituality takes form and functions in contemporary society. Neoliberal spirituality, after all, is just one form of governmentality in a wide range of forms of power relations that operate in different religious contexts; no religious complex, in other words, is immune from context-specific power relations.

Reductive Cultural and Historical Approaches to Global Spirituality

There are plentiful instances where entrepreneurs and consumers frame spiritual commodities as effective ways to escape from the stress of everyday modern life without changing one's complicity in neoliberal capitalism.

Consider, for example, the following description of the Buddha as a corporate executive:

> As the founder of a start-up that grew into a worldwide organization, Buddha knew a lot about organizational life. We can learn many lessons from Buddha because his organization was built to last—it has stood the test of time. Buddha was a wise, insightful, skillful CEO—a brilliant leader whose legacy lives on today—not just in Buddhist organizations, but in the consciousness of enlightened leaders and mindful employees in the Western workplace as well. (Gallagher 2013)

It is explicit here that Buddhism can function as a strategy through which workers can become "mindful employees."[3] There is no doubt that the rise of spiritual industries includes countless examples of facile appropriation, where the idea of mindfulness or yoga is used to brand products and activities that promise things like peace, love, and productivity, all in the service of sustaining capitalist socioeconomics and generating desire for further consumption.

Mindfulness is a massive industry in which teachers train students to focus their attention on objects of sensory experience. Consider Nhat Hanh's *The Miracle of Mindfulness*. The text promises that mundane activities, such as washing the dishes or eating a piece of fruit, can become profound engagements with the world ([1975] 2016, 5–6). Nhat Hanh describes a world in which the intensity of sensory experience, cultivated through mindfulness, transforms experience into something more. In one famous passage, Nhat Hanh sits under a tree with his friend Jim and reminds his friend that he is getting carried away in a discussion about future plans and therefore not paying attention to the slices of tangerine that he is absentmindedly popping into his mouth.

> He popped a section of tangerine in his mouth and, before he had begun chewing it, had another slice ready to pop into his mouth again. He was hardly aware he was eating a tangerine. All I had to say was, "You ought to eat the tangerine section you've already taken." Jim was startled into realizing what he was doing.

---

[3] See Wilson 2016 for further discussion of the appropriation of mindfulness for the sake of furthering participation in capitalism.

It was as if he hadn't been eating the tangerine at all. If he had been eating anything, he was "eating" his future plans. ([1975] 2016, 5–6)

Nhat Hanh suggests that if you are going to eat a tangerine, focus entirely on eating the tangerine (5). Eating the tangerine, for Nhat Hanh, is akin to every other life experience. He goes so far as to suggest the same approach to eating a tangerine should be adopted in the face of great suffering, even in the face of a situation as challenging as imprisonment:

Later, when Jim went to prison for activities against the war, I was worried about whether he could endure the four walls of prison and sent him a very short letter: "Do you remember the tangerine we shared when we were together? Your being there is like the tangerine. Eat it and be one with it. Tomorrow it will be no more." ([1975] 2016, 6)

What happens when people train themselves to mindfully consume when they already live in a culture that encourages them to constantly consume and monitor their consumption? In the prescription that one should focus on each bite of a tangerine when eating it, rather than worry about the future— and, by extension, each moment of living under the tortuous conditions of imprisonment—mindfulness reflects the salience of models of neoliberal subjectivity that prioritize the individual subject's ability and responsibility to respond to and exercise control over precariousness.

With attention to these kinds of neoliberal spirituality, some studies have bracketed the question of whether spiritual commodities inspire or help consumers suppress their capacity for critical, ethical engagement with their unjust social and economic worlds. I will call these the "bracketing approaches."

My own previous study, *Selling Yoga* (Jain 2014a), serves as an example. In that book, I bracket the question of the yoga industry's responsibility for skirting the ethical problems with neoliberal capitalism, even though I argue that the yoga industry is, in part, a product of consumer culture, which emerged out of the socioeconomic complex of global market capitalism. I acknowledge that there are indisputable ethical problems with capitalism, given its dire consequences for society and the natural environment: "The ethical implications of market capitalism in the light of modern commitments to the individual (or human rights), the social world (or social justice), and the natural environment (or sustainability) are dire. In other words, if one's ethical agenda is a modern one that includes maintaining a stable global community of equal persons and a sustainable natural environment, market capitalism is rightfully perceived as an obstacle" (Jain 2014a, 115). I do not, however, offer a critique of the commodification of yoga that brings its problems to the surface, opting instead to focus on the argument that we should analyze and critique the yoga industry as a body of religious practice.

Jeff Wilson's study of the American mindfulness industry, in which mindfulness is framed primarily as a way to cope with the rapid pace of modern life (2014, 167), similarly brackets the question of spiritual entrepreneurs' and consumers' responsibility for skirting the ethical problems with the socioeconomic realities in which they are embedded. Nonetheless, he does explain how, like yoga consumers, mindfulness practitioners sometimes call for balanced or "conscious" consumption even though they fail to critique capitalism itself as a cause of suffering (Wilson 2014, 116), instead suggesting that each individual mindfulness practitioner positively contributes to the total compassion and awareness in society. Should a critical mass come to practice mindfulness, according to proponents of the practice, then positive effects will eventually be seen in society at large (Wilson 2014, 181). Changing society, in other words, means changing consumer behavior or mindful capitalism, mindful politics, and mindful consumption. None of this, however, calls for wealth redistribution or structural changes to socioeconomic systems (Wilson 2014, 183).

Wilson describes the very landscape that so worries critics of mindfulness. Mindfulness works as a coping mechanism that allows for ever more consumerism. Mindfulness lubricates the otherwise painful tensions of living in a capitalist society. Occasionally, Wilson hints at his own critique of what he seems to think of as inauthentic adaptations of mindfulness, for example, when he refers to "crypto-Buddhism" (2014, 3, 61, 94). Yet he withholds from offering a strong critique of mindfulness, instead suggesting:

> I am neither an advocate for nor an opponent of mindfulness. . . . The encounter of cultures always results in ironies, absurdities, innovations, conflict, exaggeration—and sometimes profundity as well. You will find them all here. Mindfulness is far too large and complex a phenomenon to be reduced to any simple statement or value judgment. (Wilson 2014, 10–11)

In his study of Buddhism and modernity, David L. McMahan (2008) also brackets the ethical problems of consumer capitalism and the mindfulness industry's complicity. McMahan refuses to judge as inauthentic popular practices:

> I know people who are not interested in being Buddhists or studying Buddhist philosophy who have really benefited from stripped-down mindfulness practice. So I'm not in a position to say, "Oh no, you shouldn't be doing this unless you can read Nagarjuna!" [Laughs.] Every culture has its elite religion and its more popular folk religion; it's almost like mindfulness is becoming a folk religion of the secular elite in Western culture. We'll see whether that's a good thing or a bad thing. (2008, 43)

Other studies do not bracket the question of whether spiritual commodities inspire or help consumers suppress critical, ethical engagement with neoliberal capitalism. Instead, they ask: Do spiritual consumers ignore their own complicity in the social and economic system in which they participate by escaping into the pleasure of their present experiences? Do spiritual commodities encourage the thoughtless and uncritical acceptance of things as they are? Does spirituality leave no room for political, philosophical, or religious subversion, critique, or reflection? Many scholars address these questions head on, and they answer yes, sometimes going so far as to pit capitalist spirituality against authentic religion. These arguments suggest that when religion is reduced to the spirituality of the individual, and subsequently sold back to the public in the marketplace of religious ideas (as yoga classes, self-help books, courses on meditation, and the like), the relevant ideas, practices, and symbols become powerless to provide meaningful resistance to capitalism, instead prioritizing the individual over social and political collectivities. Spiritual methods for "personal growth," "self-care," and "liberation" function, in other words, to accommodate consumers to capitalism, pacifying or numbing the anxiety and disquiet they might otherwise feel in the face of social realities. They are nothing more than the products of marketplace logic. I will call this the "rise of spirituality as religion's decline" approach.

Such critiques share with Slavoj Žižek the view that spiritual commodities— Žižek homes in on Buddhist ones—might be too effective at bringing about equanimity in the face of the fundamentally discomforting effects of life under capitalism. As the argument goes, the more successful spiritual commodities are at addressing individuals' anxieties and discomforts, the more likely they are to contribute to political apathy, and therefore the more dangerous they become. We sometimes hear echoes of this critique in public discourse, for example, in Antonio Damasio's (2017) *New York Times* review of Robert Wright's (2017) *Why Buddhism Is True: The Science and Philosophy of Meditation and Enlightenment*. Damasio explains:

> I also wonder if, for some individuals, the successful practice of meditation and the actual reduction of the anxieties of daily life are not more likely to induce equanimity regarding social crises than the desire to resolve those crises with inventive cultural solutions. Individual therapy and the salvation of society are not incompatible, but I suspect they can be easily uncoupled. (Damasio 2017)

For the most part, these critiques strongly criticize growing spiritual industries, not only for cultivating political apathy, but also because they equate these industries' rise with religious decline. Studies that adopt this framework tend to be problematic in three ways. First, they assume traditional religious complexes are somehow more aligned with a just and equal society and a healthy natural environment; that, in contrast to commodified spirituality, religion provides meaningful resistance to capitalism. Second, they fail to account for the ways commercial spiritualities, in and through their commodities, intersect with ethical complexes, value systems, and processes of valuation, ritual praxis, shared belief systems, and other qualities usually associated with religion. Third, they assume that spiritual commodities offer inauthentic representations of the religions from which they borrow, as if those religions have ever been static entities. This is based on the assumption that there is an original tradition to be preserved (e.g., some reified notion of Buddhism, Hinduism, or yoga), and consequently they produce nostalgic representations that are out of touch with historical reality, mirroring the essentialist arguments of consumers themselves. The mistaken assumption is that it is the role of critical scholarship to demarcate authentic "tradition" from "popular innovation." The resulting missteps include a tendency to see cultural products, such as yoga or mindfulness, as timeless uniform monoliths that exist in pure form independent of the polluting act of commodification.

There is much that is correct in these studies' analyses of spiritual industries. Entrepreneurs and corporations have ransacked other cultures in order to produce spiritual commodities that help (largely) white or middle- and upper-class consumers feel better, overcome stress, or defeat illness or aging—all while making a handsome profit—and many of the activities of these entrepreneurs and corporations reflect the neoliberal tendency to value "profit over people," as Chomsky (1999) puts it.

Yet these studies also lack nuance in certain ways, for example, suggesting that those who commodify spirituality are not sincere seekers as much as they are capitalists and imperialists—in other words, the spiritual industrial complex is merely religious cover for the exploitative operations of the capitalist marketplace or Western colonialism. They paint spiritual consumers as the passive victims of the manipulation and deception of capitalist agents, cultural dopes living in a permanent state of false consciousness. Spiritual commodities, in this view, are a mere fetish, meaning a fantasy that "tricks the fetish worshipper into believing that an 'inanimate object' will give up its natural character to gratify his desires" (Marx and Engels 1957, 22).

The study *Selling Spirituality* by Jeremy Carrette and Richard King (2005) represents this tendency to write off spiritual commodities as nothing more than the products of marketplace logic. The authors suggest that the yoga industry serves as an especially apt example of the capitalist takeover of religion. According to Carrette and King, commercial yoga separates yoga practice from its religio-philosophical, ascetic, and ethical dimensions. They criticize the yoga industry for what they perceive as its reliance on physical practice exclusively and at the loss of a "complete" lifestyle (Carrette and King 2005, 117–118; see also Lau 2000, 104). They suggest premodern yoga (as if that is one thing) features a selfless ethical agenda in service to society and the environment, offering an anachronistic vision that projects modern commitments to social justice and environmental sustainability onto past ethical systems (Carrette and King 2005, 116–120). Carrette and King lament that, by means of appropriating and commodifying practices, "Yoga essentially became a form of exercise and stress-relief to be classified alongside the other health and 'sports-related' practices and fads of the late twentieth century" (2005, 119). In short, under neoliberal capitalism, yoga is appropriated, commodified, and instrumentalized at the loss of its real, authentic teachings.

Offering a similar analysis, in an essay titled "Is Mindfulness Buddhist? (and Why It Matters)," Robert Sharf addresses the separation of mindfulness meditation from Buddhist renunciatory practice, which requires practitioners "to opt out of family ties and worldly pursuits, and opt into an alternative, communal, celibate, and highly regulated lifestyle."[4] Today,

---

[4] Gregory Schopen (1997) has called into question scholars' exaggerations about the degree to which historical monks actually separated themselves from their families. One might make the

"Rather than enjoining practitioners to renounce carnal and sensual pleasure, mindfulness is touted as a way to more fulfilling sensual experience" (2016, 149). Sharf frames mindfulness advertising as a fetishization of mindfulness practice, freeing consumers to immerse themselves even more deeply in consumer culture and its pleasures.

Another recent example of this kind of critique, Peter Doran's *A Political Economy of Attention, Mindfulness and Consumerism* (2017), simplifies the consumption of mindfulness and reifies the traditions from which mindfulness consumers appropriate. Doran argues that commercial mindfulness serves simply as support for individuals' struggle to comply with pressures to enhance productivity in the capitalist workplace and has been stripped of its so-called ethical and contextual roots in Buddhism, presumably authentic Buddhism (whatever that is). Real Buddhist scholarship (as if that is one thing), according to Doran, differentiates between right mindfulness and wrong mindfulness. Right mindfulness, he argues, must be practiced with attention to the operations of power and context (again, an anachronistic envisioning of past religious traditions) if it is to lead to liberating insights. "McMindfulness," as Doran and others call commercial mindfulness, does not do that and is therefore wrong mindfulness (see also, e.g., Ronald Purser's 2019 book by that title).

The mindfulness industry is the most common target of these kinds of critiques, which generally argue that commodified meditation too often replaces intellectual or ethical complexes (Cox 1992; Braun 2013; Purser and Loy 2013; Carmody 2015; Zeidan 2015; Huntington 2015; Purser, Forbes, and Burke 2016; Repetti 2016; Wallis 2016; and Doran 2017). According to these studies of mindfulness, the industry constitutes a retreat from confronting the real causes of suffering:

> *Sati* . . . valorizes a quality of mind that remains perpetually "present," uncontaminated by "past" and "future" . . . it is a condition of undistracted myopia whereby attention is "immersed in the body." In its modern-day incarnation, it is celebrated as a condition of ostensibly non-judgmental and non-reactive "mindfulness" directed toward "just this moment" . . . this

same argument about vast generalizations concerning whether or not monks engaged in "worldly pursuits."

condition of mind is obviously neither feasible nor desirable. (Wallis, Pepper, and Steingass 2013, 146–147)

Such assessments condemn the prescription that mindfulness consumers engage with the world nonjudgmentally, without the influence of conceptual prejudgments, instead suggesting that it is problematic to cultivate such a nonjudgmental attitude in which critical thinking is shunned in favor of the peaceful or joyful appreciation of present experiences.

> The cult of mindfulness in Western Buddhism . . . serves as a blissful retreat from and compensation for a world we must always accept exactly as it is. Where once our fantasy could be a wish for unalienated labor, for the capacity to have meaningful work to do in the world . . . now we can only fantasize a retreat into infancy. (Wallis, Pepper, and Steingass 2013, 74–75)

> We are left with the logic . . . in which our thought-free contemplation of a mystical and ineffable experience can stabilize our experience of the world, but only by denying us any capacity to change it for the better. (30)

C. W. Huntington Jr. (2015) addresses the problems of mindfulness head on, arguing that it is a problem when contemporary therapists and authors, like Mark Epstein, prescribe mindfulness as a therapeutic tool.[5] Therapeutically minded teachers advocate using mindfulness to strengthen the personal self and "help make it fully functional in the world" (Huntington 2015, 632).

> The idea that the form of attention characteristic of vipassanā practice needs to be—or even can be—"put to good use" in the service of the personal self is the root error that infects much of the literature on Buddhism and psychotherapy. (638)

In contrast to psychotherapy, what Huntington calls "orthodox" Theravada vipassana programs take their goal to be the realization of the total absence of any such "personal self." By striving for healthy, functional selves,

---

[5] Huntington focuses on mindfulness within the broader context of Theravada vipassana, or "insight," meditation. He describes how the Burmese tradition of vipassana that emerged from the teachings of Ledi Sāyadaw adopted mindfulness as the primary technique for carrying out insight. He parses mindfulness as "closely focused observation" (2015, 627–628). Huntington finds fault with contemporary instructors who have learned mindfulness from this tradition but have repurposed its goals.

Buddhist-inspired psychotherapy is actually in conflict with the Theravada aim of liberation from suffering. After delineating the differences between Theravada-Buddhist and psychoanalytic-Buddhist goals, Huntington concludes that the latter is simply "narcissistic."[6]

Studies critical of such prescriptions extend Slavoj Žižek's (2001, 2005) critique of Western appropriations and commodifications of Buddhism (also discussed in chapter 1). In Žižek's argument, Buddhism serves as a palliative to Western consumers, promising the individual an escape—a therapeutic distance or coping mechanism—into the experience of the present moment. Such an escape allows them to imagine themselves as separate from the normal demands of everyday life and disconnected from the social and economic relations of global capitalist exchange. Žižek offers a referendum on commercial mindfulness, which he frames as a space in which "Buddhist subjects" nurture the feeling that they are removed from the hustle of everyday life within capitalism. In this way, they create a false inner distance from capitalism. In Žižek's words,

> No wonder Buddhism can function as the perfect ideological supplement to virtual capitalism: It allows us to participate in it with an inner distance, keeping our fingers crossed, and our hands clean, as it were. (2005)

With the inner distance from neoliberal capitalism cultivated through meditation, mindfulness practitioners can become indifferent to the grueling pace, competition, alienation, and destructive realities of the dominant socioeconomic and ideological systems. Due to its palliative power, meditators feel themselves to be the ones who maintain "mental sanity":

> The "Western Buddhist" meditative stance is arguably the most efficient way for us to fully participate in capitalist dynamics while retaining the appearance of mental sanity. . . . "Western Buddhism" is such a fetish. It enables you to fully participate in the frantic pace of the capitalist game while sustaining the perception that you are not really in it; that you are well aware of how worthless this spectacle is; and that what really matters to you is the peace of the inner Self to which you know you can always with-draw. (Žižek 2001b, 15)

---

[6] For a more polemical take on the narcissism of contemporary mindfulness from within the field of psychology, see Joiner 2017.

Buddhism and mindfulness, in this view, are a fetish that consumers choose in order to escape reality (Žižek 2001b).

Attention to the fetishization of meditation extends Žižek's analysis of the strategies of marketing and consumption at large, which impose salvific or liberatory meanings onto mundane objects, therefore spiritualizing all types of consumer activities (Žižek 1989, 50–53). For example, in contemporary advertising, a product is always promised to be more than itself. A bottle of Coke is not simply a sugary drink but also a promise of a special experience (Žižek 2013), for example, when Coca-Cola advertisements promise in their slogans, "Can't Beat the Real Thing," "Open Happiness," or "Life Begins Here."

Žižek's analysis of contemporary consumer culture raises suspicion of commercial Buddhism and its ubiquitous claims to provide access to the "more," the "greater" and the "fullness" of mindful experience (see, e.g., Kabat-Zinn 1994, 6–7). Mindfulness, including Thich Nhat Hanh's version, emphasizes nonjudgmental engagement with our present experiences, whether they are positive or negative ones, suggesting that mindfulness leads to "reality" itself: "If we're really engaged in mindfulness while walking along the path to the village, then we will consider the act of each step we take as an infinite wonder, and a joy will open our hearts like a flower, enabling us to enter the world of reality" (Nhat Hanh ([1975] 2016, 12). The goal is to access the authentic experience of reality in the present moment, a goal that many worry discourages critical reflection on the social conditions and structures that led to that moment. Is Nhat Hanh fetishizing the present? In Žižek's view, just like the strategies through which marketers encourage consumers to choose their brand of soda, Nhat Hanh invests the present with excess value.

Not all scholarship on spirituality offers polemics in the style of Žižek. Nevertheless, much of the scholarship echoes a form of reductionism that sees neoliberal spirituality as mere commodification in service to profit and as lacking many of the characteristics of traditional religions. We see similar attempts to use historical arguments to make cases against the authenticity of neoliberal yoga. The postural practice millions of consumers around the world spend money on every day is a combination of premodern asana (postures), regional Indian bodybuilding and wrestling exercises, German physical culture, Swedish gymnastics, Western metaphysical religion, and modern dance (Alter 2004; de Michelis 2004; Singleton 2010; Syman 2010; Foxen 2017; Foxen 2019) that "came into existence in a context where its goals stood at a precarious intersection between the physical and the metaphysical" (Foxen 2017b, 497). Given the complexity of its recent history, much less its premodern history, there has been great confusion and debate about its origins and authenticity, not only among practitioners and detractors, but also among scholars.

On the one hand, due to its rising cultural and economic capital, many claim yoga's origins for Hinduism and India, putting it at the forefront of Hindu identity and describing it as India's gift to the world (see chapter 5). Consequently, the daily practice of surya namaskar, the most popular sequence of modern postural yoga, is now compulsory in thousands of schools across India, the Hindu American Foundation has been promoting its "Take Back Yoga" campaign since 2010 (see Jain 2014a, 130–157), and, in 2014, the United Nations General Assembly declared every June 21 International Day of Yoga (in chapter 5, I discuss at length how Indian prime minister Narendra Modi inaugurated the event in Delhi by leading thirty-five thousand civilians through a series of yoga poses). Modi, a member of the nationalist Bharatiya Janata Party, is a vociferous proponent of yoga, not only as a health regimen, but also as a marker of Indian—and Hindu—identity.

On the other hand, scholars also debate yoga's origins and authenticity. Mark Singleton and Jean Byrne suggest that critical scholarship is the only way of distinguishing "tradition," which they admit is itself a fragmented and problematic category, from "popular innovation," before suggesting that even in this context "it might be more helpful to think of yogas, with a multiplicity of definitions and interpretations, rather than of a single yoga that we would seek to define and circumscribe" (2008, 5). Nonetheless, Jason Birch, Mark Singleton, James Mallinson, and others produce scholarship concerned with delineating the ancient "roots" of modern postural yoga for scholars and practitioners alike, without critical reflection on their own scholarly, gendered, and racial positionalities and how those might shape a particularized story of yoga's roots (see, e.g., Birch 2018; and Mallinson and Singleton 2017).

Returning to studies that broaden the scope of their critique to include spirituality at large or, even broader, the religiously unaffiliated, in 2016, director of religion research at the Pew Research Center Alan Cooperman visited my institution in Indianapolis to deliver a talk on the rise of the nones and why it is "a bad thing." He cited Pew data suggesting that "highly religious Americans" are more likely to volunteer and make donations or be involved in community groups and civil society (Cooperman 2016). Of course, his data on the "highly religious" measured religiosity in narrow terms by the standards of my discipline, religious studies. The study, for example, fails to ask whether the Americans who do not attend a church are active in other close-knit groups, such as yoga communities, book clubs, or community gardens. Many spiritual consumers are united into communities that structure their time and behavior differently than church or mosque communities. Furthermore, not everyone benefits equally from all types of donations and involvement in community groups and civil society, so why assume this behavior improves society? Are the Americans who believe in God and regularly attend church services more likely to volunteer their time or money, but on the campaigns of homophobic policymakers, for example? If so, would that constitute "volunteer" work and "donations" that would not benefit society at large? For these reasons, I did not find Cooperman's conclusions compelling and instead saw them as constituting the kind of scholarship that bifurcates between authentic religion and corrupt spirituality or non-religion.

All of the studies I have discussed offer reductive readings of formulations of spiritual commodities in the context of consumer culture by contrasting them with practices of more traditional religious communities or past ones (e.g., Sharf 2016; Huntington 2015; Carrette and King 2005; Singleton and Byrne 2008) or, in most cases and in the style of Žižek, reducing them to a form of escape from the ugly realities of contemporary capitalist society (e.g., Wallis 2016; Carrette and King 2005; Doran 2017). They attempt to affirm the value of these practices, but only according to their own standards for determining authentic practice. Critics typically note that those who commodify spirituality are not sincere seekers of religious ends as much as they are capitalists and imperialists seeking power, profit, and productivity—in other words, the spiritual industrial complex is merely spiritual cover for the exploitative operations of the capitalist marketplace or Western colonialism. Spirituality, in these analyses, does not represent a *real* or *authentic* religious complex. These are their assessments even though much of this kind of scholarship reads spirituality contra to those who describe themselves or the products they buy as *spiritual*. Alternatively, insiders often see their practices as ways of controlling desire as a sine qua non to self-actualization, self-optimization, liberation, or self-care and who locate their practices in complex "ethical and contextual roots," for example, ancient Indian or Buddhist origins.

Rejecting the Authenticity Debates

My doubts about the historical, sociological, and cultural-critical works I have outlined are not based on the critiques many of them offer of neo-liberalism, capitalism, colonialism, or imperialism. I share them. Such critiques are right to illuminate the ways power dynamics are at play in all acts of appropriation and commodification. Many such critics correctly observe that spiritual entrepreneurs and corporations ransack cultures and traditions that are not their own in order to produce commodities that help middle- and upper-class consumers feel better, as if they have overcome and defeated stress, illness, or aging—all while making a handsome profit. Spiritual appropriations and commodifications are frequently based on cultural stereotypes, and especially middle- and upper-class or white spiritual entrepreneurs and consumers appropriate from other cultures and traditions for their own utilitarian, pleasure-driven, or profit-driven purposes and reflect a colonial logic—extract from colonized people what materials and ideas are profitable without critical reflection on the history of colonialism and racism and concerted actions aimed at extending privilege or benefit to those who are the conduits.

Although such critiques are right to illuminate the ways power dynamics are at play in all acts of appropriation and commodification, I fear they often miss a lot about the nature of these activities. It is too simple to suggest that neoliberal spirituality is merely made up of commodities, easily bought and sold, and that the people buying those commodities are isolated consumers interacting with the world through consumption alone and disconnected from actual communities, or that the spiritual people are not so much seekers as consumers (as if these are fundamentally different ways of being in the world), duped by a historical narrative tying their contemporary practices to ancient roots or interested in little (and sometimes nothing) more than escaping the realities of capitalism, immersing themselves in pleasure, or achieving that coveted "yoga butt." Although it is worthwhile, in my view, to criticize the political consequences of practicing commercialized forms of yoga, mindfulness, or other appropriated practices in capitalist society, it is not helpful to question its instantiations in the present by comparing them to practices of the past or to assume all spiritual consumers hold such simplistic aims as pleasure or escape from the reality of life under neoliberal capitalism. As Featherstone explains, commodities can "receive a symbolic charge (over and above that intended by the advertisers) which makes them sacred to their users" (2007, 119).

The more illuminating approach, then—as opposed to the reduction of neoliberal spirituality to market activities or fetishization—is to avoid generalizations or assumptions about consumers' motivations and intentions as well as normative claims about authenticity or legitimation and instead analyze them as religious consumers whose behaviors relate to their values, all while embedded in the expansion of neoliberalism, consumer capitalism, and imperialism.

When we assess consumer spiritualities not as a takeover or replacement of real religion, but as a modern manifestation of religion, the following becomes apparent: on the one hand, the appropriations and commodifications found in neoliberal spirituality are frequently based on cultural stereotypes; many spiritual consumers appropriate from an exotic Other for their own utilitarian or profit-driven purposes, which often reflect a colonial logic (see, e.g., Rowell 1995; Young and Brunk 2012; and Matthes 2016). Yet what comprises spiritual perfection, union, or liberation for one community might consequently marginalize, disenfranchise, or oppress another. In other words, appropriations and commodifications are always in negotiation with power, sometimes in ambiguous and complicated ways.

Furthermore, when observers assume that there is an original, static tradition to be preserved, they produce yet another representation that is out of touch with historical reality, instead mirroring in problematic ways the essentialist arguments of spiritual consumers themselves. At the center of much of what I would characterize as an anxiety about the appropriation and commodification of religious ideas and practices lies the assumption that the nature of spiritual commodities drastically departs from traditional premodern roots. These concerns and anxieties result in investigations that reify religions in ways that simplify them and, ironically, make them easier to contain, own, discuss, or sell. Hence, it is more constructive to focus on understanding how appropriating and commodifying practices privilege certain voices while silencing others than to attempt to demarcate the ways they depart from what is perceived as the authentic or original tradition.

In other words, it is not the scholar's place to establish or verify claims about origins or authenticity. It is, however, the scholars' place, in my view, to acknowledge those claims among spiritual subjects, to analyze them as religious claims, and, in the study of religion in contemporary society, to critique their relationship to the economic and social machinations of the dominant culture of consumer capitalism. Therefore, rather than use a yard-stick derived from a certain instantiation of a particular religious tradition to measure the authenticity of spirituality or spiritual commodities, the current book uses a framework that reflects socialist and feminist values to measure its political workings.

My doubts about the adequacy of previous studies are with the extent to which this kind of polemical or reductive scholarship is "verificationist" in epistemology. In the case of scholarship on neoliberal spirituality, I mean to say that it has largely been concerned, whether implicitly or explicitly, with answering such questions as to what extent spiritual commodities, con-sumers, entrepreneurs, and corporations are authentically yogic, Buddhist, or religious at all. They seem to root themselves in the question, "Do appro-priating and commodifying activities erase any semblance of distinctively yogic, mindfulness, Buddhist, or other religiousness?" Here, I am following David Scott's argument concerning the *verificationist agenda* of scholarship on African diasporic religion. In response to "such questions as whether or not or to what extent Caribbean culture is authentically African; and whether or not or to what extent Caribbean peoples have retained an au-thentic memory of their past," Scott suggests that we refuse to address such questions since they represent an epistemologically and politically problem-atic "verificationist agenda" that arrogates the authority to demarcate what does or does not constitute authentic traditions (1999, 107–108).

The verificationist agenda is compelling only given the validity of its con-ceptual premise, namely that pasts are such as can be identified in their au-thenticity and represented in their transparency; and given a commitment to the ideological assumption that the task of critical scholarship includes corroborating narrations of the past. I reject both of these premises.

The study of neoliberal spirituality (and religion at large) should give up altogether what Scott (in his address to scholars of African diasporic reli-gion) describes as "the ideological desire to supply a foundational past and the sustained epistemological preoccupation with verification and corrobo-ration that depends for its plausibility upon the seeming oppositional virtue of that desire" (1999, 108). Whereas one of my goals in Selling Yoga was to raise suspicion about precisely this virtue (there, I treat yoga as a perpetually malleable category, consistently transforming to adapt to its context and, al-though constituting reality for its practitioners, having no authoritative or-igin point or set of roots), my goal here is to question the moral purchase it claims and, following Scott, encourage attention to the ideologies, discourses, and practices within which identities, such as *yoga* or *mindfulness*, are "animating, constitutive figures" that are deployed within "situated networks of power and knowledge" in order to produce certain types of moral communities (1999, 108).

As Scott argues concerning the study of the African diaspora, both the view that seeks to confirm continuity with ancient traditions and the one that seeks to deny or disconfirm it depend on "a single epistemic-ideological problem-space, one defined by the historically conditioned salience of the tension between the (very often racist) liberal-rationalist and the (very often emancipatory) cultural-nationalist construction (or, following V. Y. Mudimbe [1988], "invention") of Africa as an object of dispute" (1999, 109). We have occupied ourselves for too long with authenticating "origins" in methodologically questionable ways without realizing that the very trope of "origins" often encapsulates a variety of projects, beyond a historically naive proof of provenance. As discursive objects, "origins" are fundamentally emergent in nature and can be studied ethnographically as they arise, perform their moral and political work, and, at times, make way for what John Pocock (1962) usefully calls rival "past-relationships" (Palmié 2013, 46). To shift our focus away from the naive empiricism or analytical reductionism that has dominated the study of neoliberal spirituality's social and cultural formations over the last quarter-century is thus very much a task at hand for a study capable of critical engagement not only with the conceptual foundations of our discipline, but with the effects it has wrought to varying degrees on the spiritual or religious formations it purports to render.

What then of those practices and projects transnational actors like mindfulness propagator Nhat Hanh or global yoga guru Pattabhi Jois have pursued? Why do their results look so stunningly "Buddhist" or "Indian" to us, and, for that matter, anyone else who cares about such matters? Were they (and whether they knew it or not) the "carriers" of Buddhism or yoga, whose outward symptomatology cannot escape our diagnostic gaze—and, besides that, is proudly displayed under that category by their spiritual heirs practicing what is today uncontroversially called Buddhism-derived meditation or Hinduism-derived yoga? Or did their agency set into motion a train of cultural developments we might be better off studying in their proper social, economic, and historical contexts rather than referring them to ready-made solutions suggested by the historical trait-lists of a timeless Buddhism or Hinduism or yoga sprung from the latter-day historical, anthropological, as well as elite native imaginations?

It is not the scholar's place to establish or verify authenticity claims, demarcate pure and contaminated traditions, or locate the sui generis center of religious complexes. It is the scholar's place to acknowledge those claims and strategies among their subjects, to analyze them as religious claims with soteriological aims (bracketing theological questions regarding whether or not the ends are "real" or whether adherents actually achieve those ends), and to critique their subjects as engaged in collective strategies to preserve social systems, thus, in the case of neoliberal spirituality, the economic and social machinations of neoliberal capitalism. In other words, the more illuminating approach—as opposed to the reduction of neoliberal spirituality to market activities or fetishization—is to take spiritual consumers seriously as religious agents and simultaneously evaluate them, and even critique them, as complicit in the expansion of neoliberalism and market capitalism in and through their institutions and practices. As Stuart Hall articulates so well, "The notion of the people as a purely *passive*, outline force is a deeply unsocialist perspective" (1981, 186). In contrast, a Marxist socialist perspective emphasizes the importance of agency, which is exercised through critiques and diagnoses of unequal social structures, solidarity building, educational campaigns, and, ultimately, revolution. The field of culture is, therefore, more like a battlefield:

> Cultural domination has real effects—even if these are neither all-powerful nor all-inclusive . . . there is a continuous and necessarily uneven and unequal struggle, by the dominant culture, constantly to disorganize and reorganize popular culture; to enclose and confine its definitions and forms within a more inclusive range of dominant forms. There are points of resistance; there are also moments of supersession. This is the dialectic of cultural struggle. In our times, it goes on continuously, in the complex lines of resistance and acceptance, refusal and capitulation, which makes the field of culture a sort of constant battlefield. A battlefield where no once-for-all victories are obtained but where there are always strategic positions to be won and lost. (Hall 1981, 187)

When we see neoliberal spiritual subjects as religious agents, we are able to see the ways spiritual entrepreneurs and corporations work as religious leaders and institutions respectively toward containing dissent against the reigning social order and therefore maintaining the status quo. As is pervasive in the history of religions generally, the forms opposition can take shift

the language of resistance, subversion, and critique away from actual political struggles and acts and into the plane of disengaged gestures and symbols.
In many areas of contemporary culture, including spirituality, a neoliberal-
individualist understanding of "progress" largely stands in place of antihierarchical, socialist understandings of revolution. Nevertheless, the "dialectic
of cultural struggle" is in the character of very commodities themselves.

Conclusion

Apart from the verificationist agenda of much of the scholarship on neoliberal spirituality, there are also other problems, including the tendency
to reduce them to the following: appropriation or co-optation of otherwise
ancient wisdom; commodification of fast-food (e.g., "McMindfulness")
practices designed to fulfill hedonistic or utilitarian purposes; and mere
numbing devices for the pacification of angst that might otherwise cultivate
protest against conditions of exploitation, dehumanization, and assaults on
democracy. Neoliberal spirituality can be all of those things, but it is also
made up of modes of ritual and discursive agency. The people spending
their money on mindfulness, yoga, and Ayurvedic cosmetics are not passive victims of the dominant culture. I suggest we can better understand the
apparent conflicts and contradictions of the practices and commitments of
neoliberal spiritualities by approaching them as constituting both entanglements with neoliberal capitalism and the problems of cultural appropriation
and, in and through their commodities, bodies of religious practices, as well
as modes of resistance and subversion (even if merely gestural).

Analyzing spiritual commodification in terms of how religious institutions
invest power in authoritative voices (a particular guru, teacher, or tradition), it becomes clear that, stripped of that authority, practices from detox
regimens to the "adjusts" of a yoga teacher often amount not to hedonistic
immersions in pleasure, but to violent and sometimes downright abusive
rituals. Accustomed to the marketing endeavors of neoliberal spirituality,
consumers worry that anything less than expensive products associated
with ancient, credible authority will leave them at risk. Entrepreneurs use
these expectations to drive up demand and prices, and consumers, afraid and
intimidated, submit. The ways spiritual consumers assent to such spending
fit into a broader neoliberal-capitalist culture of arduous self-improvement
and neglect of social justice.

It is undeniable that spirituality industries are deeply religious—denial of illness and death, perennial concerns of religion, after all, lie at their center. We might say, then, that neoliberal spirituality is not just religious, but the paragon of religion. It just so happens that multiple vast industries rose to capitalize on it. My position, which rejects any and all claims to authenticity, lends itself, I hope, to the study of spiritual commodities in a way that illuminates the underlying social forces that produce them. From this perspective, we might treat neoliberal spirituality not as a case to be judged in terms of authenticity, but as a window into the dangerous neoliberal imagination.

3

NAMASTE ALL DAY

Appropriating and Commodifying the Ancient, Exotic, and Evocative

In the previous chapter, I discussed studies that paint spiritual consumers as the passive victims of the manipulation and deception of capitalist agents, cultural dopes living in a permanent state of false consciousness, and spiritual commodities as a mere fetish. Yet ultimately, as Stuart Hall articulates so well, "The notion of the people as a purely *passive*, outline force is a deeply unsocialist perspective" (1981, 186). In contrast, culture is more like a battlefield in which there is a continuous and unequal struggle by the dominant culture, "to disorganize and reorganize popular culture; to enclose and confine its definitions and forms within a more inclusive range of dominant forms. There are points of resistance; there are also moments of supersession. This is the dialectic of cultural struggle" (Hall 1981, 187).

I suggest we think of spiritual commodities as straddling the "lines of resistance and acceptance" in their subversions. The gestural character of spiritual consumers' resistance does not obliterate their agency. The consumer embraces the alternative, even revolutionary, values that spiritual commodities allude to, even if they function as superficial points of resistance. Therefore, choosing spiritual commodities that represent revolutionary, egalitarian, environmentally friendly, or authentically ancient values can best be understood as a form of *gestural subversion*. By gestural subversion, I mean an anticapitalist counterdiscourse widely disseminated in popular culture—these are, for example, frequently present in Hollywood movies or television when the protagonist who has been subjected to racism, sexism, or class oppression rises to the top, thanks, of course, to their entrepreneurial attitude and robust individualism. This is a by-product of *capitalist realism*, the dominant idea that there are no viable alternatives to capitalism (see Fisher 2009, 16–19). In other words, neoliberal spirituality, despite its resistant or subversive gestures, is domesticated to dominant ideologies, particularly a neoliberal rationality. Spiritual commodities engender subversions, though

Peace Love Yoga. Andrea R. Jain, Oxford University Press (2020). © Oxford University Press.
DOI: 10.1093/oso/9780190888626.001.0001

most often they gesture toward alternative values, rather than cultivate, enable, or embody political action.

Another way to put this is that consumption of spiritual commodities entails a misrecognition whereby the consumer thinks that buying the products of a particular brand name challenges certain problems the world faces under global capitalism, in a way akin to how an American consumer paying for a yoga class with a teacher who has traveled and studied in India might assume that class is closer to "authentic yoga" than one offered by a teacher who has only studied domestically, or a consumer purchasing Patanjali Ayurved NAT-URAL products might think that its instant noodles are more healthy than the noodles of other popular brands selling mass-produced products.

The authoritarian dictates and marketing strategies of spiritual corporations serve to vent attitudes of resistance while simultaneously containing them and managing desire. The spiritual corporation, then, is best understood as a religious institution that extends neoliberal governmentality through the commodities it sells. The neoliberal discourses around those commodities frame a problem, including the attribution of blame or causality for that problem, and a prognosis or intervention or set of strategies that offers a solution (Lemke 2001). The discourses of resistance, in other words, are accompanied with practices for self-care through which individuals work on themselves, not on dismantling oppressive economic or social structures. Neoliberal discourses, therefore,

> diagnose as problematic such societal conditions that prevent individual agents from effectively assuming responsibility for outcomes to themselves. As to the prognosis, the solution offered, neoliberal discourses set out to re-frame and re-configure the conditions so that the fate of the agents—and the consequences of their undertakings—would depend predominantly on their own decisions, actions and abilities" (Pyysiäinen, Halpin, and Guilfoyle 2017, 226).

The neoliberal subject, therefore, bears sole responsibility for the consequences (Lemke 2001, 201). "A paradigmatic example of such a reconfiguration through neoliberal discourse(s) would be the 'economization' of the state and societal institutions, whereby agents' previous identities—citizen or civil servant, for example—would be reframed with equivalents from the economic sphere—such as 'consumer' or 'entrepreneur'" (Pyysiäinen, Halpin, and Guilfoyle 2017, 219, citing Shamir 2008 and McNay 2009).

Discursive reframing is the mechanism for enrolling consumers in self-governance and neoliberal responsibility-taking. The operation of neoliberal governance and responsibilization, however, is "ultimately based on a positive, 'productive' form of power and government rationality, characteristic of societal rule under 'advanced liberalism'" (Pyysiäinen, Halpin, and Guilfoyle 2017, 219). In his analytics of power, Foucault (1980) formulates the productive form of power, also called "biopower," which is believed to exert a positive and productive influence, and thus is distinct from historically earlier, coercive, and negative forms of "sovereign" and "juridico-discursive" power (Pyysiäinen, Halpin, and Guilfoyle 2017, 219). In the context of neoliberal spirituality, this is all to say: if you are not performing spirituality (the right way), thinking spiritually (the right way), or eating spiritually (the right way), then there is something wrong with you as an individual, and you must make better (consumer) choices.

Spiritual consumers are known for their individualistic self-understanding and their shopping cart approach to different cultures and religious traditions in order to meet personal goals. Spiritual entrepreneurs and corporations are known for skillfully commodifying and selling spirituality as a set of tools for reaching those goals. Neoliberal spiritual tools feature evocative objects, images, or ideas, frequently appropriated from other cultures, resulting in commodities ranging from yoga pants with NAMASTE ALL DAY appliquéd across the front to NATURAL printed on the packaging.

Appropriation is indispensable to cultural change; however, in the context of consumer culture, it happens at a pace and scale never seen before, and attempts to sell products marketed as exotic or ancient are particularly profitable. When white consumers appropriate yoga, the Otherness is clearly in the exotic east. However, South Asians also appropriate and commodify yoga and other South Asian traditions in order to turn a profit. In the latter case, the Otherness of spiritual products like yoga or Ayurveda lies in their ancient origins and authenticity and therefore their distinction from contemporary, modern society and its technologies. In any case, spiritual entrepreneurs make products attractive to large target audiences of consumers who do not necessarily want to go to Hindu ashrams or Buddhist temples in order to embrace the evocative ideas, symbols, and practices associated with these cultures. Instead of relying on transmission through traditional teacher-disciple relationships, most spiritual consumers prefer easily accessible commodities that embody the enlightenment-ethics popularly deemed "spiritual."

When we explore religion in consumer culture, we are frequently talking about behavior or practice, that is, the ways commodifying, marketing, selling, and purchasing collectively deploy and act on religious discourses, images, ideas, and values. In this chapter, homing in on the American yogaware corporation Spiritual Gangster and the Indian NATURAL foods and medicine corporation Patanjali Ayurved, I ask how spiritual entrepreneurs, corporations, and consumers relate religious discourses, images, ideas, and values to ethical values through marketing and consumer activities. What we find is that the commodities of neoliberal spirituality often enact an orientalist fantasy of enlightenment-ethics that is especially seductive in a world of ever-expanding obligations and needs. Profiting from popular orientalist stereotypes, corporations and entrepreneurs combine the imagery and discourses of spirituality with the transmission of neoliberal values. Dissent against the problems of colonialism and capitalism, from inequity to environmental degradation, is contained in spiritual commodities, therefore serving the reigning and totalizing framework of a global neoliberal rationality.

Are brands like Spiritual Gangster and Patanjali Ayurved (subversively even if *not so subversively*) performing a parody of the orientalist fantasy of enlightenment-ethics? I suggest that, in and through its creative and exaggerated usage of orientalist tropes, the text of spiritual commodities provides a theoretical model and ideological justification for a neoliberal capitalist ethic. I seek to demonstrate how the powerful expressions appliquéd across yogaware or printed on food and health products and the industry's "do good" discourse are attractive to the consumer who believes that the products are intrinsically characterized by "yogic" or "natural" values. Yet for all of the self-actualization it offers through PEACE LOVE YOGA or NATURAL HEALTH, the industry also plays a game that thrives on nostalgia about lost cultural norms, as well as neoliberal narratives about the capitalist market and the individual's responsibility for self-care and personal growth.

Finally, I ask if we can learn anything about globalization by analyzing the aim of enlightenment-ethics in the commodities of spiritual brands. I am following Tulasi Srinivas, who argues,

Whereas globalization was incontrovertibly dominated by Western economic and ideological structures, in actuality the data suggested that India had "emitted' cultural goods, ideologies and ways of being regularly into the network—that cultural goods, services and ideas flowed *out* of

India—though little attention was paid to analyzing how cultural ideologies and forms *from* India *engaged* and *affected* the global network. (2010, 29)

Understanding how neoliberal spiritual ideas, practices, symbols, and discourses flow both throughout and out of India through commodifying practices helps illuminate how India influences the global flow of neoliberal spiritual commodities.

Spirituality, Identify Formation, and Neoliberal Politics

Neoliberal spirituality is not merely spiritual cover for the economic operations of capitalism. Rather, it is also a discursive network that is a part of a larger complex grounded in the shared aims of self-care, personal growth, and even liberation. Yet, as noted in the previous chapter, what comprise these for one community might consequently marginalize, disenfranchise, or oppress another. Appropriations and commodifications are always in negotiation with power, sometimes in ambiguous and complicated ways. They build identities, from national and religious identities to consumer groups, in part through the creation of out-groups. Hence spiritual appropriation and commodification often entail an orientalist portrait of Indian culture as spiritually rich but otherwise inadequate and despotic or, in the case of Indian spiritual commodities, of Indian culture rooted in an essentialized portrait of pure, "classical" Hinduism.[1]

We might compare, for the sake of illustrating this point, twenty-first-century identity formations among spiritual consumers to twenty-first-century political ones. Consider the Bharatiya Janata Party (BJP) and Narendra Modi's successful 2014 campaign for prime minister of India. Modi was elected based on his neoliberal economic vision despite being known as complicit with communal violence against Muslims in Gujarat (see chapter 5). He succeeded under the slogan "Ek Bharat, Shreshtha Bharat," or "One India, Great India," which, in the context of the BJP and Modi's historical and ongoing economic and political activities, can be taken to mean unifying India under a blanket of neoliberal capitalist economic policies and an exclusivist right-wing Hindu identity. Also consider 2016, a year of political

---

[1] See my discussion of guru sex scandals and the problems with blaming the "guru model" in chapter 4.

upsets that stunned policymakers and citizens across the world. In June 2016, British citizens voted to withdraw from the European Union, an economic, political, and social community to which they had belonged for decades. The Brexit referendum had not been expected to pass, yet the "leave" campaign succeeded, and thus the experiment of European integration began to unravel. As with the "leave" campaign, real estate developer and media personality Donald Trump was not expected to win the 2016 US presidential election, yet he did so by promising to "Make America Great Again."[2] Both of these campaigns featured "calls to build walls, erect fences, and fortify physical and cultural barriers between a national 'Us' and nonnational 'Them'" (Croucher 2018, 86).

Furthermore, building identities, whether in terms of consumer groups, political affiliations, or otherwise, involves appropriating, commodifying, and even mythologizing practices that are often fragmented, even appearing as contradiction or discontinuity. Hence the contradictions in Modi's divisive Hindutva rhetoric and his call for "One India" or those in Patanjali Ayurved's marketing strategies, for example, combining English and Hindi to mark its products as MADE IN BHARAT (using the Hindi instead of the English name for India). But the cultural analyst must reclaim the multiplicity of collective fantasy life from the "merely subjective" (Jameson 1981, 22). In other words, the analyst must avoid reducing social dynamics, conflicts, and contradictions to a function of individual psychology or projection. The text of neoliberal spirituality, for example the expressions appliquéd across yogaware or natural food products, is often a contradictory process of the production of meaning given that it includes the situation and intention of the marketer, relations within society, ideological, economic, political, and psychological articulations, and relations between consumers and with other texts. In spiritual commodities, private consumption and personal fulfillment, on the one hand, and the desire to challenge inequality, environmental toxins or pollution, or other pervasive global crises with subversive gestures or the false promise of charity, as well as appropriating practices that fulfill a desire for access to the exotic, mystical, or ancient authenticity, on the other hand, are all material for overdetermined, that is, multidimensional and often contradictory images within the text. Consumers actively participate

---

[2] I am indebted to the students who participated in a master class I led at the Australian National University on August 1, 2018, for helping me uncover the parallels between the community- and identify-formation discourses of neoliberal spirituality and those of the Trump campaign.

in the creation of the text, yet the text does not reflect any single consumer's behaviors or values.

Strategies for Selling Spiritual Commodities

In the second half of the twentieth century, yoga was transformed from a largely countercultural phenomenon to a part of pop culture when entrepreneurial gurus succeeded in selling yoga to the masses by tapping into dominant trends in global consumer culture (Jain 2014a, 42–72). The yoga industry has become pervasive in global popular culture, primarily among middle- or upper-class consumers. Beginning in the late twentieth century, a consumer mode of spirituality became common among bourgeois urban dwellers, and an orientalist gaze that pictured yoga as spiritual filler to a modern, industrialized, or Western cultural void became pervasive in what would become a multi-billion-dollar global industry. That industry profits from the union of appropriation, commodification, and liberation embodied by yoga teachers, gurus, and wares ranging from yoga classes to spandex pants and rubber mats. The industry is also known for its focus on self-care and personal improvement, more specifically, adopting a neoliberal privatized and personalized notion of lifestyle and worldview; wedding an orientalist nostalgia for ancient symbols and traditions to white supremacist and patriarchal ideals of beauty, fitness, and well-being; and valorizing and profiting from the capitalist free market.

By charging for teacher trainings, retreats, apparel, and other spiritual accoutrements, yoga entrepreneurs "lock in" consumers, meaning they decrease the likelihood those consumers will pursue alternative, competing wares, since they have invested energy, time, and money in a particular practice, system, or brand.[3] In short, spending on spiritual commodities serves to "lock in" consumers.

The yoga and wellness industries in particular are enormous. American yoga practitioners alone reported spending over $16 billion on yoga apparel, equipment, classes, and other accoutrements in 2016, which is up from $10 billion in 2012 (Yoga Journal and Yoga Alliance 2016). Baba Ramdev is the co-founder, with Acharya Balkrishna, and brand ambassador for and CEO of Patanjali Ayurved, a corporation with over two hundred thousand outlets,

---

[3] On consumer lock-in see Zauberman 2003.

and sales of products reached over $1.5 billion in the 2017 fiscal year (Scroll Staff 2017). Although Acharya Balkrishna serves as the CEO, Ramdev is the face of Patanjali Ayurved and continues to lead executive-level decision making. Ramdev is the most influential among many of India's well-known yoga gurus who are also spiritual entrepreneurs. Although the Patanjali spokesperson is perhaps the most popular yoga guru involved in business, in recent years a significant number of others have emerged as entrepreneurs in their own right, for example, Sri Sri Ravi Shankar and Sadhguru Jaggi Vasudev. None of these men describes himself as an entrepreneur. Ramdev, in fact, has no executive position at Patanjali, nor does he own any shares. That said, they run consumer goods companies and serve as their spokespersons, reflecting a corporate logic whereby they sell goods and services in high demand in India's ever-rising spiritual marketplace.

Whether selling home, self-care, and wellness products or yoga and meditation, spiritual entrepreneurs of all kinds and around the world work to meet consumer demands and therefore sell products. On yoga gurus in India, Meera Nanda explains:

> The modern gurus, who are practically CEOs of huge business empires, know that they operate in a highly competitive spiritualism market and try to differentiate their products and services accordingly. Spiritual seekers, too, shop around for just the right guru, often trying out many before settling on one. Depending upon their bent of mind and their spiritual needs, they go for one of the three main types of gurus: type I, the miracle-making gurus; type II, the philosophical gurus who specialize in expounding on Vedic wisdom; and type III, the yoga-meditation-alternative-medicine gurus who may or may not combine yogic postures and breathing techniques with new age techniques of astrology/tarot, vastu/feng shui, reiki, pranic healing, aromatherapy, etc. (2011, 92)

Neoliberal yoga, from India to the United States, is especially known for a consumer idiom that attempts to sell evocative objects, images, or ideas that evoke yoga's ancient and authentic "motherland," India, resulting in countless commodities guaranteed to purify and enhance the mind, body, and society. Although the yoga industry is largely made up of forms of postural yoga, a twentieth-century transnational product that focuses on the health and fitness benefits of certain postures, it thrives on widespread orientalist stereotypes of India as spiritually rich and pure.[4] Marketers capitalize on those stereotypes, suggesting consumers buy authentically Indian products or, if they live outside of India, to go to India on pilgrimage (but for god's sake do not stay there—simply extract spiritual goods and come home). Branding and commodifying processes are framed within a well-worn binary that positions the rational West in opposition to the spiritual East.

Repeated images of India as abundant in spirituality and purity are pervasive, for example, in one of the most powerful mouthpieces of commercial yoga among white consumers, *Yoga Journal*. *Yoga Journal* is also the go-to brand for orientalist images of India. Consider this excerpt from a *Yoga Journal* article that tries to convince readers to go on a pilgrimage to India:

> A pilgrimage to India promises an adventure like no other. India is a beautiful, colorful, loud, sacred, magnificent and dirty country. India is yoga incarnate, it is the unification of opposing forces in every way. The amount of grit is equal to the amount of grace and the poverty of pocket is no match for the abundance of spirit. India is often called "the Mother" and is true to her nickname. She fully embodies the qualities of a mother in that she is benevolent, fierce, and inspiring. She serves as a catalyst, asking you to engage, surrender, and transform your body, mind, and spirit. (C. Brown 2015)

Though the industry generally profits from such a narrative about ancient spiritual Indian origins, consumers choose from a variety of yoga systems, products, and teachers in part based on their spiritual (or nonspiritual) fit.[5] Although some consumers prefer yoga systems focused almost exclusively on fitness, for example the American yoga studio chain CorePower Yoga, which prescribes intense strength-building exercises, others choose more explicitly spiritual varieties, such as Jivamukti Yoga. On the one hand, a student attending a yoga class at a more fitness-oriented studio might witness a teacher immediately distance themself from any "spiritual" dimensions of yoga by following the greeting of "namaste" with the caveat that there is nothing religious about the expression. On the other hand, a student at a more intentionally spiritual yoga studio might find their teacher pausing

---

[4] For a history of modern yoga, its transnational construction, and globalization, see Sjoman 1996; de Michelis 2004; Singleton 2010; and Jain 2014a.

[5] I have argued elsewhere that the industry at large, even when spiritual aims and content are not explicit, constitutes bodies of religious practice (Jain 2014a).

between yoga postures or sequences to deliver spiritual discourses on karma, dharma, or enlightenment.

Jivamukti Yoga is an American-based studio chain with global reach. Founders David Life and Sharon Gannon ground it in the position that postural practice is one step on the path to enlightenment, a path that also includes devotional practices. Though Jivamukti Yoga has the aim of enlightenment, consumer choice remains important. At its New York City studio, for example, the student can choose from a variety of classes, including Jivamukti Spiritual Warrior, advertised as a yoga class for "busy people." This is "a fully balanced class which includes asana warm up, chanting, setting of intention, surya namaskar, standing poses, backbends, forward bends, twists, inversions, meditation and relaxation" all packed into one hour. Alternatively, a more serious student or one with more time might choose to attend a Jivamukti Yoga retreat, such as the 2020 workshop with Gabriel Cousens on holistic health and Ayurveda, in which students could "explore the theory and practice of holistic liberation and cultivate an environmentally conscious and individual ayurvedic vegan diet" (Jivamukti Yoga 2019). The most serious students might opt for a Jivamukti Yoga three-hundred-hour teacher training, with boosted authenticity points, given it is held in India. "If you have an interest in yoga," according to Gannon, "then India's the place for you. To take a yoga teacher training course in India is a great privilege." Faculty member Jules Febre explains, "This training is going to push you to ask fundamental questions about who you are, how you see the world, and is that bringing you happiness?" Gannon concludes the video, "You become a part of this worldwide satsang, changing the world for the better" (Jivamukti Yoga 2017).

The teacher-training industry is the bedrock of commercial yoga and serves as the primary source of transmission for modern yoga teachings. Those interested in teaching yoga attend a wide range of certification trainings, from one-time eight-week, two-hundred-hour trainings offered through yoga studio chains such as CorePower Yoga, or famous yoga institutes, such as the Kripalu Center for Yoga and Health, to repeated, intensive trainings at Indian yoga institutes, such as Patanjali Yogpeeth (Haridwar), the Shri K. Pattabhi Jois Ashtanga Yoga Institute (Mysore), the Ramamani Iyengar Memorial Yoga Institute (Pune), or the Sattva Yoga Academy (Rishikesh). When some of these institutes opened in the 1970s, this step not only served to fortify particular systems of modern yoga, it also greatly augmented the amount of yoga teachers getting official training (Jain 2014a, 82–85). Teacher trainings facilitated the expansion of postural yoga, which could now be constructed, marketed, and perpetuated across product lines offered by yoga teachers who commodified yoga practices for consumption in urban spaces around the world.

Consider the American ashtanga yoga teacher and entrepreneur Kino MacGregor. Having received certification to teach ashtanga yoga by Pattabhi Jois in Mysore, she became one of the most successful yoga teachers to deliver those teachings to Americans on readily accessible social media channels. Her website features an eclectic array of products, including DVDs, books, yoga mats, towels, malas, and "Kino's favorite vanilla scents" (Kino Yoga n.d.a.). Profiting from her associations with an Indian yoga master, unsurprisingly, this white American yoga entrepreneurial teacher also profits from a discourse based on the appropriation of key orientalist tropes, in several settings describing her yoga-marketing career, for example, as her "dharma."

Bikram Choudhury (discussed at length in chapter 4), like Kino, does not require students (who are largely white Americans) to travel to India for intensive teacher trainings. Instead, in 1994, he began training them in Los Angeles. These training programs would eventually boast upwards of six hundred registrants and cost as much as $16,600. Teachers who have completed the training have opened over five thousand yoga studios worldwide. In addition to charging for his yoga classes and teacher-training programs, Bikram merchandise has included CDs, DVDs, apparel, towels, mats, books, and water bottles.[6]

Other modes of transmission for neoliberal yoga include various forms of media, including magazines (e.g., *Yoga Journal*) and corporate television. *Yoga Journal* boasts of nearly two million readers. The average reader is a college-educated, middle-aged, employed woman who makes nearly $100,000 per year. The 2019 media kit sets out the journal's mission: "Yoga Journal is the go-to brand for inspiration and guidance on how to live an authentic, happier, healthier, and more peaceful life. We believe that yoga can help heal the world" (Yoga Journal 2019).

Baba Ramdev's two-hour-long yoga television program is the most popular program on Indian television, attracting more than twenty-five million viewers on an average morning (for comparison, that's five times the

[6] Consider the self-proclaimed guru of Bikram Yoga, Bikram Choudhury, as a prime example of this consumer-religion overlap. Bikram's efforts to establish himself as the living embodiment of an authoritative lineage that offers salvation through a healing kinesthetic ritual are mutually constitutive with his entrepreneurial, profit-driven activities (see chapter 4 and Jain 2018).

viewership of *Good Morning America*). The guru has also made appearances on other popular television programs, including *On the Couch with Koel*, on India's leading English news channel, India Today TV (more discussion on this appearance in chapter 4).

Marketing yoga works through several strategies prototypical of neoliberal spirituality at large. As appropriating and commodifying practices have become increasingly central to the constructions of spirituality, tensions between profit-driven competitive capitalist exchange and spiritual ideals have become the norm, but so has selling creative resolutions. Founder and co-CEO of Whole Foods Market John Mackey suggests it is possible for conscious entrepreneurs to produce an "intelligent design," an operating system for a capitalist organization to function in harmony with human nature and the environment (Mackey and Sisodia 2014, 236). The product of Mackey's "intelligent design," Whole Foods Market, is arguably the largest retailer known for products that fit squarely within neoliberal spirituality, from health foods to yoga mats and magazines on meditation and yoga.

At Whole Foods Market, consumers can purchase yogaware made by the transnational corporation Satva Living, the tagline for which is SUSTAINABLE ACTIVEWEAR. While working in the fashion industry in New York City, the Indian co-founder of Satva Living, Puja Barar, struggled with a "disconnect in the way these big fashion houses were producing their garments"; namely, there was a disconnect between the use of toxic chemicals, poor treatment of labor, and negative environmental impact and her personal "values." The solution: an athleisure fashion line for the "conscious" consumer, consumers who want a fashion line that is "respectful to people and the planet" (Chhabra 2018). In 2012, she partnered with the Mumbai-based managing director of Suminter India Organics, Sameer Mehra, to launch Satva (Sanskrit for "pure"), an athleisure brand using organic cotton. The two built a supply chain, working with Indian organic cotton farmers, focusing on organic certification. They settled on the GOTS certification, or Global Organic Textile Standard, which has increasingly attracted consumers to particular products sold in many parts of the world. Working directly with Indian farmers, they eliminated intermediaries between farmers and retail, paying the farmers directly for their crop instead. According to Barar, the farmers use non-GMO seeds, practice all-natural growing methods, and earn up to 40 percent more revenue than conventional Indian cotton farmers. On the Satva retail website, this approach is dubbed "creative capitalism" (Satva 2018a).

Consider also the Canadian yogaware corporation Lululemon, which in 2011 controversially printed on its retail bags WHO IS JOHN GALT?—the question that appears throughout Ayn Rand's famous libertarian text, *Atlas Shrugged* (Austen 2011, 2012). The question was meant to remind consumers that socioeconomic class, careers, incomes, and even bodies are not the outcomes of forces beyond their control, of social structures, of systemic racism or sexism, or of any other form of oppression or privilege. They are the outcome of personal effort and choice. Hence, the solution to unhappiness is to *choose* better. "We are able to control our careers, where we live, how much money we make, and how we spend our days through the choices we make . . . many of us choose mediocrity without even realizing it" (Austen 2011).

In addition to convincing the consumer that success is a matter of (consumer) choice, the marketer must also convince the consumer that buying its products is itself a spiritual act. Consider Karma Keepers, an online retail website for ritual accoutrements that puts this bluntly. Its motto poses the following question: "What side of karma are you on?" (Karma Keepers 2018). This question assumes consumer activities go hand in hand with advancement along the spiritual path and reflects a larger social pattern: through the production and management of desire, the marketplace creates a religious sensibility by which commodities can attract spiritual energy. Consuming spiritual commodities—regardless of the tradition or culture from which one appropriates—entails accumulating spiritual energy or becoming more spiritual.

The Politics of Appropriating and Commodifying Practices

In consumer culture generally, selling products requires marketers to uniquely package them by "mythologizing" them, a process that serves to "position" them in consumers' minds (Einstein 2008, 12). By purchasing books and other media grounded in a narrative guaranteeing authenticity, anyone can enter into and perform other cultures. These products, like others in consumer culture, are not tied to particular times and places, such as church on Sunday morning, but can transport the consumer to an authentic landscape, Native American or ancient Indian, for example, independent of actual time and place (Einstein 2008, 7).

Analyzing the politics of appropriating and commodifying activities in neoliberal spirituality is complex. There are forms of appropriation that most people would not find objectionable, for example, an individual saying a prayer from another culture in the privacy of their home. But there are many other cases in which individuals borrowing from other traditions exploit or even destroy those traditions, for example, by using Hindu imagery, such as the image of a Hindu goddess, on objects considered polluting in certain Hindu contexts (see Ramachandran 2015). Even the appropriation and commodification of nontangible cultural objects, such as stories about deities or ancient origins, can be seen as cultural imperialism, theft, rape, or inappropriate poaching. To be sure, cultural appropriation can sometimes harm the appropriated community, compromise its integrity, transform cultural objects in ways that offend the community that produced them, or allow some to benefit to the financial detriment of others.

Another way to articulate these concerns is to point out that spiritual consumers usually ignore context, history, and politics when they appropriate and commodify spirituality. There are several relevant contexts to consider, including of course the history of the white genocide of Native Americans and white British colonial control of India. The appropriation of cultural symbols and practices from Native Americans or South Asians is situated within a history of colonialism and capitalist exploitation. Social inequalities, colonial histories, racism, and nationalism all shape our ways of understanding who uses Native American or South Asian practices and why. A white woman might be viewed as bold and fashion forward for donning a GOOD KARMA T-shirt; but when a South Asian woman wears a sari, she might be viewed as fashionably backward or failing to assimilate. This reflects a sanitization of cultural practices—appropriate only those parts of others' cultures that can be cleansed of unwanted or unpopular cultural baggage. For global consumers to widely appropriate religious images or practices, they need to be rendered spiritual in the sense of free of unwanted cultural baggage, reflecting only prevailing spiritual trends and not traditional understandings, orientations, or commitments. Although many spiritual entrepreneurs, corporations, and consumers might resist critical reflection on these matters, preferring instead to speak of their spiritual products as if they represent static essences that can be seamlessly transmitted from one consumer-practitioner to another, transmission is far messier and usually does not take place between social equals.

People appropriate cultural products because there is something evocative about them (Einstein 2008, 4). Among consumers of spiritual commodities, for example, middle- or upper-class people living in the globalized twenty-first century often imagine themselves as materially rich but spiritually poor and, in turn, see the cultures represented by the products they buy, especially when ancient Indian sources are cited, as materially poor but offering great spiritual wealth or wisdom.[7] In these representations, it becomes clear how capitalism, colonialism, racism, nationalism, and orientalism engender and reify one another by discouraging reflection on historical and contemporary systematic forms of oppression.[8]

Ashtanga yoga teacher Kino MacGregor describes India as "a place where you are free to discover yourself on your own terms." She imagines it as a place radically other, encouraging westerners to "go to India and lose all the accoutrements of the Western world to see what's underneath and just be yourself" (MacGregor 2015, para. 4). John Mackey suggests that leadership in conscious capitalism "integrates Western systems and efficiency with Eastern wisdom and effectiveness" (Mackey and Sisodia 2014, 194).

Using cultural products like yoga or notions of "Eastern wisdom" as tools through which to romanticize the exotic other, while ignoring the problems of colonialism and imperialism, is not exclusive to white consumers' relationship with India. We also see it in the Africa Yoga Project (AYP). Consider this excerpt from a list of testimonials about the Project's "seva safaris":

Falling in love with Kenya has nothing to do with the tangible aspects of the experience, I fell in love with Kenya because she taught me to be the person I have always wanted to be, igniting my truth. . . . AYP Teacher Training

---

[7] This binary vision of the East as materially poor but spiritually rich and the West as materially rich but spiritually poor has a long history in metaphysical religion. Vivekananda, for example, openly proclaimed, "I have come to America, to earn money myself, and then return to my country and devote the rest of my days to the realisation of this one aim of my life. As our country is poor in social virtues, so this country is lacking in spirituality. I give them spirituality, and they give me money" (Vivekananda 1894).

[8] Edward Said defines orientalism as "a system of representations framed by a whole set of forces that brought the Orient into Western learning, Western consciousness, and later, Western empire . . . a product of certain political forces and activities" (1978, 202–203). In the colonial period, orientalist scholarship legitimated colonial rule by bifurcating the world into the Orient and the Occident. The Orient and the Occident were defined in terms of perceived essences, and thus each was considered a homogenous, static system. Because orientalist thinkers have defined the Orient vis-à-vis the Occident, the system of representation Said calls orientalism reveals more about Occidental subjectivity than about any reality underlying representations of the Orient. Although these representations do not directly serve colonial rule, the regime of knowledge they support perpetuates divisive attitudes toward colonized cultures.

gave me the ability to see the courage, the beauty, the work, the rhythm and the joy of Kenya in my own soul. The motherland pulls back hard because it is there, on her soil, with her people, I have found the strength to be the teacher, leader, sister, daughter, wife, friend I always wanted to be. The paradox is not lost on me, even though I am there to teach, assist, educate . . . it is the people of Kenya that have taught me how to live my life. ON FIRE. (teacher-training assistant Laura Tropea, quoted on Africa Yoga Project 2019)

We do not just hear these stereotypes in the voices of white entrepreneurs and consumers either. Voices of Hindu nationalism, for example, often echo orientalist stereotypes in their attempts to privilege a particular envisioning of Hindu and Indian identity, often for the sake of growing markets and turning profits. Consider, for example, the Indian Ministry of Tourism's Swadesh Darshan Scheme, launched under the Modi government, which includes a "spiritual" tourism circuit, arguing that India is "the land of spirituality" and therefore is in need of "tourist facilities across the country" to accommodate spiritual travelers (Ministry of Tourism, Government of India 2018). Such orientalist dialectics or win-win narratives free spiritual consumers to purchase spirituality without attention to their embeddedness within social structures based on power inequities and histories of colonialism (O'Reilly 2006, 1003).

Given the historical dominance of white, Western discourses and the legacy of colonization, it is not surprising that contemporary commentators have seen cultural appropriation as disturbing and problematic. In addition to the scholars arguing against the authenticity of spiritual commodities, especially yoga and mindfulness (discussed in chapter 2), the scholar Lisa Aldred targets appropriators of Native American spirituality, describing the New Age as a "consumerist movement," its leaders as "plastic," and its rituals as "bastardized versions" of authentic practices (Aldred 2000). In short, these appropriations are dangerous fakes. Her analysis assumes a clear demarcation between authentic and inauthentic spirituality, including her suggestion that the new groups that emerge are "mistaken" for real spiritual communities (Aldred 2000, 346). Other scholars describe the performance of Native American identity and spirituality (usually by white appropriators) as "playing Indian."[9] In his book by that title, Philip Joseph Deloria assumes a clear demarcation between authenticity and inauthenticity when he suggests

[9] See, for example, Green 1988 and Deloria 1998. On ethnic impersonations by white appropriators, see also Browder 2000.

that, in the appropriation and commodification of Native American cultural products, authenticity loses its material or social forms and is replaced by fanciful subjective interpretation.[10]

There is no doubt that large-scale interest in the spiritual products of cultures, including Native American, Buddhist, or South Asian ones, is built on exoticized and romanticized images and a distorted view of history. Often the history and lived political and social realities of colonized or formerly colonized peoples are conveniently forgotten. Furthermore, opposition to spiritual commodifications are, in part, based on sound objections to popular stereotypes and to what Renato Rosaldo has described as "imperialist nostalgia," in which other cultures are romanticized. According to Rosaldo, "Imperialist nostalgia uses a pose of innocent yearning both to capture people's imagination and to conceal its complicity with often brutal domination" (1993, 68–87). This kind of forgetting is destructive in many ways.

That said, as I argued in chapter 2, when observers, scholarly or otherwise, assume that there is an original, authentic tradition to be preserved, they produce yet another representation that is out of touch with reality. In other words, these approaches mirror in problematic ways the essentialist arguments of spiritual consumers themselves. They reify other traditions in ways that simplify them and make them easier to contain, own, discuss, and sell. As articulated by Bruce Ziff and Pratima Rao, "Just as defining the parameters of a cultural group is difficult, so, too, is establishing a theoretical basis for connecting a particular cultural practice to that group. If cultural practices develop from an amalgam of influences, it becomes difficult to assign these to one group over another" (1997, 3). Hence, it is more constructive to focus on understanding how appropriating practices and relevant discourses buttress dominant ideologies and social structures, for example, neoliberal capitalist ones, while silencing or containing others, especially those resistant or alternative to the dominant ideological or socioeconomic orders, than to argue on behalf of demarcating what constitutes an authentic or original tradition and, in turn, "fake" ones.

---

[10] Deloria (1998, 176) notes the 1992 series of articles in the Indian-published newspaper *Indian Country Today* that denounced many New Age "medicine people" as frauds and invited responses by those commercial shamans marketing themselves as authentic. Most failed to respond. Deloria suggests, "The newspaper's detailed investigative reporting had no appreciable effect on New Age audiences. Indian presence was noted. Complaints, however, were ignored and suggestions rejected" (177).

Be a Gangster, Wear Yogaware?

Donning yogaware or other spiritual clothing (e.g., T-shirts with OM appliquéd across the front) is a key ritual of neoliberal spirituality, and the garb of spiritual and athleisure industries illustrates the appropriation-commodification-religion overlap. Corporations deliver authoritarian prescriptions and prohibitions through the often-orientalist expressions printed across T-shirts and yoga pants or product descriptions. Expressions frequently entail egalitarian messages of peace and love that counter the neoliberal value of competition, but these amount to a form of gestural subversion. They do not actually entail political action to dismantle oppressive social structures and challenge class, race, gender, or sexual divisions. Instead, they contain dissent in the threads of clothing products. In other words, dissent is contained when the expressions printed across yogaware and the industry's do-good discourse attract the consumer who believes the products are intrinsically characterized by a social ethic of PEACE LOVE YOGA.

Among yogaware corporations and consumers alike, this is not regarded as morally problematic; rather, advertising discourses apotheosize the apparel, so donning it alone is a spiritual and ethical act. Satva Living advertises its apparel by suggesting that wearers make a "happier planet," which, in turn, "produces a happier you" (Satva 2018a). Lululemon describes its products as making the wearer "free to move, free to be yourself" and as "gear for staying present during speed workouts." If you wear its running gear, you can "run better. Practice mindfulness" (Lululemon n.d.). The relationship between the consumer and the corporation is a religious one—the corporation serves as an institution that grounds a consumer identity through commodities that help the consumer assert and embody their values, beliefs, and aims.

The commodities of the high-end yogaware company Spiritual Gangster capitalize on consumers' aspirations for enlightenment-ethics by appropriating provocative cultural imagery and symbols. The consumer is given a choice when it comes to yoga apparel. Spiritual Gangster, which has been described as "a hip yoga line with a twist of social good" because it donates some of its profits to various "organizations that are close to [its] heart," makes it possible for the consumer to "give back" and send GOOD VIBES into the universe.[11] In this way, its charitable gestures are similar to those of

---

[11] Spiritual Gangster was described as "a hip yoga line with a twist of social good" on Trendhunter (Bianca 2011, para. 1). For the corporation's own understanding of its charitable giving, see Spiritual Gangster 2018b.

Satva Living. On the surface, choosing Spiritual Gangster (or Satva Living) products seems a potentially more spiritual and ethical prospect. Some of the organizations that benefit from Spiritual Gangster's charitable giving include Feeding America, Cambodian Children's Fund, Make a Wish Arizona, and Phoenix Children's Hospital.

However, the relationship between giver and recipient is reduced to an exchange between what Herbert Marcuse describes as "animate and inanimate things—all equally subject to administration" (1955, 103), the terms of which are the instrumental relations of the late capitalist market. The individual's discomfort at thoughts of people starving or seriously ill children is alleviated even as subversion and critique shift away from actual political struggles and acts to change the social structures and environmental conditions that cause suffering into the plane of disengaged gestures and symbols, in this case, a charitable gesture and donning T-shirts with something like MAY WE ALL BE HAPPY AND FREE or BELIEVE IN MIRACLES printed across the front.

Can giving to charity collapse common critiques of charity (which would require it to be neither "charity" nor "charitable")? Can it disrupt the liberal conceit of compassion or the neoliberal imperative of self-care? Can it avoid charity's condescending dimensions—what Mary Douglas, in her fore word to Marcel Mauss's *The Gift*, calls charity's "wounding" character (1990, ix)? Do the recipients have to be grateful? Do they have to reciprocate? Is it just another form of humanitarian giving that responds to, and therefore demands, a "spectacle of suffering"?[12]

In marketing materials, silences, gaps, or omissions are sometimes more revealing than overt message content (see Macherey 2006 and Moi 1995). In order to demystify the ideological function of a text, buried processes of class, race, and gender conflict and struggle must be illuminated. In yogaware advertisements, privilege and hierarchy are clearly illustrated when one takes note of the absences of darker-toned bodies, fat bodies, atypical or disabled bodies, queer bodies, and class differences. For example, in Spiritual Gangster advertisements, (usually white) models are never working but always in leisure, positioned at sites of exotic retreat.

Among Spiritual Gangster's many products are the YANTRA MANDALA T-shirt for $50, the GURU T-shirt for $48, and the NAMASTE ALL DAY T-shirt for $56. The Spiritual Gangster's motto reads: "We are all one." Another reads,

---

[12] There has been a substantial amount of scholarship critiquing charity and the politics of charitable giving. See, for example, Boltanski 1999, 3 and Bornstein and Redfield 2011.

"Raise your vibration," a motto that echoes the tendency in metaphysical religion to envision the divine as vibratory or energetic and testifies to the infiltration of this notion into popular discourse.[13] The Spiritual Gangster website claims that it is "designed to join ancient wisdoms with modern culture" and that it aspires to "create collections to encourage the high vibration practices of living in gratitude, giving back and choosing happiness" and to inspire "positivity, generosity, kindness and connectedness" with the goal that "all beings everywhere be happy and free" (Spiritual Gangster 2019).

In Spiritual Gangster, orientalist imagery and a do-good discourse establish the brand's authenticity and ethics while obscuring the neoliberal governance that goes hand in hand with the kind of consumer spirituality it represents. In the SELF LOVE CLUB and EVERYTHING YOU CAN IMAGINE IS REAL T-shirts, the consumer hears echoes of Lululemon's neoliberal responsibilization—your situation in life is your (consumer) choice, not the result of social structures. There is, therefore, no reason to challenge or subvert social or economic structures, even if you are uncomfortable or troubled by the social and economic outcomes of those very structures. Simply change your own personal habits, including consumer choices. This individualized approach to social change echoes the famous lines attributed to Mahatma Gandhi: "Be the change you want to see in the world." Unsurprisingly, that same quotation is incessantly quoted by spiritual consumers; it can be seen printed on T-shirts and coffee mugs and quoted in memes shared across social media.

Yogaware is concerned with the individual's desire and its management rather than revolutionary social action. The practice of donning clothes with spiritual expressions (e.g., YOUR EGO IS NOT YOUR AMIGO), which include a litany of authoritarian statements, prescriptions, and prohibitions, functions to affirm the very desires they publicly denounce. The appropriation of terms associated with revolutionary or nonconformist dispositions and even something that has been historically a space of Black resistance (e.g., GANGSTER) makes it possible for the privileged consumer to express transgressive or subversive desires while simultaneously containing them. In other words, whereas Spiritual Gangster consumers might see the text of the corporation's yogaware as acknowledgment of social maladies, such materials just exacerbate those maladies by enforcing neoliberal responsibilization and skirting systemic forms of oppression or environmental degradation.

[13] On energy as a defining metaphor in metaphysical religion, see Albanese 2007.

Given the wide range of products and retailer descriptions, the consumer is free to choose based on a variety of aesthetic, spiritual, and functional needs and preferences, but the spirituality industry also features certain patterns in the production and management of desire. Spiritual Gangster aptly captures those patterns. The brand offers a mix of charitable giving, dissent and rebellion, and ancient and exotic authenticity for the modern consumer. The popularity of Spiritual Gangster products may be attributed to the powerful contradictions they represent and contain through strategies of desire management. Private consumption and personal fulfillment (e.g., in SELF LOVE CLUB T-shirts), on the one hand, and concern about inequality and the false promises of charitable giving (e.g., in PEACE LOVE YOGA—as if these three were inherently compatible and mutually reinforcing commitments—T-shirts), on the other hand, as well as appropriating practices that fulfill a desire for access to ancient authenticity (as indicated, e.g., in GOOD KARMA or OM T-shirts), are material for multidimensional and even contradictory images within the text.

As a neoliberal strategy manual, the text offers consumers products for achieving aims set by the late capitalist marketplace, but coded in terms of enlightenment-ethics: means-to-ends relations motivated by self-interest, especially leisure and sex appeal. The goal of enlightenment-ethics, in fact, must be honed through consumer practices. You can pursue things like leisure and sex appeal and still feel good about yourself because you are also sending GOOD VIBES into the world. Desire to be a rebellious GANGSTER is subsumed within the fantasy in familiar codes of alternative, antiauthoritarian, social-service enlightenment-ethics. Yet the repetitive, authoritarian tone of the text attests to the instability of the resolutions it offers.

Spiritual Gangster's products contain dissent. Marketing devices convince the spiritual consumer that its products, made from such concrete materials as cotton and spandex, represent such abstract values as peace, love, and "giving back" in a world where people unjustly suffer or are imprisoned. Spiritual Gangster covertly defines selective consumerism as a form of civic participation and social activism that addresses those problems, yet purchasing its products does not entail any effort to actually dismantle social structures. Their products, however, halt resistance to inequity because, having purchased T-shirts that gesture toward dissent and commitments to equality, consumers feel as if they have done their part in making the world a better place. Spiritual consumers need not ignore or be numbed to the violence of neoliberal capitalism; rather, they can acknowledge the realities of

suffering, inequality, and oppression and feel more spiritual and more ethical by donning Spiritual Gangster commodities without actually engaging
in revolutionary acts.

Be Pure, Eat Ayurvedic?

We have all heard the expression "You are what you eat." Historically, the
extent of religious concern about what, when, or how a person eats is met
only by concerns about with whom, when, or how a person has sex, hence
attention given in many religious traditions to purifying the body through
rigorous control over diet and fasting alongside celibacy. Today, especially
among those living in global cities, religion is as much about what a person
buys, another kind of consumption. Spiritual adherents are in most cases full
participants in the global consumer economy, marking their worth by purchasing expensive or otherwise authenticated brands.

Consider what spiritual consumers eat and return to Baba Ramdev and
his consumer goods company Patanjali Ayurved. As mentioned above,
Ramdev is a megacelebrity and major ally of India's ruling right-wing political party, the BJP, as well as the cofounder of the NATURAL consumer goods
company Patanjali Ayurved. Patanjali Ayurved products are marketed as the
natural and authentic Indian alternatives to products sold by transnational
consumer goods corporations, hence the title of the company; *Patanjali* is
the name of the person believed to have authored the fourth-century Yoga
Sutras, the most frequently cited source on "classical" yoga, and *Ayurved* is
the name used for the "traditional" Indian medical system.

Ramdev is not known for donning sexy spandex or T-shirts with witty
spiritual expressions printed across the front. He wears the traditional saffron robes of an Indian monk, but he is famous nonetheless. In addition to
running Patanjali Ayurved, Ramdev is known as a yoga guru who teaches
yoga as a self-optimizing health and fitness method—it is the panacea, according to Ramdev, for illness and disease (and even, as discussed later, the
"disease" of homosexuality).

As mentioned in the previous chapter, rising spiritual industries like yoga,
traditional medicine, and natural foods seem solidly in the domain of political progressives. Sure, the natural foods movement and corporations
like Lululemon have a libertarian streak, and Republicans do attend yoga
classes, but spiritual consumers are heavily urban, educated consumers

who voice concerns about a wide range of progressive topics, from environmental sustainability to food justice. Paying close attention to the discourses of neoliberal spirituality both within the United States and across national boundaries, however, reveals that the ethos with which they are engaging lends itself not only to neoliberal, but in some cases conservative, agendas. In other words, some of the very things that animate global manifestations of neoliberal spirituality—the obsession with purity, the nostalgia for a glorified, preindustrial past, the pride in the local—also animate Ramdev's political campaigns, more specifically, the guru's efforts to criminalize homosexuality in India and for the institutionalization of, not only neoliberal economic policies, but also the right-wing social policies of the BJP, which are rooted in Hindu nationalism (for more on these political efforts, see chapter 5). Ramdev's rise illustrates a worrying turn in Indian politics. But it can also help us understand the appeal of nationalism in the twenty-first century, and to see the unexpected connections among neoliberal spirituality, natural products, and conservative politics.

In 2003, Ramdev was offering yoga *shivirs* (basically, yoga retreats) to large audiences in the "holy city" of Haridwar when he took over the daily morning yoga program on Aastha TV, "India's leading Socio-Spiritual-Cultural Television Network." Ramdev became the face of yoga in India. It is no surprise that, as a right-wing televangelist whose success is tied to his unapologetically conservative Hindu nationalist politics, Ramdev has been described as a Jerry Falwell of India—a Falwell who wears saffron robes and teaches yoga (see Thomas 2012, 242; see also Sanghvi 2017). This is partly what makes the Indian yoga teacher and megacelebrity such a fascinating figure. He is at once a source, reflection, and distortion of what feels familiar in global neoliberal spirituality.

Ramdev's fame grew, and, as if the Indian version of Bikram Choudhury (or perhaps Bikram is the North American version of Ramdev), he hosted even bigger yoga camps. He traveled the world and taught yoga to Bollywood stars. The guru-entrepreneur quickly became a familiar figure in India, and one in a wave of spiritual leaders who sell yoga as a spiritual fitness method. But his story came to include other consumer goods when, as the origin story goes, a group of gooseberry farmers visited Ramdev in 2005 and told him that their farms were going to be destroyed; there was not enough demand for the fruit.[14] In response, Ramdev started a small operation to make *alma*, or gooseberry juice. Business boomed, and before long, he and a business

[14] This story is widely told among Ramdev's supporters and enthusiasts but cannot be confirmed. After an initial reply from a spokesperson to inquiries by my coauthor of an earlier essay on this

partner, the Ayurvedic guru Acharya Balkrishna, started the company, Patanjali Ayurved, and began selling other goods.

It is difficult to confirm this story, but the results are apparent all over India. Having already become a yoga celebrity, Ramdev now took on major global consumer goods companies with products ranging from cornflakes and fruit juices to toiletries. Patanjali Ayurved has steadily grown, and sales of products reached over $1.5 billion in the 2017 fiscal year (Scroll Staff 2017). (Ramdev claims not to have any direct financial stake in Patanjali Ayurved since he is, technically, a Hindu renouncer.)

The frank alliance between spirituality and capitalism here might be unexpected. Monks tend not to appear in television commercials, but Ramdev frequently does (e.g., Ramdev 2014). Then again, plenty of religious figures around the world make aggressive financial appeals, and plenty of commercial icons seem to have a spiritual vibe. Just consider Steve Jobs, who, as the famous myth goes, had one book on his iPad: *Autobiography of a Yogi*. In the case of Ramdev, it is impossible to disentangle the entrepreneurial and commercial from the spiritual.

It is also impossible to disentangle both from the political. Ramdev got started in politics by campaigning against corruption. He held hunger strikes in Delhi in 2011 and 2012, which did not endear Ramdev to the ruling Congress Party. A contingent of police broke up a public protest and kicked Ramdev out of the city after the ninth day of his 2011 strike. They tracked him down even after he tried to escape dressed as a woman. Ramdev was caught when police noticed his beard, which the guru had tried to hide under a dupatta, a shawl-like scarf that women commonly wear in India. Police efforts to break up the protest, which included killing at least one protester, attracted global attention and served to validate Ramdev's claims of government corruption.

Is Ramdev just a conglomeration of contradictions, or does something unify his work? If any theme is strung throughout and is consistent with other discourses of neoliberal spirituality, it is the quest for purity: pure foods, pure medicines, pure health, pure yoga, pure sexuality, pure politics, and a pure nation (Jain and Schulson 2016). "Because of pollution in food, thought, mind and behaviour, disease, fear, corruption, crime and anarchy are spreading in the entire country," writes Ramdev in *Jeevan Darshan* (2008),

subject (Jain and Schulson 2016), Patanjali Ayurved's representatives did not respond to multiple interview requests.

a booklet translated and published by his yoga trust as *Complete Guidance to Yog-Discipline, Self-Righteousness & Nationalism.*

In the twenty-first century, purity has its appeal in neoliberal spirituality as well as mainstream politics. Just witness the success of Donald Trump's nativist rhetoric, with its promise to scrub America free of filth and foreign contagion (and sometimes protect it from actual illness) (Trump 2014). Or look at the way that activists have marshaled fear of contamination into powerful movements against vaccines, fluoride, and GMOs.

Similar politics often succeed in India. Ramdev's rise has been closely tied to the ascent of BJP politician Narandra Modi to prime minister of India in 2014. In the popular imagination, a pro-Gandhi outlook might be pervasive in India, but it was a member of the powerful Rashtriya Swayamsevak Sangh (RSS), a right-wing Indian paramilitary organization that now comprises the BJP's activist wing, that assassinated Gandhi in 1948. Although the BJP was a force in national politics for years, it was never more powerful than it became in 2014. Under Modi, India has seen sustained economic growth (along with some massive protests) (Jilani 2016). Yet a joint report by the Mumbai-based Centre for Study of Society and Secularism and the UK-based Minority Rights Group International accuses the BJP and its active promotion of Hindu nationalism for the spike in communal violence in India since it came to power in 2014 (Center for Study of Society and Secularism and Minority Rights Group International 2017). Scholars note that the rise of the BJP to power represents the culmination of many years of Hindu nationalist activism and threatens the ongoing struggle to maintain a modern liberal democracy in India.[15]

Ramdev is widely thought of as one of Modi's spiritual advisers, and they have made several public appearances together in an effort to promote yoga and Ayurveda as indigenous Indian strategies for strengthening individuals and the nation. Modi appointed India's first minister of yoga to the "yoga ministry" or AYUSH (Ayurveda, Yoga, Unani, Siddha, and Homeopathy) in 2015. The ministry's strategy to reclaim the yoga industry for India includes the expansion of yoga's role in key areas of Indian civil society, including schools, hospitals, and police training centers. Ramdev advises the government on how to design government-sponsored yoga programs.

As discussed more in chapter 5, yoga (as conceived by Modi's government) signifies Hindutva, the position that the strength and unity of India depend

---

[15] See, for example, Vajpeyi 2014, 2016; Doniger and Nussbaum 2015; and Kingston 2017.

on its "Hindu-ness," therefore the growth and influence of social practices and religions deemed unorthodox or foreign should be resisted.[16] Although Modi's government claims that its yoga campaign is rooted in historical facts insofar as it aims to return yoga to its pure origin point, they actually reconstruct history to reflect an inaccurate and unified vision of India's religious history and yoga as Hindu, all of which serve to further marginalize India's religious minorities.

Long before Modi's rise, however, Ramdev had already promoted an exclusionary social agenda. The yoga guru entered sexual politics in 2006, when he claimed he could treat HIV/AIDS patients using yoga and Ayurvedic medicine. He has prescribed yoga as a cure for the disease of homosexuality, which, he suggests, is in conflict with the Indian family and "Vedic culture."[17] In 2009, after the Delhi High Court decided to decriminalize homosexuality, Ramdev was instrumental in pressuring it to reverse that decision, which the court did in 2013. The guru celebrated with a public response that described homosexuality as "unscientific," "unnatural," "uncivilized," "immoral," "irreligious," and "abnormal."

Ramdev and his vision of Ayurveda and yoga continued to increase their power, influence, authority, and monetary worth. This new influence was on display, for example, in 2015 in the small coastal state of Goa, where the state's minister for sports and youth affairs, Ramesh Tawadkar, announced that the government would host a program to "cure" young gay people of what are perceived as deviant sexualities. The minister explained that the government would work with Ramdev to incorporate the guru's yogic methods into the gay-reversal program. In a *New York Times* interview following the announcement, Tawadkar warned, "We will definitely use law as a tool to teach them what is right and what is wrong" (Najar and Nida 2018).

The entrepreneurial guru has not only targeted sexual minorities; he also targets religious ones. In 2016, Ramdev publicly announced that only

---

[16] A nativist critique of religious minorities emerged in the colonial era but gained significant traction in the 1920s. Proponents of Hindutva argue that the strength and unity of India depend on its "Hindu-ness" (Hindutva). In 1925, the Rashtriya Swayamsevak Sangh (National Volunteer Organization) became the first organization founded on Hindutva and remains the "sangh" of the Sangh Parivar (Family of the Sangh), a conglomeration of social, religious, and political organizations rooted in Hindutva (and including the BJP). Proponents consider Islam and Christianity to be foreign, predatory religions and have resisted their growth in India.

[17] Ramdev also made medically dubious claims during the global COVID-19 pandemic when he claimed he could cure COVID-19 with a medicinal plant sold by Patanjali Ayurved; he also urged people to practice yoga in order to boost their immunity, using the hashtag #YogaForCorona (Ulmer 2020).

a respect for the Indian law kept him and his followers from decapitating hundreds of thousands of Muslims for refusing to recite the Hindu nationalist mantra "Bharat Mata Ki Jai," meaning "Honor to Mother India" (some Indian Muslims consider the mantra incompatible with their religious commitments, since it personifies India as a goddess). Given Ramdev's popularity as a yoga guru, the consequences of his sustained campaign against India's religious minorities could be devastating: India has more than two hundred million religious minorities, the majority of them Muslims. Alone, they would form the sixth largest country in the world.

There is a kind of paradox in Ramdev's work. On the one hand, Ramdev's stance seems fundamentally nationalist and conservative. He profits from products marketed as traditional, natural foods, and ancient medicinal practices. In Ramdev, Patanjali has a strong brand ambassador, one credited with bringing yoga to the mainstream in India. He has supporters across the country who choose Patanjali products because of the yogic authority they invest in its ambassador as well as the nationalist associations of the brand. Ramdev consistently positions Patanjali Ayurved as a homegrown Indian company fighting global multinational competitors with natural, indigenous alternatives. All of Patanjali's products are marketed as SWADESHI (meaning "one's own country," or indigenous to India). Products include Patanjali Dant Kanti dental cream, with the acacia babul, neem, turmeric, cloves, and other herbs; Mukta Vati Extra Power capsules, a product that "completely cures" high blood pressure and heart disease "if it is taken along with the practice of Yoga." Patanjali also makes food products, from cornflakes to instant noodles, with the BLESSINGS OF NATURE (or PRAKRITI KA ASHIRWAD), the brand's tagline. Ramdev is piggybacking on Modi's "Made in India" campaign to promote his goods. His company's logo and packaging use the orange, white, and green of the Indian flag, and although packaging information is written in English, it says MADE IN BHARAT, using the country's Hindi name, rather than "Made in India."

But, like other entrepreneurs selling yoga and associated products globally—think Bikram Choudhury or Kino MacGregor—Ramdev is also building a massive corporation selling packaged, branded, and commercialized products with sleek modern advertising, and he thrives in a modern neoliberal health-and-wellness sector that is growing globally, a sector that calls on consumers to take responsibility for their health, wellness, success, and empowerment. His products include skin-whitening cream, and he has even announced plans to compete in the athleisure apparel industry with MADE IN BHARAT yogaware.

Ramdev helped accelerate yoga's and Ayurveda's entry into the twenty-first-century neoliberal capitalist global economy. He plays an urban, right-wing, and neoliberal game that thrives on nostalgia about lost cultural norms, as well as self-governance narratives about self-care and personal improvement. Entrepreneurial gurus like these might be appealing in part because they successfully appropriate and commodify the "ancient" and even subversive (e.g., resisting Western colonialism and imperialism) ideas and symbols, but they also represent one expression of a global shift toward a form of spirituality that is deeply exclusionary, creating out-groups perceived as moral failures facing related health crises because they are not choosing the right consumer products.

Conclusion

Bodies of religious practice are social. They demarcate social structures and organize social interactions and are therefore political insofar as they assign authority and frequently organize people and other living beings into hierarchies. Appropriation, commodification, and purchasing are a part of identity formation in contemporary consumer culture. Individuals build identity and gain a sense of belonging to communities through participation in a consumer group. Spiritual consumers fashion identities based on romanticized and sometimes orientalized images of certain cultures and their ideas, practices, and symbols. Identity formation through these practices facilitates the creation of communities, but they also sometimes pose serious ethical problems when they elide contemporary and historical forms of oppression or unfair social structures, even though they frequently gesture toward subverting or resisting them.

Some critics of neoliberal spirituality suggest that it can be reduced to market practices. A more nuanced approach, however, is necessary for understanding neoliberal spirituality's dynamism, internal diversity, religious creativity, and connections to consumer culture. Any linear narrative that imagines "authentic" religions inexorably giving way to market-driven rivals is misleading: it underestimates the religious aims, motivations, and ambitions of spiritual consumers who drape their bodies in the T-shirts and yoga pants from Spiritual Gangster or consumers loyal to Patanjali Ayurved or to the products of any other such spiritual entrepreneurs or corporations. The fact is there is a wide range of cultural products and services that are both deeply religious, subversive, and commodified or exploitative. In other words, commodified spiritual products are not one thing—there are many varieties—and their religious qualities do not stand in opposition to consumer activities. Consumer culture has not *replaced* religion; rather new religious forms and products have emerged in the context of global consumer culture.

In this chapter, my goal was to contribute to our theorization of neoliberal spirituality as consumer religion. Understanding this phenomenon necessitates, not contrasting authentic cultural products with capitalist commodified ones, but rather examining how spiritual products, practices, identities, and communities are created within networks of commodification and exchange. I focused on the ways dissent against inequality, the status quo, or colonialism and imperialism is often contained in spiritual commodities, ideas, or practices at the cost of sustained protest or non-cooperation. Political dissent has been largely contained in contemporary spiritualities, which instead use commodities to gesture toward alternatives to reigning and totalizing frameworks of neoliberal and capitalist rationalities. In other words, the subversions of spiritual commodities—against global violence, hunger, suffering, globalization, colonialism, imperialism, and inequality—actually return to a neoliberal ethic of individual responsibilization, therefore functioning as a superficial point of resistance.

It is easy to think of market capitalism and religious nationalism as the targets of spiritual entrepreneurs or corporations, who opt for approaches they dub "conscious capitalism," self-care, SWADESHI, or NATURAL. Yet the opposite is true: neoliberal trends and calls for self-governance feed into capitalist and even conservative sentiments; cultural appropriation drives backlash against social justice; and, in a shifting and globalizing world, there is a profound, sometimes violent, draw toward purity.

4

SELF LOVE CLUB

Neoliberal Feminism and the Call to Heal the Self, Not the System

The commodities of neoliberal spirituality are often means of body maintenance and enhancement; they overlap with sport and are, therefore, cultural
productions entangled with the construction of sex, sexuality, and gender.
"Besides making money," Shari L. Dworkin and Michael A. Messner point
out, "making gender may be sport's chief function" (2002, 17). In the late
nineteenth and early twentieth centuries, white men were largely responsible for creating sport culture in order to support the reconstitution of hegemonic masculinity, boosting men's claims of superiority over women and
other groups that were disenfranchised based on race or class. "Sport is organized to sell masculinity to men" (Dworkin and Messner 2002, 17; see also
Hall 1994; Young et al. 1994). This is all to say that, although often imagined
as based on natural physical qualities, sport was socially constructed out of
gender, race, class, and nationalist identities and structures.

Speaking primarily about North American sport contexts, David Whitson
adds that it is important to note that the increasing legitimacy of noncom-
bative sports, including yoga, for men, has created space in which men "can
experience different kinds of physicality and ways of being strong other than
through use of force" and therefore freed them to exercise "other ways of
being male" (Whitson 2002, 236). Modern postural yoga, on the other hand,
was largely constructed in India by men for men as a way to promote "muscular Hinduism," a masculinized ideology incorporating issues of health,
strength, and vital energy (Alter 2004, 146; see also Alter 1994). This new
form of yoga functioned as a means to physical vigor, which symbolized the
power of Indian men in resistance to colonial powers. Yet, in North Atlantic
contexts, it is more often performed by women.

Nevertheless, the ascent of the global yoga industry, which largely sells yoga
as a sport (if a spiritual one), no doubt represents a part of the realization of
the feminist project. When women participate in sport, they are empowered

Peace Love Yoga. Andrea R. Jain, Oxford University Press (2020). © Oxford University Press.
DOI: 10.1093/oso/9780190888626.001.0001

through the active use of and control over their bodies (see, e.g., MacKinnon 1987). In fact, as a gendered "model of bodily action," sport opens up opportunities to critically analyze the social construction of gender (Connell 1987, 84–85) as well as to deconstruct the "shifting imagery of physical femininity" as it is sold to women through sport (Dworkin and Messner 2002, 17).

Although yoga can be empowering for women and men, it is also a site of rampant and various manifestations of sexual violence, usually committed by men against women or sexual minorities. Because of the ways it embodies these contradictions, yoga is a fascinating space in which to explore feminist questions of power and agency. And the framework of neoliberal capitalism, within which I locate the yoga industry, provides a unifying context in which to understand sexual violence by spiritual entrepreneurs.

On the one hand, Baba Ramdev was instrumental in recriminalizing same-sex sex in India, which exacerbated the social and physical vulnerability of LGBTQ Indians. In 2009, after the Delhi High Court decriminalized same-sex sex in India, Baba Ramdev publicly criticized the High Court's decision and filed a petition demanding homosexuality's recriminalization in the Supreme Court, which was successful.[1] On the other hand, since the October 2017 *New York Times* publication of investigative work into the decades of sexual harassment allegations against Hollywood producer Harvey Weinstein (Kantor and Twohey 2017), hundreds of women participants in the yoga industry, either as teachers or students, stepped forward to say, "Me too." Most notably, in December 2017, Rachel Brathen collected more than three hundred #MeToo stories and posted them on her Yoga Girl website (Yoga Girl 2019). The hundreds of #MeToo exposés shared on Yoga Girl and elsewhere chronicled (mostly) women's stories in which they accused (mostly) male yoga teachers and gurus, most notably the famous yoga guru responsible for inventing ashtanga yoga, Pattabhi Jois, of exploitative and sexually violent conduct.

The #MeToo yoga narratives are not all the same, but they do share certain prototypical qualities. On the one hand, there are patterns regarding the role of power imparity—most of these women experienced abuse in structurally hierarchical institutions and at the hands of their teachers or gurus.

---

[1] Protest arose from those representing a variety of conservative religious communities. For example, Maulana Abdul Khaliq Madrasi, a vice chancellor of Dar ul-Uloom, the main university for Islamic education in India, lamented the decision, stating it would "corrupt Indian boys and girls"; and Joseph Dias, general secretary of the Catholic Secular Forum, warned Indian Christians were in danger of being lured by the "glamour of the gay world" (Timmons and Kumar 2009).

In many cases, they complained at the time of the violations, but their efforts to challenge abusers were obstructed, either by the perpetrator, by others in positions of power, or by their own peers. And in several cases, individual perpetrators were identified by more than one woman.

Following the explosion of #MeToo exposes, Caitlin Flanagan wrote the following in an op-ed in the *Atlantic*:

> The most remarkable thing about the current tide of sexual assault and harassment accusations is not their number. If every woman in America started talking about the things that happen during the course of an ordinary female life, it would never end. Nor is it the power of the men involved. History instructs us that for countless men, the ability to possess women sexually is not a spoil of power; it's the point of power. What is remarkable is that these women are being believed. (2017)

This points us to another prototypical quality of the yoga narratives: the sameness is in part in the ways these women exercised their own privilege. It took hundreds of (mostly) white women publicly sharing stories on the internet and social media to draw mainstream attention to the pervasiveness of sexual violence against women, not only in the yoga world, but in every industry. That this is what it took is no surprise. After all, race, gender, sexuality, and class converge in people's lives and have created the social conditions under which many are excluded from institutions or practices (from sport, for example) or are included but under conditions of coercion and the expectation to suffer harassment or abuse.

Understanding #MeToo, therefore, is not only about combating sexual violence; it is also about witnessing to relations of power and analyzing how they work. Those relations of power are relevant, not only between perpetrator and victim, but also between victims. In other words, understanding #MeToo requires us to pay attention to the ways some people do not have the privilege to speak or, having spoken, to be heard. We must reflect on the ways #MeToo narratives highlight affinities in experiences of sexual violence and, in so doing, obscure differences. We should ask, for example, whether we acknowledge the pervasive threats of sexual violence and the different kinds of threats against women of color or sexual minorities (Crockett 2016; Wilson 2018).

When we analyze sexual violence in the global yoga industry—attending to similarities as well as discrepancies—we can better understand the relationship between spiritual industries and corporations, the abuse of power, and neoliberal capitalism at large. The ways contemporary yoga gurus and teachers are perpetrators of or are complicit in sexual violence reflect the troubling gender and sexual politics long embedded in neoliberal spirituality and pervasive in the dominant global culture.

The symbolic opposition of "alternative" spirituality, presumably characterized by gender and sexual equity, to "traditional" culture, characterized by heteropatriarchy, operates within a troubling theoretical framework that misses much about the ways spirituality perpetuates dominant cultural modes. When confronted with the abuses in neoliberal spirituality, attempts to diagnose the problem tend to range from blaming the "guru model"—pointing to the flawed attribution of infallibility and insistence on submission to gurus—to blaming the conservative sexist and heterosexist ideals certain individual teachers and gurus represent. I think these are accurate in capturing the authoritarian dysfunctions of particular guru-disciple or teacher-student relationships; however, none of them sufficiently explains the unique strategies through which power is abused and how so many industry leaders and gurus get away with violence against women and sexual minorities, especially when, in the popular imagination, spiritual practices, such as yoga, are associated with goals that are seemingly disruptive to the violence of inequitable power structures, goals such as universal health and wellness or empowerment and liberation.

Alternative genealogies around sexual violence can be narrated not only through attention to individual incidents of sexual harassment and assault, but also by reading the texts of popular publications, such as *Yoga Journal*, or listening to widely disseminated yoga discourses, such as those of Baba Ramdev. In these, we learn that single women, queer people, fat people, sick people, people of color, differently abled and disabled people, and poverty-stricken people are real problems. We learn that yoga practitioners, should they want to survive and thrive, must avoid, call out, and regulate those problems. Industry leaders learn that its prescriptions about how to govern bodies and sexuality has a productive energy that can be harnessed to convince consumers to buy more spiritual commodities and therefore support the industry even when that support also cultivates discrimination, exclusion, and abuse. Spiritual corporations run only by convincing consumers that they are imperfect, flawed, and that they can be healed if only they purchase the right products. And as much as consumers are not in control over their own conditions, they struggle to convince themselves that, through spiritual and wellness consumption, they are in fact in control. The burden of healing rests solely on individual consumers and their purchasing activities, and the industry's neoliberal discourses of self-care and personal growth help consumers avert their eyes from disturbing and at times violent power dynamics playing out in yoga classes, mindfulness manuals, festivals, and retreats.

In this chapter, I argue that attention to different and conflicting narratives of sexual violence in the yoga industry sheds light on larger systemic issues in neoliberal spirituality and the dominant capitalist culture at large, particularly by illuminating the following: a globally pervasive neoliberal logic whereby control over one's body is valued, but is defined as an individual responsibility and achievement; and capitalist strategies of commodification that contain dissent by putting the burden of healing on individual consumers, including victims of sexual violence or heteropatriarchy. Together, these brew an industry that neither challenges dominant sexist and heteropatriarchal ideologies nor holds industry leaders accountable for sexual violence. Subsequently, I analyze this toxic brew through attention to the ways neoliberal spirituality, with its emphasis on self-care, and neoliberal feminism, which encourages individual women to focus on themselves and their own aspirations, combine to make yoga more easily popularized, circulated, and sold in the marketplace, since it dovetails with neoliberal capitalist meritocracy.

#MeToo has been a ritual exercise through which people express disdain for the oppression of women and sexual violence, but it sometimes simultaneously ignores the very social and economic structures that buttress heteropatriarchy and sexual violence in many forms and that put the burden of healing and self-care on individual victims. In other words, like the text printed across yogaware, discourses on sex and gender in the yoga industry often acknowledge and even challenge social and economic inequity or other failures of neoliberal capitalism, but usually by recreating an industry in a neoliberal image in which empowerment is about individual consumer choice and empowerment, not revolutionary restructuring.

Sexual Violence in the Yoga Industry

If global spiritual industries impart deep and lasting significance and even healing and liberation to consumers, at the same time asymmetrical relationships riven with power inequities pervade them. Unlike the spiritual entrepreneurs themselves, the targets of their marketing campaigns are often overwhelmingly women, middle class, or both. Far from erasing such distinctions in the name of universal and transformative practices and products, the rituals of spirituality inscribe the marketer-consumer relationships with the covert mark of difference and sometimes overt subordination.

In the yoga world, even as industry leaders brand themselves as embodiments of ethical integrity, many late-twentieth-century and twenty-first-century scandals have revealed sexual corruption, violence, and abuse. A number of yoga gurus and teachers have been outed as sexually active with students, usually with young, white women. Among modern gurus, sex scandals are ubiquitous. In most cases, these gurus claimed to be celibate. Therefore, whether they engaged in consensual sexual activities or repeated, systematic patterns of non-consensual sexual abuse, scandals erupted at the very least in light of the breach of celibacy. Although there is much scholarship on late-twentieth-century scandals, scholars are just beginning to analyze more recent ones among contemporary mainstream gurus or teachers of modern postural yoga schools and systems, most of whom do not claim to be celibate. These have included Rodney Yee of YeeYoga and Gaiam, Ruth Lauer-Manenti of Jivamukti Yoga, Pattabhi Jois of Ashtanga Yoga, John Friend of Anusara Yoga, and Bikram Choudhury of Bikram Yoga.

Yoga's Bad Boy

Here I will focus on Bikram Choudhury (born in 1946 in Kolkata). Bikram is the CEO of Bikram Yoga Inc. and founder of Bikram's Yoga College of India, which provides certification in Bikram Yoga, a school of modern postural yoga performed as a series of twenty-six postures (each of which is performed twice) and two breathing exercises in a room heated to 105 degrees. Bikram is a multimillionaire who has exploited the cultural cache and economic capital of yoga, claimed copyrights on yoga postural sequences, pursued litigation against rival yoga studio owners and teachers, and battled allegations of sexual harassment and rape, all while serving as the self-proclaimed guru of Bikram Yoga and a teacher of spirituality.[2]

---

[2] Parts of this chapter first appeared as a conference paper titled "Being a Superman Who Can't Be

Bikram has been accused of serious abuses of power, especially sexual misconduct. For years, a general reputation as "yoga's bad boy" (as *Yoga Journal* dubbed him in 2000) (Despres 2000) was a part of, not damaging to, Bikram Yoga's brand image. In 2013, however, a *Vanity Fair* article titled "Bikram Yoga's Embattled Founder: The Alleged Rapes and Sexual Harassment Claims against Guru Bikram" shifted the public's perception of the guru. His sex life went from being an enticing part of Bikram Yoga's mischievous brand image to being a damaging public scandal. The success of Bikram Yoga's brand image steadily declined, and many of the yoga studios that promoted themselves as offering Bikram Yoga rebranded as "hot yoga" studios.[3]

Increasingly, women publicly accused Bikram of harassing them and, in some cases, raping them. Several filed lawsuits. In 2016, a Los Angeles jury ordered Bikram to pay over $7 million to his former head of legal and international affairs Minakshi Jafa-Bodden, who said the guru sexually harassed her and wrongfully fired her for investigating another woman's rape allegation. Shortly after the ruling, Bikram left the country and went into hiding. In 2017, a California judge issued an arrest warrant for Bikram, stating that he had yet to pay any of the nearly $7 million awarded to Jafa-Bodden. Later that year, Bikram Choudhury Yoga Inc. filed for bankruptcy.

Analyzing the values, ontology, rituals, aesthetics, mythology, and community-making activities promoted through Bikram Yoga illustrates the ways neoliberal spirituality often represents, in and through its commodities, bodies of religious practice that perpetuate neoliberal enlightenmentethics and lend themselves to other dominant ways of thinking, including heteropatriarchal ones. In many ways like Baba Ramdev, Bikram is the paragon of neoliberal spirituality. He is one among many entrepreneurs in the global spiritual marketplace who have become front-line agents of commercial empires. He is also a yoga guru worshiped by adoring disciples and a purveyor of spiritual commodities that transform the bodies, lives, and relationships of those who consume them.

F*$#d With: Bikram Choudhury, the Yoga Industry, and Neoliberal Religion," delivered at the "Being Spiritual but Not Religious: Past, Present, and Future(s)" conference in 2016 at Rice University (Jain 2016), in another incarnation as "The Case of Bikram Yoga: Can 'Pop Spiritualities' Be Truly Transformative," *Tricycle* (Jain 2017), and finally as "Yogi Superman, Master Capitalist: Bikram Choudhury and the Religion of Commercial Spirituality" in *Being Spiritual but not Religious: Past, Present, and Future(s)* (Jain 2018).

[3] For example, in 2017, the first Bikram Yoga studio in New York City (founded in 1999 as "Bikram Yoga NYC") dropped the Bikram name in its rebranding efforts. It was renamed "Bode NYC" (see Bode NYC 2017).

Like many insiders to the yoga industry and neoliberal spirituality at large, Bikram avoids the category *religion*, which in the popular imagination is narrowly defined primarily in terms of shared belief, implying that a person cannot rationally adopt two or more religions at the same time because that would entail commitment to different and incompatible belief systems. Bikram himself has proclaimed, "I teach spirituality. I use the body as a medium. I use the body to control your mind, to make your spirit happy" (Staskus 2012). Bikram forcefully rejects that Bikram Yoga is *religious*: "Religion is the biggest piece of shit created in all time!" (Martin 2011). The relationship between religious, spiritual, and consumer behaviors in neoliberal spirituality, nonetheless, is a dynamic and mutually constitutive one. Bikram's efforts to become a yogi superman are concurrent with his efforts to be a spiritual leader and simultaneously with his work toward becoming a master capitalist. In all of these ways, Bikram believes he has become more powerful than Superman. In his own words, "I'm beyond Superman. . . . Because I have balls like atom bombs, two of them, 100 megatons each. Nobody fucks with me" (quoted in Keegan 2002).

Biographical details about Bikram depend heavily on his autohagiography (see, e.g., Choudhury 2007). Having practiced yoga since age three, at age five he began studying with Indian physical culture advocate Bishnu Ghosh (younger brother of Paramahansa Yogananda, who in 1920 traveled to the United States, where he founded the Self Realization Fellowship and authored the acclaimed book *Autobiography of a Yogi* (I mentioned this book earlier because it is believed to have been the only one on Steve Jobs's iPad). Bikram won the Indian National Yoga Competition at age thirteen. He likes to tell a story of how, as a teenager, he dropped a nearly four-hundred-pound weight on his knee, shattering his patella. Doctors said Bikram would never walk again, but he turned to Ghosh, who used yogic techniques to rebuild the young man. Bikram emerged completely cured after only six months. He moved to Bombay, where he became immersed in Bollywood culture, which remains a central part of Bikram Yoga teacher-training programs to this day (trainees gather at night to watch Bollywood films until two or three in the morning) and a daily pastime of Bikram himself.

Soon after Bikram's guru's death in 1970, having been charged with the mission to finish Yogananda's project of delivering yoga to the world, Bikram left for Japan, where he used heated rooms to replicate the conditions of Calcutta. He also claims to have aided Japanese scientists studying tissue regeneration and to have healed Richard Nixon of chronic phlebitis using nothing but Epsom salt.

In 1973, Bikram came to the United States and opened a small yoga school in the basement of a Beverly Hills bank building, where he taught a twenty-six-posture yoga program, which he claimed would maintain and restore health even to those with grave injuries and illnesses. There he very much represented the ascetic ideal of a traditional celibate yogi, sleeping on the studio floor and offering donation-only classes.

According to Bikram, all that changed when one of his students, the famous actress Shirley MacLaine, approached him and advised, "In America, if you don't charge money . . . people won't respect you" (Choudhury 2007, 32). Rather than have capitalism restrain him, Bikram became a master capitalist. He changed his approach, becoming one of the first entrepreneurs to build a commodified, franchised, and merchandized yoga brand.

The growth in demand was exponential, and Bikram's overt economics, rooted in the neoliberal emphasis on the individual, came to embody a lifestyle of physio-therapeutic consumption. In 1994, Bikram hosted his first teacher-training program in Los Angeles. Training programs would eventually boast upwards of six hundred registrants. The cost for training steadily rose; a 2019 training, for example, cost $16,600. If, as Lofton suggests, "Religion manifests in efforts to mass-produce relations of value" (2017, 2), then Bikram Yoga teacher-training programs represent consumer religion. Teachers who have completed the training have opened over five thousand yoga studios worldwide. In addition to charging for his yoga classes and teacher-training programs, Bikram merchandise has included CDs, DVDs, apparel, towels, mats, books, and water bottles. In Bikram's rise-to-the-top story, we witness what Philip Goodchild describes as a general consequence of neoliberalism: "The spheres of piety . . . have been increasingly appropriated by finance capital itself. Religions adapt to make themselves more appealing in a competitive market" (2002, 248).

The convocational meetings of Bikram Yoga teacher-training programs occur in front of wreathed portraits of Bikram, Ghosh, and Yogananda, a devotional gesture that situates Bikram within an authoritative and presumably authentic, Indian yogic lineage and narrative. Though it has been suggested that religiously unaffiliated "spiritual" communities are averse to history (Courtney Bender, for example, suggests that "narrating spirituality in a way that gives it a past and affords it a tradition makes it unrecognizable to those who practice and produce it" [2010, 185]), Bikram Yoga clearly illustrates that narrative mythology indeed can serve as spirituality's very nucleus. Multiple intersecting narratives about free enterprise and ambition, the individual and their well-being, and long Indian lineages or ancient origins shoulder commercial spirituality (for additional examples, see Jain 2014a and Aschoff 2015). Bikram is among the many charismatic entrepreneurs responsible for producing the narratives that sustain capitalist empires today.[4] In other words, branding and mythologizing go hand in hand.[5]

Though some might retort that "fitness," "stress-relief," and "health" are the "final objectives" of Bikram Yoga and serve utilitarian or hedonistic self-interest as opposed to salvation or other truly religious aims, as I have argued elsewhere (Jain 2014a, 105–106), a full understanding of the global yoga industry qua religion requires reflection on the human tendency to seek resolutions to the problems of weakness and suffering. On New Age healing systems, Wouter J. Hanegraaff suggests that they are not concerned only with the utilitarian aims of physical and psychological healing, but also with the religious problem of human weakness and suffering: "In a general sense, 'personal growth' can be understood as the shape 'religious salvation' takes in the New Age movement" (1998, 46). In turn, "Religious salvation in fact amounts to a radical form of 'healing'" (Hanegraaff 1998, 44). Like new age religious complexes, adherents of Bikram Yoga set out to resolve the problems of weakness and suffering. And like neoliberal spirituality at large, they buy and sell Bikram Yoga simultaneously as a commodity and a radical form of healing. Bikram's Yoga College takes seriously the charge to sell universal healing through yoga, proclaiming on its website, "We are fully dedicated to the wellness of the millions of people around the world" (Bikram Yoga 2016a).

On the one hand, at times Bikram resorts to overtly religious terms to convey the purpose of yoga: "The spirit is nothing without the body. And the body is nothing without the spirit. Our body is God's temple. We must take care of it, keep it healthy, by coming to yoga class every day" (Despres 2000). On the other hand, Bikram has denied that many practitioners of Bikram Yoga are capable of "spiritual growth," telling one American journalist, for example, "You Westerners are like spiritual babies. You were born in the wrong

---

[4] Ardent procapitalists in the spirituality industry, as Aschoff (2015) demonstrates, situate their products within narratives about self-improvement and actualization.

[5] Mara Einstein (2008) suggests that mythologizing is at work in branding, which requires marketers to uniquely package their products. On mythologizing practices in the yoga industry at large, see Jain 2014a, 95–129.

country, with the wrong skin color, in the wrong culture. You can never be spiritual! It is not your fault. I'm sorry about that. If you can even get the body right, that much is good enough for you!" (Martin 2011). But getting the body "right" is itself a form of radical healing, as Bikram adds: "It is very simple. Go do good in the world, like me. Teach them their mind has a screw loose. It hates itself, it hates its body. But the lotus can grow in the garbage! Make them fall in love with themselves! That is the secret" (Martin 2011).

The constant efforts to situate Bikram Yoga within larger narratives testify to the importance of those stories to identity construction for teachers and other practitioners. At teacher trainings, lecturers deliver complex, intersecting narratives on Bikram Yoga's capacity to prolong youth and heal the body of disease as well as its rootedness in allopathic medicine, nutritional sciences, pathology, subtle energy, and the chakra system. Bikram and the most advanced teachers in Bikram Yoga lecture on the theory and practice of yoga, yoga therapy, and setting up and marketing a yoga studio.

If the mythological narratives underlying Bikram Yoga reconcile the contradictions between unquestioned devotion to youth, the pervasive yet impossible aim, and the inevitability of aging, then it is the Bikram Yoga rituals that unite individuals into a community of assent. Bikram Yoga's rituals are in large part concerned with activities through which yoga practitioners conceptualize and reinforce their value systems, goals, space, and relationships. Bikram's Yoga College of India provides teachers with "basic guidelines" for constructing and managing a predetermined ritual space and ritual process. All Bikram Yoga–approved studios, for example, are required to meticulously follow a particular format. All teachers must memorize a forty-five-page script, which they call the "dialogue," to be recited verbatim so that classes across studios are identical to taking a class with Bikram himself. Every class is supposed to follow additional specific requirements and contain a series of postures instructed in the same way every time, all of which buttresses the concentration of authority in Bikram and, as an extension of Bikram, Bikram Yoga–trained teachers. The guidelines include the following excerpts:

> Carpet is the only approved flooring. No other flooring is allowed. . . .
> Mirrors must be on the front wall. . . .
> Temperature: 105 degree heat / 40% humidity.
> Only Bikram certified teachers can instruct classes.

Bikram's Beginning Yoga Class of 26 postures and 2 breathing exercises is
permitted. No other styles of yoga . . . can be conducted. . . .

No physical contact, hands on corrections or adjustments of students is
permitted (with the exception of Bikram). . . .

Do not turn yoga mats at any point during the class. (Bikram Yoga 2016b)

One Bikram Yoga–trained teacher testified to the power of that space to
transform the practitioner: "Those who ignore the Bikram types of yoga may
not understand what yoga is—there is something very real that happens in
there once you overcome your self (lower case) and that real thing is yoga
pure and simple. You connect to truth."[6] *Religion?*
Healing through Bikram Yoga requires hard work. In fact, Bikram calls
approved Bikram Yoga studios "torture chambers." Although critics are
quick to write off yoga practitioners as hedonistic or utilitarian consumers,
ascetic behaviors are essential to advancement in Bikram Yoga.[7] One student
describes a not uncommon experience in a class led by Bikram himself:

Before I can do the Head-to-Knee Pose . . . I have to wipe the sweat out of my eyes
and dry my hands and foot to stop them from slipping. Even so, I topple over immediately. I look around. A few of the students can hold the poses until the bitter
end, but most, like me, are tortured and teetering while Bikram urges us on,
admonishing us to work harder, stretch harder. "Pain is good. You Americans
taught me, no pain no gain. In India we say, No hell, no heaven." (Despres 2000)

All that suffering is for the sake of miraculous healing, enhanced life expectancy, and bodily perfection as embodied by Bikram himself. Bikram frequently enrobes his muscular body in little more than his signature speedo.
He wears a diamond-encrusted watch, and, until a California judge issued
a warrant for his arrest in 2017, with bail set at $8 million, which led to
his fleeing the country, he lived in an eight-thousand-square-foot Beverly
Hills mansion, drove a Rolls-Royce, and had a Bentley collection. Bikram's
skimpy speedo bears some resemblance to the emblematic loincloth associated with the master yogis of South Asia and, when he sits to rest at
teacher-training programs, the guru reclines on a chair covered with an
ochre-colored towel, resembling the ochre-colored robes donned by many

---

[6] Anonymous source, email correspondence, February 28, 2014.
[7] Many of the ascetic dimensions of Bikram Yoga are present in other schools of modern yoga (see
Jain 2014a, 95–129).

of those renunciates. Yet Bikram's consumer behaviors are a far cry from the renunciatory behaviors we envision when we think of a South Asian master yogi who is poor, celibate, free of superfluous possessions, and, as a consequence of his ascetic behaviors, has developed his powers to the point of being nearly superhuman, from being able to read minds to living for extraordinary lengths of time.

Although Bikram's biography is often interpreted as a tale of an ascetic yogi turned capitalist entrepreneur (Anya Foxen describes him, for example, as evoking the "ascetic-turned-capitalist Maharaja" [Foxen 2017a, 180]), I would suggest that the guru does not represent a shift from the yogi to the entrepreneur; rather, he represents the juxtaposition of the two. In other words, however much Bikram serves as an entrepreneurial guru, he is also a supernatural yogi. Bikram claims to eat only one meal a day (only chicken or beef), drink nothing but water and Coke, and sleep only two hours per night (Martin 2011). In a claim evoking images of yogis believed to have transmuted their semen into soma by means of their extreme *tapas* or ascetic activities, Bikram once claimed he had no need to sexually harass or assault women because "People spend one million dollars for a drop of [his] sperm."[8] Based on calculations of the average time human beings spend sleeping, Bikram once determined that he was approximately 220 years old (Lorr 2012, 140).

These narratives serve to vindicate Bikram's authoritative excesses. The famously intensive Bikram Yoga teacher training has a schedule that starts daily at 7:00 a.m. and ends at 10:00 p.m. The schedule includes classes in the postures, lectures, and demonstrations. During postural classes, Bikram alternates between standing and hollering corrections, oftentimes with expletives, into his headset and lounging on his throne set upon a stage at the front of the class. Beautiful women comb his hair and massage his feet. There are other physical and verbal gestures of devotion. One of Bikram's employees told an interviewer, "I'm in love! I'm in love with Bikram! I'm in love with our life! I'm in love with what we are doing for people!" (Martin 2011). Others declare the supernormal nature of Bikram Yoga and the superhuman nature of Bikram more publicly. When Bikram asked students to introduce themselves at a 2002 teacher training in Los Angeles, one student

---

[8] For Bikram's interview in which he makes this claim, see HBO 2016. For examples of myths about the yogic transmutation of semen, see Doniger 1980, 20, 43–47.

rose and exclaimed, "I'm from San Diego. I've been doing yoga for 11 months. I love Bikram. He is God" (MacGregor 2002).

Like other areas of neoliberal spirituality, the story of Bikram Yoga entails all sorts of contradictions. In 2002, there was a transnational public outcry in response to Bikram and Bikram's Yoga College when they attempted to enforce copyrights over Bikram Yoga's sequence of twenty-six postures on yoga studios claiming to teach Bikram Yoga but not conforming to Bikram's standards. Bikram's attorney, Jacob Reinbolt, commented, "Many people think yoga belongs to the world. That is wrong" (MacGregor 2002). In February 2003, Reinbolt announced that Bikram secured federal copyright registration for the very same series of twenty-six postures and two breathing exercises he claims could bring about universal healing and transformation.

Bikram threatened to pursue legal action against anyone who copied his sequence or created a derivative work that used even a small number of consecutive postures; the addition of different postures or breathing exercises to the sequence (with or without the dialogue); or the introduction of elements, such as music, to the sequence. Bikram sent "cease and desist" letters, warning yoga studio owners and teachers not to teach his style or anything derivative unless they graduated from his teacher-training program and paid a franchise fee. By means of these actions, Bikram maintained, for a while, an iron grip on the hot yoga industry. Teachers had to undergo a nine-week, costly teacher training offered by Bikram Choudhury Yoga if they wanted to teach the same postural sequence or something derivative. Bikram and his Yoga College were involved in two US federal court lawsuits, which were settled out of court under nondisclosure agreements, and they threatened many more around the world (Fish 2006, 192).

Allison Fish (2006) suggests this case serves as an example of how the yoga industry, given the difficulty in locating and defining yoga, has consequences for how open source and intellectual property rights are defined and how information management strategies emerge. The case, indeed, forced those concerned with who owns yoga to take a stand with regard to how to define and categorize new conceptualizations or applications of what are popularly considered preexisting materials, traditional knowledge, or spiritual practices.

In 2012, however, the US Copyright Office slighted Bikram's claims of ownership, concluding that the copyrights issued to him were issued in error (Office of the Federal Register 2012). Neither Bikram and the Yoga College nor any other individual or organization could copyright yoga postures or their sequences. In response to the question of whether "the selection and arrangement of preexisting exercises, such as yoga poses" are copyrightable, the answer was a definitive no (Office of the Federal Register 2012, 37607). The refusal to grant copyrights to yoga posture "compilations" or sequences is based on the idea that "exercise is not a category of authorship" (Officer of the Federal Register 2012, 37607). Therefore, it is based on the assumption that postural yoga, by definition, is "exercise."[9]

The government of the United States was not the only one to respond to Bikram and the Yoga College's efforts to establish and enforce copyrights on yoga postural sequences. In 2002, in part as an act of resistance to Bikram's attempts to claim yoga ownership, the Indian government-run Traditional Knowledge Digital Library created a database of thirteen hundred yoga postures believed to be documented in ancient Indian texts (Sinha 2011). The Indian government's agenda, which has expanded to include many strategies on the part of Prime Minister Narendra Modi to "reclaim yoga for India" (discussed at length in chapter 5), is akin to that of Bikram's in the sense that both betray a corporate logic in claiming some kind of ownership of yoga and to prevent what they perceive as the inequitable profiteering off knowledge they perceive as belonging to them.

From one perspective, Bikram joins rank orientalists, essentializing yoga and profiting from the exploitation of yoga's cultural cachet for the purposes of power and profit. He sees yoga as a commodity that can be bought and sold and reflects the neoliberal emphasis on corporate rights over respect for community rights. From another perspective, as Foxen notes, his claim to ownership can also be read as an attempt to control a model of initiatory yogic transmission through modern structures of economic and legal power (2017a, 182).

Though they earned him many adversaries, tensions and debates over copyright issues did not lead to the complete demise of Bikram Yoga's brand image. His reputation as a womanizer did not either. In a 2011 interview, when asked if he has sex with students, Bikram exclaimed, "Only when they

---

[9] In the view of the Copyright Office, a selection, coordination, or arrangement of exercise movements, such as a compilation of yoga poses, may be precluded from registration as a functional system or process in cases where the particular movements and the order in which they are to be performed are said to result in improvements in one's health or physical or mental condition. See, for example, *Open Source Yoga Unity v. Choudhury*, 2005 WL 756558, *4, 74 U.S.P.Q.2d 1434 (N.D. Cal.) ("Here, Choudhury claims that he arranged the asanas in a manner that was both aesthetically pleasing and in a way that he believes is best designed to improve the practitioner's health"). Although such a functional system or process may be aesthetically appealing, it is nevertheless uncopyrightable subject matter (Office of the Federal Register 2012, "Registration of Claims to Copyright," 37607).

give me no choice! If they say to me, 'Boss, you must fuck me or I will kill my-self,' then I do it! Think if I don't! The karma!" (Martin 2011). Despite such explicit confessions to sexual exploitation, Bikram Yoga continued to grow and expand. It was not until there were legal proceedings that delegitimized Bikram's abuses of power that the obliteration of the brand image became inevitable.

The Nuanced Modes of Sexual Violence

Not all cases of sexual violence in the yoga industry involve an openly sex-ually active yoga guru and a preponderance of white students practicing in urban neighborhoods of places like Los Angeles. Consider Krishna Pattabhi Jois, who died in 2009. Millions of people practice a form of yoga derived from the ashtanga yoga Jois disseminated in the late twentieth century across the globe. Hundreds of yoga studios exclusively teach Jois's ashtanga method—students and teachers gather at these sites before sunrise six days a week—whereas thousands of others offer classes inspired by ashtanga yoga, frequently described as "vinyasa," "flow," or "power" yoga.[10] Today, many of those teaching ashtanga yoga studied with Jois himself at his yoga institute in Mysore.

Jois is known for his disciplined and rigorous approach to yoga, which requires practitioners to move through a sequence of difficult postures with precision, often with the help of a teacher who "adjusts" students as neces-sary. According to Jois, cultivating a yogic practice requires "99% practice, 1% theory." His adjusts, however framed as strategies the teacher could use to help students in their practice, were instruments of sexual abuse. With the #MeToo campaign, several students went public with accounts and photographs of Jois sexually touching female students under the guise of adjusts. Jois regularly assaulted students by groping their breasts, pinning them down under the weight of his body, humping and rubbing their bodies, and using his fingers to penetrate their vaginas. Jois's legacy was significantly damaged in the wake of #MeToo when several women publicly accused the guru of having sexually assaulted them in these ways when they were his students.[11]

---

[10] As one *Yoga Journal* survey testifies, vinyasa or "flow" is the favorite style of yoga among their readers (Yoga Journal Editors 2015).

[11] For a summary of the accusations against Jois, see Remski 2019.

Now consider Baba Ramdev, a very different case since there are not allegations that Ramdev sexually abused or harassed students. However, I would argue he has been complicit in sexual violence. On the one hand, Ramdev is a successful entrepreneur and runs a massive corporation selling packaged, branded, and commercialized yoga, food, and wellness products with modern advertising, and, like the yoga teachers spread across the world profiting from the ashtanga yoga of Pattabhi Jois, he thrives in the global health-and-wellness market sector. His company, Patanjali Ayurved, profits from products marketed as traditional, natural foods, and ancient medicinal practices, and Ramdev frames it as a homegrown Indian one fighting global multinational competitors. On the other hand, Ramdev is an ally of the right-wing politician and prime minister of India, Narendra Modi, and was instrumental in recriminalizing same-sex sex in India. As mentioned in the previous chapter, he is known for describing homosexuality as a "disease" and prescribing yoga as its cure. His efforts exacerbated the social and physical vulnerability of LGBTQ Indians.

Although a celibate monk himself, Ramdev is happy to endorse sex and even prescribe yoga as a means to enhance its pleasure and thrill; he does so, however, only when it upholds a heteronormative and neoliberal ethic. For example, consider his guest appearance in 2016 on *On the Couch with Koel*, a popular television program on India's leading English-language news channel, India Today TV. Ramdev told the host, Koel Purie Rinchet, about how yoga can enhance sex (India Today 2017). The beautiful, slim Koel sat gracefully in a yoga asana across from Ramdev. She perfectly embodied a heteronormative and neoliberal feminist ideal, a highly successful professional woman who is beautiful, fit, healthy, and also a mother who has, as far as anyone can tell, perfectly achieved work-family balance. In fact, before asking Ramdev about yoga's sex-enhancing effects, Koel carefully situated herself directly within this ideal by assuring him that she was the appropriate age to have sex and is married. Ramdev then described how yoga not only enhances the quality of sex, but heals a variety of sexual disorders, including low sperm count, and cultivates control over sexual urges, so that a person can avoid the dangers of what he calls "free sex"; given Ramdev's long history of homophobia, the implication was that this included any form of sex that was not heterosexual. Ramdev, therefore, uses sex as a means to sell yoga, but in a strategic way whereby it perpetuates a heteronormative morality and, simultaneously, a neoliberal feminist ethic.

Neoliberal Feminist Rationality

In *Justice Interruptus: Critical Reflections on the "Postsocialist" Condition*, Nancy Fraser critiques the decoupling of "cultural politics from social politics" (1996, 2), the increasing tendency of social movements and feminists to privilege recognition over redistribution. In later work, she argues that this privileging has intensified over the years, and she targets second-wave feminism for having failed to sustain a critique of capitalism, suggesting second-wave feminism, by giving up the demand for economic redistribution, ended up as a key enabler for "the new spirit of neoliberalism" (2013, 220).[12] Fraser also adopts a three-dimensional account of injustice. In addition to her insistence that an emancipatory feminism must integrate demands for redistribution and recognition, she adds the demand for political representation (2013, 225).

Other feminist scholars have joined the conversation about the unfortunate compatibilities between mainstream feminism and the values of neoliberalism (see Eisenstein 2013, 2013; Fraser 2013; Kantor 2013; Huffer 2013; and Rottenberg 2014). Catherine Rottenberg explains that *neoliberal feminism* represents a shift "from an attempt to alter social pressures towards interiorized affective spaces that require constant self-monitoring." Feminism then becomes a "mode of neoliberal governmentality" (2014, 424). The discourses of neoliberal feminism utilize feminist terms—*liberation, empowerment, freedom*—but are ultimately informed by a market rationality. Whereas radical, revolutionary, and social feminist analyses tend to reveal and critique "the gendered exclusions within liberal democracy's proclamation of universal equality, particularly with respect to the law, institutional access, and the full incorporation of women into the public sphere," mainstream feminism is "in sync with the evolving neoliberal order" (Rottenberg 2014, 419). Neoliberal feminism, in other words, shifts the focus from a critique of social or economic structures toward self governance, self monitoring, and self critique, therefore compromising the demand for radical social or economic change.

---

[12] Fraser blames second-wave feminism, which privileged recognition (i.e., identity claims) over materialist critique (i.e., economic justice), arguing that, when feminists abandon economic analyses, they strengthen neoliberal capitalism. I agree with Rottenberg and with Ozlem Aslan and Zeynep Gambetti, who disagree with Fraser's ascription of culpability, arguing that to place the blame on second-wave feminism is to "misrepresent the 'cunning of history,'" while subscribing to a causal view of the past that "constructs unitary subjects" (Aslan and Zeynep 2011, 145).

Neoliberal feminist discourses are deeply individuated; they convert gender inequality from a structural problem into an individual one. Each individual woman must take full responsibility for her own livelihood, lifestyle, and place within unequal power structures. On the one hand, there is awareness and recognition of inequalities between men and women. In this way, neoliberal feminists gesture toward the problems of heteropatriarchy. On the other hand, each individual woman must accept full responsibility for how she responds to those problems, for her own well-being and self-care, which are predicated on the need to cultivate work-family balance based on a constant cost-benefit analysis.

What does it mean that a movement once dedicated to women's liberation is now being framed and commodified in individualistic terms, consequently ceasing to raise the specter of *social* justice? Some feminists decry the emergence of a mode of feminism profoundly informed by a neoliberal rationality. This mainstream movement contributes to a public discussion about gender inequality, for example, bringing to light the pervasiveness of sexual violence in countless industries, yet it also ignores the issues that concern the overwhelming majority of women around the world, for example, women living in poverty or women of color (see, e.g., Kantor 2013; Huffer 2013; Eisenstein 2013; Rottenberg 2013, 2014; and Fraser 2013).

According to Rottenberg, a new neoliberal feminist subject emerges in the twenty-first century that is so individuated that it has been "completely unmoored from any notion of *social* inequality and consequently cannot offer any sustained analytic of the structures of male dominance, power, or privilege" (2013, 424–425). Her description of the neoliberal feminist subject is worth quoting at length:

> The contemporary convergence between neoliberalism and feminism involves the production of a new kind of feminism that is eviscerating classic, mainstream liberal feminism. This neoliberal feminism, in turn, is helping to produce a particular kind of feminist subject. Using key liberal terms, such as equality, opportunity, and free choice, while displacing and replacing their content, this recuperated feminism forges a feminist subject who is not only individualized but entrepreneurial in the sense that she is oriented towards optimizing her resources through incessant calculation, personal initiative and innovation. Indeed, creative individual solutions are presented as feminist and progressive, while calibrating a felicitous work-family balance becomes her main task. Inequality between

men and women is thus paradoxically acknowledged only to be disavowed, and the question of social justice is recast in personal, individualized terms. (Rottenberg 2018, 59)

Rottenberg asks why neoliberalism spawned a feminist rather than simply a female subject. The answer, she suggests, is that although feminism is "yet another domain that neoliberalism has colonized by producing its own variant, [neoliberal feminism] simultaneously serves a *particular* cultural purpose: it hollows out feminism's potential to underscore the constitutive contradictions of liberal democracy, and in this way further entrenches neoliberal rationality and an imperialist logic. Rottenberg is focused on neoliberal feminism in the United States, where she argues each woman's success becomes a feminist success, which is attributed to the nation's enlightened political order, as well as to its moral and political superiority" (Rottenberg 2013, 420).

In their recognitions and celebrations of women's successes, for example, American neoliberal feminists conveniently ignore the emerging disruptive protests in places outside the United States that represent an unprecedented surge of feminist response to the dominant culture of sexual violence, the ways twenty-first-century millennial Indian women, for example, used social media campaigns against the culture of sexual violence to launch a radically new kind of feminist politics. As scholars chronicling these disruptive feminist solidarity movements note, they are inspired, not by neoliberal modes or discourses, but by a vocabulary of rights and modes of protest similar to those used in the Occupy Wall Street and the Arab Spring movements (see Kurian 2017). Examples from the past fifteen years include the 2003 Blank Noise Project against eve-teasing, the 2009 Pink Chaddi (underwear) movement against moral policing, the 2011 SlutWalk protest against victim-blaming, the 2011 Why Loiter project on women's right to public spaces, the 2015 Pinjra Tod (Break the Cage) movement against sexist curfew rules in student halls, and the 2017 Bekhauf Azadi (Freedom without Fear) March.

Is the Guru Model the Problem?

Returning to the sex scandals and abuses within the yoga industry, we find that yoga insiders and academic outsiders alike tend to blame the guru model and its devotional culture for the various ways yoga gurus have recently been agents of or complicit in sexual violence. Scandals involving Indian male spiritual leaders exist within networks of discursive formations that narrate gurus as despotic, abusive, and sexually dangerous.

In the Indian media, the guru model is not envisioned as unsalvageable, but those gurus enmeshed in sex scandals are usually represented as con men, inauthentic, or unorthodox. In that same television interview discussed previously, Ramdev warns Koel, for example, that the gurus entangled in sexual abuse scandals "are neither spiritual nor religious. They are crooks, criminals and rapists. They are like demons disguised as saints . . . [They are] frauds."

In Western media representations, gurus enmeshed in sex scandals are often situated within orientalist narratives about the hypersexualized Indian man and his undemocratic leadership style (see, e.g., the famous expose of Sathya Sai Baba in the BBC 2004 documentary, *The Secret Swami*) (BBC 2004). Non-Protestant forms of spirituality are envisioned as inevitably despotic and abusive, and the relevant gurus and their organizations are labeled *spiritual cults*. As in Western media representations, Western scholarship usually imagines the "guru model" as inherently problematic for its undemocratic tendencies, suspecting the model is an extreme form of authoritarianism that inevitably leads to demise. The guru is positioned as a fraudulent religious leader who sexually and financially preys on disciples.

Much of this thinking can be located in a framework that characterizes the work of Joel Kramer and Diana Alstad (1993) in which they warn against the dangers of the guru-disciple relationship, suggesting it displays "the seductions, predictable patterns, and corruptions contained in any essentially authoritarian form" and "the epitome of surrender to a living person, and thus clearly exhibits what it means to trust another more than oneself" (Kramer and Alstad 1993, xiii).

More recently, the Canadian high-profile yoga blogger and public speaker Matthew Remski, having interviewed nine women alleging Jois sexually assaulted them, suggested the violence was due to the "devotional culture that saw [Jois] first and foremost as a benevolent father figure" (Remski 2018). Remski explains that Jois's students "have gone on to normalize these interventions—even when intrusive, forceful, or painful—as a common feature of the yoga mainstream" with "the implicit expectation among some that a yoga master should know students' bodies better than they do and that discipline and sometimes pain were necessary to further their practice. One result of this mindset is a culture in which a prominent book on yoga adjustments contains neither the words 'consent' nor 'permission' within its 184 pages."[13] One informant immersed in the ashtanga yoga world once told me that he regularly and unquestionably submits to his teacher as she contorts his body into a position in which she could easily break his back and that "her body becomes so entangled with [his] that if she was having sex with [him,] it would take half an hour before [he] would even realize it."[14]

Remski suggests that Jois's status allowed the guru "to manipulate a cultural aura of spiritual authority and implied consent." He poses the question, "Is the yoga studio consistently the healing space it is advertised to be? Or has it engendered a culture in which spiritual surrender can be conflated with physical submission? . . . It's now worth asking whether the encouragement to submit to physical intrusion and pain through adjustments disarmed resistance to sexual abuse." Remski, therefore, paints the guru model as one that results in an inevitably authoritarian culture in which sexual assault is more likely to occur.

Religious studies scholar Amanda Lucia offers another argument:

> There are three influential reasons for the ubiquity of sexual scandals in guru movements: (1) like other new religious movements, guru movements are fields of sexual experimentation; (2) guru transgressions are regarded as evidence of their divinity; and (3) the haptic logics of proxemic desire, that is, the rules and regulations managing the proximity a disciple has to their guru, lead to social relations in which physical contact with the guru is sanctified and thus the rejection of that contact becomes heresy. (Lucia 2018, 975)

In other words, guru movements are rich soil for sexual assault.

These explanations approach sexual transgressions as a failure of either individual corrupt or inauthentic gurus or as consequences of the guru model itself. All of them are at the loss of a sustained analysis of larger social and historical contexts in which sexual assault is ubiquitous and in which individual perpetrators or institutions are embedded. We have no reason to believe that those situated within particular religious institutions or movements (Indian or otherwise) are more likely to be victims of sexual violence. As the #MeToo campaign revealed, sexual violence is pervasive in every industry where women work and where hierarchical structures prevent accountability and transparency. In other words, a focus on "the monster" diverts attention to larger issues around gendered power. One might compare the view that sex scandals are

---

[13] Remski is referring to the book *Yoga Assists*, which was written by the founders of the Jivamukti Yoga School, a key institution in making the Jois method famous worldwide.

[14] Anonymous source, email correspondence, July 1, 2019.

more of a guru problem than a larger social problem or a problem with religious or spiritual authoritative models generally to the view that child sexual abuse is more of a problem with the Catholic Church than with religious institutions generally. Experts suggest there is little reason to conclude that sexual abuse is mostly a Catholic problem (Wingert 2010). As Catholic priests may appear more likely to sexually abuse children because cases of abuse come to light in huge waves, so with guru scandals. This might be in part because of delayed reporting: "What looks like high concentrations of abuse may simply reflect long and diffuse patterns of abuse that mirror those among all males" (Wingert 2010).

Furthermore, although the #MeToo campaign was instrumental in revealing the pervasive nature of sexual violence across industries, it also misses a lot about sexual violence. Yolonda Wilson has noted that, although #MeToo has been successful in bringing down several high-profile assailants, it has been monopolized by middle- and upper-class white women. This, despite the fact that a Black woman, Tarana Burke, created the Me Too campaign more than a decade ago. Black women in the United States, she adds, have experienced sexual violence differently than white women, given that race and gender converge in Black women's lives and have created the social conditions under which Black women are coerced and expected to suffer sexual violence, often with the support of the state.

Many white liberal academics and political pundits were shocked that Donald Trump was elected to the presidency and that white women voters were key to his election even after recorded statements aired on news media that he admitted to habitually grabbing women by "the pussy" without their consent and numerous accusations of sexual assault surfaced. In response to that shock, Melissa Harris-Perry proclaimed that racism and pussy grabbing had never been a disqualifier even for the American presidency. In fact, she argued that for the majority of US history, it had been a requirement. As Harris-Perry noted, "pussy grabbers"—that is, white cisgender heteromen sanctioned and celebrated for their assaults on women—founded this country: except the acceptable pussy usually belonged to Black and Brown women. Indeed, Harris-Perry asserted that white women have always supported white male pussy grabbers, even despite their own interests. And Trump's election was telling not because it was distinct from American historical politics, but rather because of its consistency with a history of white supremacist patriarchy (Crockett 2016).

Women in many parts of the world, furthermore, are regularly subjected to forms of gender inequality and sexual violence, including the everyday, supposedly harmless, and largely sanctioned practice of eve-teasing, a form of sexual harassment and abuse that affects women on the streets and at work.

Given these realities, it would be misguided to respond to the explosion of #MeToo exposés in the yoga industry by blaming the guru model, as if this is what cultivates the richest soil for sexual violence. In other words, we should avoid falling into dichotomous traps by too simplistically subsuming gurus and their sex scandals into "guru scandals" as if sexual violence is simply a result of an essentialized "guru model" or, more generally, of religious authoritarianism. The appeal to the dangers of guru charisma and devotion as an explanation for sexual violence pulls our attention away from larger social structures and norms that cultivate a dominant global culture of sexual violence. Though yoga gurus can no doubt behave in an authoritarian fashion and there are dynamics that are common to the guru-disciple relationship that could exacerbate the abuse of power, the assumption that the model lends itself to abuse, in my view, lends itself to an orientalist stereotype of South Asians, their religions, and other cultural products as despotic in contrast to white, so-called democratic religions or cultures.

Although #MeToo narratives do important cultural work by bringing attention to the pervasiveness of sexual violence in the yoga industry, they run the risk of blaming the "guru model" in that both displace efforts to offer solutions, diverting attention away from the social structures that created a culture of sexual violence and toward the individual perpetrator and the individual victim, their suffering, and their strategies for healing. In other words, a structural problem becomes highly individualized, so that blame for the act is directed exclusively toward the sexist teacher or guru, and the victim accepts full responsibility for their own healing and self-care.

In these ways, certain narratives of sexual violence perpetuate a neoliberal feminist avoidance, one that does not target the structural causes of suffering and instead puts the burden on the individual to take responsibility for their own suffering and its solutions. As one self-proclaimed "feminist" yoga entrepreneur explains, women are indeed oppressed but, more importantly, women "internalize that oppression" and engage in "self-oppression" (Scott 2017, 98). There are countless examples of this attitude toward gender discrimination and sexual violence in the industry since the #MeToo campaign. On a relatively small scale, for example, two London yoga franchises cohosted an event titled "#metoo in yoga" with the explicit intention "not to offer solutions, but instead to create an independent, safe and sacred space and time in which we can acknowledge that we are facing some serious problems in the yoga world" (#metoo in yoga n.d.). On a much larger scale, *Yoga Journal* acknowledged that sexual assault is a common occurrence in the yoga world, but responded simply by publishing a selection of #MeToo narratives, offering no discussion of structural causes, solutions, or interventions.

As an alternative approach, I suggest we use the frameworks of neoliberal capitalism and neoliberal feminism as unifying concepts with which to understand sexual violence involving the abuse of power in spiritual contexts. If we focus on global structural problems, for example the neoliberal emphasis on extreme investments and returns, which results in consumer "lock-in," a more nuanced understanding of sexual violence by spiritual entrepreneurs and other industry leaders or yoga teachers and gurus is possible. Large-scale investments in a particular form of spirituality, its teacher or guru, and its various commodities, from yoga classes to expensive teacher trainings and special equipment, "lock in" practitioners, meaning they decrease the likelihood that students will pursue some other yogaware or yoga community, for example, in the marketplace, given what has already been a large investment of energy, time, and money. #MeToo testimonies from the yoga industry show patterns of neoliberal governmentality in which women are responsible for adapting their behavior and movements, habitually limiting their own freedom, in order to prevent, avoid, ignore, dismiss, and ultimately heal from abuse.

One of Jois's students, Marisa Sullivan, for example, describes how she stayed with Jois even after she witnessed him assault other women and after he assaulted her: "She had also prepared for years for this opportunity, had come a long way from New York City, where she lived, and felt socially invested. 'I feared my position in the community if I spoke out.... I said, "I'm here. I'm just going to dive in. Enough with this questioning." I'd always been on the outside of communities'" (Remski 2019). Another student, Anneka Lucas, describes how she was assaulted but decided not to publicize the abuse, sharing, "I thought I might be banned from my community that had come to feel like home." Yet another Jois disciple notes, "I do not see Jois's behavior as a flaw in the system, but a flaw in the man." She then recognizes that it is this very mentality that prevented her from speaking out sooner: "I think this is part of the reason why, until now, I have only spoken privately to students who ask about this. I have such deep love for the practice—a practice that has saved my life" (Yoga Journal Staff 2018).

The ways in which a neoliberal rationality puts the burden of healing on the individual has consequences for the culture of sexual violence in spiritual industries. Abuse, in fact, is often imagined as something that can cultivate personal growth. One of Jois's victims explains, "My experience of Jois and the abuse actually helped propel me in a different direction with yoga and bodywork. It was a springboard to find something that originated from within, rather than from teachers who sought control over their students in ways that did not feel safe, spiritual, kind, or compassionate" (Remski 2018).

Ramdev's instrumentalization of dominant discourses of sexuality and their notions of gender in order to prevent the legalization of same-sex and transgender sex in India is also best understood as a form of neoliberal governmentality under which discursive reframing is the mechanism for enrolling agents in self-governance and neoliberal responsibility-taking. Spiritual leaders like Ramdev begin from the assumption that there is something wrong with our bodily and mental capacities, and that, through discipline and practice, a person can gain everything from self-control and inner peace to increased productivity and pleasure. Of course, these spiritual disciplines are only available at a price to the consumer. The operation of self governance and responsibilization are forms of power—forms of what Foucault calls "biopower" (1978)—believed to exert a positive and productive influence on individuals and therefore society at large.

Spiritual entrepreneurs and corporations exercise neoliberal biopower in all sorts of ways. Ramdev justifies hostile political policies and discourses by referring to an assumed heterosexual imperative between women and men. His comments reflect a naively essentialist view that heterosexual desire could be coaxed out of any person who identifies as homosexual or transsexual. Furthermore, Ramdev carefully weds neoliberal feminism to heteropatriarchy such that it hollows out feminism's potential to underscore the constitutive contradictions of liberal democracy, and in this way further entrenches neoliberal rationality in a Hindutva logic. Similarly to what Rottenberg pointed out with regard to American neoliberal feminism (2013, 420), in the case of Ramdev's influence in India, each woman's success becomes the success of the Hindu nation and its moral and political superiority.

Ritualized and hierarchical relationships between teachers, gurus, or spokespersons and disciples or students are essential to the maintenance and growth of neoliberal spirituality. They attract people to spiritual products and discipline them in ways that keep them coming back for more. However, if one imagines these figures—yoga gurus, health food gurus, and mindfulness trainers, just to name a few—as entrepreneurs who offer a profile of neoliberal spirituality, it becomes readily apparent that their modes of sexual violence are as much a reflection of capitalist corporate culture as a reflection of patriarchal religious hierarchy.[15] And it frees us to see the culturally systemic issues involved.

In a just social system, neoliberal spiritual leaders, gurus, and teachers would face career-ruining social and professional consequences for sexual assault and harassment or for open complicity with sexual violence. There would not be circumstances in which abuse remained an open secret for decades while the perpetrator was left free to chew through generation after generation of students, trainees, or members of the public. But many of these stories are not stories of downfall but stories of gurus and teachers who got away with sexual violence, and discourses of neoliberal governmentality were critical to their ability to do so.

Conclusion

In feminist discourse we talk about rape culture, but the people we most need to reach—those who are the perpetrators and those who protect them—are often resistant to the idea that rape culture even exists. And then an icon of spirituality like Pattabhi Jois is revealed as a sexual predator. The open secret stops being a secret. More women are emboldened and share their own experiences with the predator or another like him. They share their experiences because they know this moment demands their testimony. However, rather than attend to the structural hierarchies of corporate culture or the neoliberal conditions under which victims feel responsible for their own healing, attention is placed on the guru system as if the flaw resides there, letting the dominant social structures, the neoliberal capitalist ones, that largely determine our lived experiences off the hook.

Neoliberal spirituality provides an apt example of an individualized religion of the self, packaged over and over again as a commodity to be sold to consumers for their own perfection according to capitalist-consumer standards and at the cost of social equality, not to mention environmental

---

[15] I first started developing this lens on guru sex scandals in *Selling Yoga* (Jain 2014a) and then again in "Yogi Superman, Master Capitalist" (Jain 2018).

costs. Many yoga commodities, from ashtanga yoga classes to the yoga retreats of Ramdev's Patanjali Yogpeeth, are methods for gesturing toward alternatives to the reigning order of global neoliberal capitalism and imperialism, while simultaneously containing that dissent through commodification and mass consumption so individuals can continue to live embedded within consumer culture.

The #MeToo campaign and its impact around Pattabhi Jois and ashtanga communities, the rise and then demise of Bikram Yoga, and the rise of Ramdev, not only as a yoga guru, but also as an advocate for the criminalization of homosexuality, expose how heteropatriarchal entitlement saturates every industry, including spiritual ones. Although #MeToo exposed the pervasiveness of sexual violence in yoga, which served to bring down a handful of industry leaders (or, in Jois's case, his reputation), it did not bring about systemic change. Rather, participants in a global system are still free to instrumentalize heteropatriarchy toward systemic oppression and violence. This, I suggest, is possible because neoliberalism represents the neglect of social concerns in favor of individualism, a logic whereby control is defined as an individual achievement, and capitalism depends on demarcating outsiders, moral failures. There is nothing inherent to #MeToo that threatens the structural hierarchies that allow those at the top to abuse those at the bottom and to contain or colonize their protest in wellness and self-care discourses. In other words, although it challenges individual perpetrators or oppressive institutions, it fails to challenge an increasingly dominant neoliberal system that puts power and profit over people.

The majority of yoga entrepreneurs and consumers are complicit in upholding harmful power structures. With the rise of neoliberal spirituality, with its emphasis on self-care, and neoliberal feminism, which encourages individual women to focus on themselves and their own aspirations, yoga and other spiritual commodities can be more easily popularized, circulated, and sold in the marketplace since they dovetail with neoliberal capitalism. An unabashedly exclusionary spirituality encompasses only so-called aspirational consumers in its address, thereby reifying white and class privilege as well as heteronormativity, lending itself not only to neoliberal but also to conservative agendas.

The reigning public discourse about sexual violence drives radical social critique underground. Too often, the emphasis from large- and small-scale entrepreneurs and corporations and prominent yoga figures tends to be placed on the individual perpetrator and victim. The dominant message echoes a long-standing one among spiritual consumers: the social, cultural, and economic forces producing gender inequality are real, but the individual is fully responsible for what they do about it in order to cultivate peace, love, balance, and happiness in their life.

Sexual assault is rampant in neoliberal spirituality, like everywhere else, and neoliberal structures and mechanisms, designed to transfer the locus of control away from the worker or otherwise disenfranchised, enforce the power relations that make it possible.

In sum, I suggest we avoid falling into orientalist traps by too simplistically subsuming gurus and teachers and their sex scandals into "guru scandals," as if this is simply a result of an essentialized "guru model" or, more generally, of religious authoritarianism. Although there are undoubtedly devotional components at play in acts of sexual violence in neoliberal spirituality, this is not sufficient in explaining the pervasiveness of sexual violence in industries like the yoga industry or the extent to which industry leaders get away with sexual violence. It is more illuminating to evaluate perpetrators as both front-line agents of capitalist commercial empires and simultaneously gurus or spiritual icons worshipped by adoring disciples.

Corporate control of the globe is at an all-time high, and the superwealthy, more than religious authorities, have little reason to fear the average global citizen. CEOs, after all, regularly get away with making over three hundred times the average wages of workers. Yet some of Jois's and Bikram's disciples bemoan that hearsay is destroying the reputation of their beloved teachers and possibly the healing systems they created; likewise, disciples of Ramdev decry accusations that their beloved guru is a homophobic, right-wing entrepreneur, motivated primarily by political power and profit, arguing that these are merely meant to taint the image of their holy teacher.

Well these concerned students and disciples can rest assured that such accusations are often not sufficient to destroy powerful industry leaders in the neoliberal age. In fact, as we have learned from Donald Trump, a pussy-grabbing entrepreneur who openly boasts about committing sexual violence can rise to one of the most powerful positions in the world. And considering that in the United States police arrest someone for marijuana charges every forty-two seconds (Ferner 2012), many of whom, especially Black youth, end up serving prison time, the costs to someone of Jois's, Bikram's, or Ramdev's magnitude are strikingly minor for allegations of serious, violent, harmful behavior.

5

MADE IN BHARAT

Yoga as Political Ritual

"The neoliberal state," according to David Harvey, needs nationalism of a certain sort to survive" (2005, 85). A conservative nationalist rationale for why citizens should be loyal and obedient to the state, rather than undermine neoliberalism's "thoroughgoing individualism," can actually bridge neoliberal individualism and a strong state by providing citizens with a "point of identification" (Kotsko 2018, 23). Conservativism is not, as Wendy Brown puts it, simply "a supplement, something outside of its terms, yet essential to [neoliberalism's] operations" (2015, 210). Rather, the two are "deeply intertwined," for "every neoliberal regime has witnessed the expansion of police powers and surveillance—and in the United States in particular, this has led to a vast intensification of the carceral state, implemented in part through innovations in the private prison industry" (Kotsko 2018, 23) (I discuss the US prison system at length in the conclusion).

In this chapter, I analyze the Indian state's uses of spirituality in order to illustrate that neoliberalism and conservativism are not just related but that they lean on one another. In other words, I use India as a foil that might help us see beyond the surface progressive gestures of spiritual industries, corporations, entrepreneurs, and consumers in North Atlantic contexts and to underscore the conservative character of global spirituality. Spirituality relies on the selective deployment of key neoliberal assumptions, such as the importance of self-governance and individual responsibilization. It privileges meritocracy insofar as many activities revolve around discerning and certifying the merit that leads to the envied lifestyle of personal growth, self-care, health, and success. At the same time, spiritual texts and commodities reify racial, religious, gender, and class privilege as well as heteropatriarchy, lending themselves not only to neoliberal, but in some cases to conservative social agendas. Subsequently, I investigate how yoga, "the calling card of global Hinduism" (Foxen 2017b, 495), serves a right-wing agenda in India. When we critique neoliberal spirituality

Peace Love Yoga. Andrea R. Jain, Oxford University Press (2020). © Oxford University Press.
DOI: 10.1093/oso/9780190888626.001.0001

and even yoga, we are not just investigating Western appropriations and commodifications. Neoliberal spirituality is a global phenomenon, and the current Indian government and its allies instrumentalize the rhetoric of yoga as a unifier toward a neoliberal shift in "lifestyle" for the sake of increased productivity, all while reifying boundaries between social groups and privileging a Hindu heteropatriarchal elite.[1]

This chapter builds on my analysis elsewhere of the "Take Back Yoga" (for Hinduism) campaign, which was launched by the Hindu American Foundation (HAF) in 2008 (Jain 2014a, 2014b). I have argued that, in its challenge to Western co-optations of yoga, rather than offering a robust political critique of cultural appropriation, the campaign offers just one more articulation of what I call the Hindu Origins Position, an essentializing and exclusionary take on yoga, which defines it as a Hindu practice.

Prime Minister of India Narendra Modi, whom I largely focus on in this chapter, does something similar. When he was elected as prime minister in 2014, he joined the HAF in offering his own version of the Hindu Origins Position (though it largely mirrors the HAF's) in an attempt to benefit from yoga's rising cultural and economic capital. A member of the right-wing nationalist Bharatiya Janata Party (BJP), Modi is a vocal proponent of yoga as a health practice and marker of Indian and Hindu identity. His efforts to prescribe yoga as a daily practice for all Indians and promote it as India's gift to the world go hand in hand with and profit from orientalist stereotypes of India as "spiritually rich." In fact, immediately following his election, the country's Ministry of Tourism launched the Swadesh Darshan Scheme, a program for developing theme-based tourist circuits. The ministry includes a "spiritual" circuit, arguing that India is "the land of spirituality" and therefore is in need of "tourist facilities across the country" to accommodate spiritual travelers (Ministry of Tourism, Government of India 2018).

Modi strongly differentiates his yoga campaign from that of the Western appropriators who commodify yoga and sell it to white consumers, yet the assumption underlying many of the conversations on neoliberal spirituality, especially yoga and mindfulness industries, and cultural appropriation, including much of the work cited in chapter 2, is that it is simply a Western phenomenon, a matter of white appropriators illegitimately co-opting and

---

[1] A flurry of scholarship over the past twenty years has addressed the notion of Hindu pluralism and tolerance (Fisher 2017; Adcock 2014; Nicholson 2010; Long 2007; Clooney 2003; also Halbfass 1988) as well as the political role of tolerance in postcolonial India (e.g., Nandy 1998; Chatterjee 1998).

commodifying the East. In this chapter, I hope to demonstrate that neoliberal spirituality is far more decentralized, multifocal, and multidirectional, emerging from multiple locales across a shifting, interconnected global marketplace, and that its marketplace in many ways intersects with the rise and success of conservatism, including the 2014 success of the BJP in India.

In late 2014 in his first speech to the United Nations General Assembly, Modi requested an International Day of Yoga be marked every June 21. Nearly two hundred countries expressed their support for the proposition, and it was approved. The newly established Yoga Day led to mass gatherings in 2015 and every year since across the world. In the city where I live, Indianapolis, the Yoga Day event is held at the city's infamous Monument Circle, where thousands of practitioners spread their mats with the massive Soldiers' and Sailors' Monument as the iconic backdrop. Before or after their practice, attendees visit vendors at the "Yoga Village," where they can purchase a vast array of products, including yoga apparel, jewelry, and healthy foods.

There is a ritual quality to mass yoga demonstrations.[2] Held at iconic locations across the world, they echo social narratives concerning beliefs about the self, the body, and salvation, conceptions of reality, and shared values and aims. Their public and massive character can serve to mainstream those narratives. At these sites, consumers purchase evocative, self-care products and experiences, replete with motifs of self-control and self-optimization. These discourses converge in a neoliberal narrative of responsibilization, a form of subjectivity whereby agents produce the ends of the dominant culture by fulfilling themselves rather than being merely obedient to the government. In other words, neoliberal governmentality is exercised by individuals acting on themselves, rather than giving way to some externally enforced, active government (Rose, O'Malley, and Valverde 2006, 89). The burden of achieving health and wellness, in turn, lies with the individual rather than the state. It is precisely this close and complex relationship between self-control, self-optimization, self-care, and neoliberal governmentality through which entrepreneurs, corporations, and state governments alike exploit yoga's positive associations in the popular imagination. By practicing yoga, an individual presumably exercises their freedom to become a better person through a self-care regimen.

---

[2] Later I will draw heavily on Stephen Lukes's theory of political ritual to understand the 2015 Yoga Day demonstration. I use *ritual* in the way Lukes defines it: "rule-governed activity of a symbolic character which draws the attention of its participants to objects of thought and feeling which they hold to be of special significance" (1975, 291).

The conservative and neoliberal underpinnings of yoga were on display at the brink of dawn on June 21, 2015, during the mass yoga demonstration along Delhi's main thoroughfare inaugurating the International Day of Yoga.[3] There, Modi set the world record for leading the largest yoga demonstration in a single venue. Following a scheduled speech at the Yoga Day event, Modi surprised the tens of thousands in attendance and the countless viewers watching it broadcast on television by spreading his mat at the head of the crowd and leading over thirty-five thousand people through the rules laid out in the Common Yoga Protocol (Ministry of AYUSH 2017a), formulated by the government's yoga ministry, in a vast public ritual that lasted thirty-five minutes.

Aerial images showed a sea of bodies clad in white Yoga Day T-shirts and seated on yoga mats with the famed India Gate monument as a backdrop. More than twenty state-run television cameras captured the event and broadcast it all over the country. Similar rituals were held in all Indian state capitals, and Indian bureaucrats participated in demonstrations at several locations around the world. The demonstration was one part of Modi's larger political agenda, which aims to position yoga as a special part of Indian identity and reclaim it from foreign appropriators. This goes hand in hand with Modi's larger capitalist economic plan, energized by the slogan "Make in India," to get investors and entrepreneurs to transform India into a manufacturing hub.

Despite Modi's efforts to claim yoga for India, the findings of historical and social scholarship on yoga suggest it cannot be said to definitively originate or belong to anyone or to any particular state or religion.[4] A historically and

---

[3] The cost of the Delhi event was over $4.5 million (Express News Service 2015).

[4] The last twenty years have produced several scholarly studies on yoga that attend to the particularities of premodern yoga systems, which vary in religious commitments, communities, and practices across social and ideological contexts. See White 1996; Davidson 2002; Chapple 2003; Bronkhorst 2007; Samuel 2008; White 2009; Chapple 2011; Wallace 2011; Larson 2012; White 2012b; Mallinson and Singleton 2017. A quick review of research on modern yoga helps illuminate the fact that most of the instructions found in the protocol for Yoga Day bear scant resemblance to the yoga traditions going back thousands of years in South Asia. What many scholars call *modern postural yoga*, which includes movement through yoga postures that are usually synchronized with the breath, makes up the bulk of the protocol. Postural yoga cannot be defined as either Hindu or Indian. Scholars doing historical and anthropological research, including Joseph Alter, Anya Foxen, Elizabeth de Michelis, Mark Singleton, and Norman Sjoman, have shown that yoga proponents constructed modern postural yoga systems in response to early-twentieth-century transnational trends, including military calisthenics, modern medicine, western metaphysical religion, and the physical culture of gymnasts, bodybuilders, and contortionists. Postural yoga's methods and aims, which include health, stress reduction, beauty, fitness, and overall well-being, all according to modern medicine and standards, were specific to the time period and would not have been considered yoga prior to the twentieth century. See Sjoman 1996; Alter 2004; de Michelis 2004; Singleton 2010; Foxen 2020. In *Selling Yoga*,

socially informed approach to yoga would capture the historical and lived reality that yoga is an ongoing process, not a static object. Yoga includes a variety of historical as well as living, dynamic traditions, hence the divergences between many premodern Buddhists, Jains, and Hindus, among others, who practiced yoga both within and beyond the borders of what is today the Indian state, as well as living yoga giants, from Baba Ramdev to Kino MacGregor and Bikram Choudhury. Any attempt to demarcate what counts as yoga based on particular national or religious identities, themselves constructed long after the historical emergence of yoga and the majority of its history, is historically and socially misguided.

Situated within any particular time and place, however, yoga can come to signify certain ideologies and values specific to that context, yet spiritual entrepreneurs, corporations, and consumers largely fail to see themselves from a distance, either historical or from the vantage of another race, gender, or class, and therefore they do not recognize the contingencies of their own yoga politics, ideology, commodities, or regimen.

In this chapter, I suggest that the first Yoga Day demonstration signified Hindutva, the position that the strength and unity of India depend on its "Hindu-ness," and that therefore the growth and influence of social practices and religions deemed unorthodox or foreign should be resisted; the Hindu nation should be purified of their cultural corruptions.[5] This is the ideology underlying the nationalist call by the BJP in alliance with the Vishwa Hindu Parishad and the Rashtriya Swayamsevak Sangh (RSS), collectively referred to as the Sangh Parivar. Their efforts to reconstruct India's social landscape mainly occur through two strategies that Geeta Chowdhry succinctly summarizes:

> The reconstruction of religious identities in which a monolithic, victimized, Hindu identity is juxtaposed against a monolithic, villainous, Muslim identity; and second, accompanying historical revisions, because religious reconstruction has required a rewriting of history in essentially communal ways. (2000, 98)

I noted that the religious dimensions of postural yoga are also specific to varying social contexts and, therefore, take different forms across contexts; see Jain 2014a, 95–129.

[5] In 1925, the RSS (National Volunteer Organization) became the first organization founded on Hindutva and remains the "sangh" of the Sangh Parivar (Family of the Sangh), a set of social, religious, and political organizations united by a shared adherence to Hindutva.

Specific examples include enveloping Hindu texts, such as the Bhagavad Gita or Yoga Sutras, into a national canon. Furthermore, in addition to juxtaposing a monolithic Hindu identity against a monolithic Muslim one, strategies also include advancing conservative sexual politics—in Hindutva, Hindu-ness is heteropatriarchal—that does not extend the benefits of full citizenship to LGBTQ Indians and, instead, propagates a frightening story of how the heteronormative majority is imperiled by corrupt, morally sick homosexuals (Sharma 2017; Jain and Schulson 2016).

In what follows, I will contextualize the first Yoga Day demonstration within Modi's conservative, nationalist, and neoliberal political career. Although Modi has largely governed on a neoliberal platform of economic growth and efficiency, he has subtly introduced a divisive social agenda, in part, through political ritual. Drawing on Steven Lukes's (1975) theory of political rituals, which suggests they manipulate a political agenda in order to make it appear that community power is at play when in fact they were generated by and empower a select few, I will then argue that the demonstration was crucial in demarcating out-groups and empowering a heteronormative Hindu chauvinist elite. It did not promote social integration and value consensus, as Modi's rhetoric around the event implied and as civil rituals are often perceived to do. Although the yoga demonstration produced an element of *collective effervescence*, it served as a key ritual through which Modi's government extended a characteristically neoliberal narrative on the centrality of Hindu-ness (narrowly defined) to the Indian nation and its identity.[6] In other words, Modi and his Yoga Day demonstration evoked a representation of the social and political order that advanced an authoritarian and exclusionary social agenda aimed at maintaining social and economic differentials in citizenship.

Yoga, almost de rigueur in urban areas across the world, became an instrument of neoliberal governmentality through which Modi could burden individual citizens with the responsibility for their self-optimization, all while mainstreaming Hindutva and broadening the BJP's constituency. The 2015 Yoga Day demonstration was a public and political ritual that essentialized that which, from a historical perspective, cannot be essentialized.[7] It was a

---

[6] *Collective effervescence* is a sociological concept used by Émile Durkheim (2001) to refer to a social setting outside of ordinary individualistic economic activity in which members of society become "concentrated and condensed" in a particular place where they participate in the same action and come into contact with the "world of sacred things" (162–164).

[7] The fear that an essentializing approach to yoga could be used to impose a Hindu nationalist agenda is not new to Indian politics. For several years, some members of the parliament have attempted to make yoga compulsory in public school physical education, angering certain Muslims

carefully choreographed ritual gesturing toward unity in reclamation of the Indian roots of yoga, yet it further demarcated out-groups, including LGBTQ and Muslim Indians, and aligned with Modi's neoliberal capitalist policies. In short, when one considers the demonstration within the context of social conflict and asymmetrical power relations in the 2015 BJP-governed India, and especially in light of Modi's longer political career, it becomes apparent that it perpetuated social disunity.

Contextualizing Yoga Day: Communal Violence, Hindutva, and Homophobia

Understanding Yoga Day requires close attention to its political context, especially Modi's career and his complicity in social conflict and asymmetrical power relations. The RSS ignited Modi's political career and campaigned to get him elected as prime minister. Modi's training with the RSS started when he was just eight years old and began attending its local *shakhas,* military-style daily drills. Yoga is a part of those drills, so this also began Modi's yoga education. He worked full time for the RSS from 1971 until 1987, when the organization assigned him to the BJP. Modi rose to the rank of general secretary and then became chief minister of Gujarat, serving in that position until 2014.[8]

Modi's administration during his term as chief minister of Gujarat has been considered complicit in the 2002 Gujarat riots and has been widely cited as having an exclusionary social agenda (Nussbaum 2007, 50–51). The riots were prompted after a train carrying Hindu pilgrims returning from

---

who suggest that teaching yoga in schools is a part of a Hindu nationalist agenda and tantamount to religious indoctrination. Another public campaign beyond India courts fear of yoga, arguing that people have been duped into thinking yoga is merely a consumer product. The movement warns that yoga has its origins in India and is essentially Hindu. The most suspicious and fear-inciting critics include certain Christians, including Albert Mohler (president of the Southern Baptist Theological Seminary), Pat Robertson (television evangelist and founder of the Christian Coalition of America), the Congregation for the Doctrine of the Faith of the Roman Catholic Church, and even some parents in Encinitas, California, who sued their public school district for teaching students yoga. Some Hindus join these Christians in defining yoga as Hindu, most notably the HAF. Such attempts to define yoga in terms of some national or religious identity are alive and well despite the lived and historical reality that yoga has never been a static and unified system. Rather, it has varied in its premodern and modern forms, featuring different practices and aims, many of which appeared both within and beyond Hindu traditions and the borders of what is today the state of India. On these debates, see Jain 2014a, 130–157; Jain 2014b; Brown 2019.

[8] For a biography of Modi, see Marino 2015.

Ayodhya, a pilgrimage site cloaked in a history of violence and fierce debates between Muslims and Hindus over its rightful ownership and religious significance, burned at the hands of a group of Muslims, killing about sixty people. Reprisal riots spread throughout Gujarat. They involved anti-Muslim violence, including murders, rapes, and mutilations. Unofficial estimates put the death toll as high as two thousand (Human Rights Watch 2002, 21). According to government reports, around ninety-eight thousand people were driven into refugee camps (Human Rights Watch 2002, 52). Under Modi's leadership, the state looked on without intervention. Although the Supreme Court found no evidence of Modi's direct responsibility for the violence, many political scientists, economists, historians, and other scholars, human rights organizations, and governments have claimed there is sufficient evidence to conclude Modi was complicit.[9] In Martha C. Nussbaum's (2007) words:

> There is by now a broad consensus that the Gujarat violence was a form of ethnic cleansing, that in many ways it was premeditated, and that it was carried out with the complicity of the state government and officers of the law. (51)

Despite (or perhaps because of) the fact that Modi was most widely known for his complicity with the anti-Muslim pogrom and, therefore, with communal violence, in 2013, the BJP selected him as its candidate for prime minister. Violence against Muslims is one of the BJP's ongoing political strategies. As Christophe Jaffrelot explains, "This violence in effect polarises society along a religious line of cleavage, which generally leads the Hindu majority, with a heightened sense of Hindu identity, to vote more in favor of the BJP" (2003, 8).

During the campaign, Modi largely dodged criticism of his government's complicity in the riots by focusing on the corruption scandals surrounding the previous Indian National Congress government (the electorate denounced years of corruption and inefficiency under the Congress Party's leadership) and projected himself in a neoliberal framework, highlighting

---

[9] For example, Modi was barred from entering the United States under a provision of the Immigration and Nationality Act banning violators of religious freedom. The State Department judged sufficient evidence of Modi's complicity in the communal violence even though he had not been convicted in court. Likewise, the United Kingdom and the European Union barred him. As Modi rose to prominence in India, the UK and the EU eventually lifted their bans in October 2012 and March 2013, respectively, and after his election as prime minister, he was invited to Washington.

the high rate of GDP growth in Gujarat during his service as chief minister. Modi expressed interest in attracting investment and manufacturing and reviving the capitalist economy through development and accelerated privatization.

Indeed, during Modi's service as chief minister, the GDP growth rate of Gujarat averaged 10 percent, a value above that of the country as a whole. Despite its growth rate, however, his government had a poor record on human development, poverty relief, nutrition, and education. Under Modi, the number of families below the poverty line increased, and conditions for rural populations, in particular, declined (Jaffrelot 2013). In other words, growth was unevenly distributed, as inequality increased. The high-profile Indian economist Amartya Sen criticized the BJP's appointment of Modi as its candidate for prime minister, arguing that Modi privileged Hindu religious communities and that the development in Gujarat benefited some, but not the majority. He rebuked Modi for his poor record on education and healthcare, especially inequity with regard to minority groups, and said he made minority groups feel "insecure," describing the 2002 riots as "organized violence" (Sen 2013).

Despite such criticism, Modi was elected the fourteenth prime minister of India in 2014. Scholars noted that the rise of the BJP to power represented the culmination of many years of Hindu nationalist activism by the Sangh Parivar, and that it threatened the ongoing struggle to maintain a modern liberal democracy in India.[10] As Doniger and Nussbaum put it immediately following Modi's election, "The moment is an ominous one, for pluralism and amity between groups, for the freedoms of press and scholarship, and for India's very future as a democracy" (2015, 1).

Leading up to the first Yoga Day, many of the policies Modi supported in his role as prime minister and his rhetoric on social conflict went hand in hand with a Hindu chauvinist and exclusionary social agenda consistent with his RSS training and membership in the BJP. Though attention to the exclusionary nature of Modi's social agenda tends to focus on his complicity in Hindu-Muslim conflict, it does not end there. For example, his complicity in the ongoing criminalization of same-sex and transgender sex has continued to allow the BJP and other conservative organizations to propagate a story of how the heteronormative majority is imperiled by LGBTQ communities. Most significantly, Modi was silent on Section 377 of the Indian Penal

---

[10] See, for example, Vajpeyi 2014; Doniger and Nussbaum 2015; Vajpeyi 2016; and Kingston 2017.

Code, which prohibited "carnal intercourse against the order of nature with any man, woman or animal." The law was historically interpreted to criminalize homosexual and transgender sex.[11] Opponents of the law viewed it as a callous, Victorian vestige of the colonial era; it was enacted by the British in 1860. Though the law was rarely enforced, those seeking reform claim LGBTQ people frequently faced prejudice, discrimination, harassment, and blackmail as a consequence of the law (Harris 2013).

Building on the momentum of the recently accelerated expansion of LGBTQ activism, the Naz Foundation, an Indian NGO that advocates for those impacted by HIV/AIDS, filed a petition with the Delhi High Court in 2001, stating that the law allowed state agencies to discriminate against sexual minorities and deny them basic human rights. In other words, the challenge represented an attempt to access the benefits of full citizenship for sexual minorities.

In 2009, Chief Justice A. P. Shah and Justice S. Muralidhar of the Delhi High Court declared Section 377, as it pertains to consensual sex among people above the age of eighteen, in violation of the following articles of the Constitution: Article 21 (right to life), Article 14 (right to equality), and Article 15 (nondiscrimination on grounds of sex and gender) (Delhi High Court Judgment on Homosexuality and IPC 377 2009). Advocates for sexual minorities thought the decision would thenceforth support a progressive direction for the national conversation on sexual rights (Timmons and Kumar 2009).

The decision was indeed groundbreaking, not only in its recognition of LGBTQ rights, but also in the resistance it engendered from right-wing religious and social activists. Immediately, the effects of the High Court's decision were felt across India when antigay rights protesters deployed a homophobic rhetoric of mental disease, family protection, and "Vedic culture," a reference to what some Hindus consider traditional Indian culture as determined by heteronormative interpretations of a carefully constructed Hindu canon. They also argued that the High Court's ruling overstepped its jurisprudential role by trying to demarcate moral norms.[12]

---

[11] Section 377 termed same-sex and transgender sex an "unnatural offence" and provided punishment equivalent to that for the offense of rape under Section 376. Offenders could be imprisoned for ten years to life.

[12] Anticipating negative responses to the decision in the name of "morality," the Delhi High Court stated, "Moral indignation, howsoever strong, is not a valid basis for overriding individuals' fundamental rights of dignity and privacy. In our scheme of things Constitutional morality must outweigh the argument of public morality, even if it be the majoritarian view."

Baba Ramdev, the very person who would become Modi's most high-profile spiritual advisor following his election to prime minister, publicly criticized the High Court's decision and filed a petition in India's Supreme Court demanding homosexuality's recriminalization.[13] Stating that the court inappropriately intended to change moral norms, he suggested that the right to privacy should not include the right to deviant sexual behavior and that yoga could cure the disease of homosexuality. He described homosexuals as antisocial and said that legalization would negatively affect India's youth, damage the institution of marriage, and increase the prevalence of HIV/AIDS. Ramdev used his celebrity and moral authority to make a compelling threat that there would be nationwide protests if the Supreme Court did not strike down the High Court's decision (Nelson 2009).

Conservative responses delimited publicly sanctioned and state-protected sexuality to heteronormativity and modeled a right-wing strategy for opposing the civil rights of sexual minorities. "Deviant," "diseased," and other descriptors of sexual minorities were code words for homophobia and transphobia. Moving the discussion of Section 377 away from systemic inequality and toward the putative best interest of Indian society, which coincided with a Hindu nationalist envisioning of "Vedic culture," was emblematic of the conservative attempt to police morality and erase sexual diversity.

Decriminalization failed when, on December 11, 2013, the Supreme Court reinstated the law following numerous appeals. The Court ruled that the High Court struck down Section 377 improperly and only parliament had the power to change it.[14] Ramdev celebrated with a press conference where he again prescribed yoga as a cure for the disease of homosexuality (NDTV 2013).

Two years later, the idea that yoga cures homosexuality would appear in the rhetoric of another of Modi's associates and advisors. In a 2015 interview for an article on Yoga Day, H. R. Nagendra—a prominent yoga researcher and teacher; nephew of the former general secretary of the RSS, H. V. Sheshadri;

---

[13] Protest arose from those representing a variety of conservative religious communities. For example, Maulana Abdul Khaliq Madrasi, a vice chancellor of Dar ul-Uloom, the main university for Islamic education in India, lamented the decision, stating it would "corrupt Indian boys and girls"; and Joseph Dias, general secretary of the Catholic Secular Forum, warned Indian Christians were in danger of being lured by the "glamour of being gay world" (Timmons and Kumar 2009).

[14] Supreme Court of India, Civil Appeal No. 10972 of 2013, http://courtnic.nic.in/supremecourt/temp/41-55201492812014p.txt. This was unprecedented, according to the additional solicitor general of India, Indira Jaising, as the court had never been deterred by the argument that the legislature should make a decision in place of the court (Harris 2013).

Modi's long-term spiritual advisor; and chairman of the committee for the International Day of Yoga—spoke to the *New York Times* journalist Ellen Barry about the importance of Yoga Day because of yoga's universal benefits, including its power to make homosexuality disappear (Barry 2015).

Although three major political parties, the Congress Party, the Aam Aadmi Party, and the Communist Party of India, pledged to decriminalize consensual same-sex and transgender sex if elected in 2014, the BJP did not. Although Modi refused to take an official stance on Section 377, he let his associates, including his spiritual advisors, Ramdev and Nagendra, as well as representatives of the BJP, speak for him. These included Home Minister Rajnath Singh, who said the BJP would not support such "unnatural" acts, and member of parliament Subramanian Swamy, who, in the week after the 2015 Yoga Day, said, "Our party position has been that homosexuality is a genetic disorder" (Hussain 2015). Most significantly, following his election as prime minister, Modi and other parliamentarian members of his party had the legislative power to initiate concrete action to decriminalize same-sex and transgender sex, yet they did not do so.

When in 2018 the same Supreme Court that recriminalized LGBTQ sex in 2013 agreed to reconsider Section 377 in response to a petition claiming it violated sexual minorities' rights to equality and liberty, most of the religious and political voices that had advocated for retaining it fell silent. Although some of India's Christian organizations appeared in court in defense of the law, arguing that sexual orientation was not innate and that decriminalizing LGBTQ sex would lead to the transmission of HIV, the large, mainstream religious organizations and most high-profile figureheads, including Ramdev, did not participate in the debate. And when the Supreme Court unanimously voted to extend all constitutional protections under Indian law to LGBTQ Indians and that any discrimination based on sexuality would be illegal, those voices remained largely silent. There were few exceptions. For example, Swami Chakrapani, president of the right-wing organization All India Hindu Mahasabha, said, "It's shameful. We are giving credibility and legitimacy to mentally sick people" (Gettleman, Schultz, and Suhasini 2018).

Did religious voices largely drop out of the debate because they knew it was a lost cause? The Supreme Court's decision to end the use of Section 377 to discriminate against, harass, and threaten LGBTQ Indians after nearly 160 years is no doubt worthy of attention. Modi's silence and that of his religious allies, therefore, could be interpreted as progress when contrasted with the vocal homophobic and transphobic pushback that the initial 2009 decriminalization decision engendered. Yet I would argue that the silence actually signals a calculated decision in favor of continued discrimination and oppression. Conservative opponents to decriminalization likely knew that pushback on the categorization of LGBTQ sex as "unnatural" would fail, and anticipated that their silence would be interpreted as a gesture toward equity. They remain unmoored, however, from social ideals like religious, gender, and sexual equality and economic justice. The kind of neoliberal capitalism Modi represents relies on the very differences it sows—it needs racial, sexual, gender, religious, and ethnic conflict to fuel competition and create new markets, and a division of labor in order to maximize the output from the working classes. Under Modi's neoliberal capitalism, individuals are construed as automatons, ideally self-optimizing and entrepreneurial. Economic success is measured in terms of the growing GDP even though the fruits of economic growth are not reaching all social strata (Reuters 2017). India's human development index ranking, which measures life expectancy, education, and per capita income as calculated by the United Nations Development Program, has dropped while Modi has been in power. According to a 2017 report by ratings firm CRISIL, "Persistent inequality reflected in the low human development attainments of the most marginalised groups, including scheduled castes, tribal and rural populations, women, transgenders, people living with HIV, and migrants, have [sic] brought down India's HDI score" (Karnik 2017). Another 2018 CRISIL study reported, "Inequality is set to rise as the return on capital will increase compared with the return on labor. This will continue to concentrate wealth in a few hands, [and] can be socially disruptive and pose a major policy challenge for a country like India, which already has high inequality and is set to add millions to the workforce in the coming years" (CRISIL 2018).

Under Modi's neoliberal rule, citizens are incessantly incited to accept full responsibility for their own well-being and self-care. This worldview is an unabashedly exclusionary one, encompassing only the Hindu, heteronormative capitalist classes, the so-called aspirational adherents, in its address, effectively erasing the vast majority of India's population from view. Hence the Modi government avoids concrete actions to achieve social equality, including support for the expansion of antidiscrimination laws.

Other outcomes of Modi's right-wing agenda included state-sanctioned historical revisions. As Mukul Kesavan (2011) notes, "Hindutva seeks to remake the diversity of Hindu narratives and practices into a uniform faith based on standardised texts" (as quoted in Simeon 2015). A group of over

130 scholars of South Asia lamented Modi's historical revisionist strategy, saying it involved "underqualified or incompetent key appointments" to the Indian Council of Historical Research, among other government institutions (Academe Blog 2015). For example, shortly after his election, Modi appointed RSS member Yellapragada Sudershan Rao to the position of chairman of the Indian Council of Historical Research, which funds all major historical scholarship in India. Rao recruited three RSS officers to the council and proposed that the council view the Ramayana and the Mahabharata, both considered by Hindu nationalists to be a part of an orthodox canon, as historical fact. Modi's strategy to lift up a reified Hindu narrative about India's past is echoed in his elevation of the Bhagavad Gita, a Hindu scripture, to a national text. Modi gifted the Bhagavad Gita to world leaders on official visits as prime minister and, in so doing, joked about bothering his "secular friends" (Kesavan 2015).

Modi's yoga campaign was one more part of the strategy to ground Indian identity in a Hindu narrative. As a part of Modi's cabinet reorganization, he established a yoga ministry (AYUSH) and appointed another RSS-trained politician, Shipad Yesso Naik, to head it. AYUSH has been known to make historical revisions, publishing on its website that yoga is a system of Vedic philosophy. There is no mention of the many non-Vedic systems of yoga. It also demarcates the bounds of yogic authority by stating that Patanjali (author of the Yoga Sutras, which includes a concrete theology and identifies samadhi, a state of absorbed concentration on the immaterial self, as the end goal of yoga) is the "Father of Yoga" (Ministry of AYUSH 2017b). Naik is committed to Modi's goal to make yoga readily available to Indians across the nation and credits Ramdev for his major advances toward that end by making yoga popular in India. As mentioned in chapter 3, Ramdev's two-hour-long yoga television program is the most popular program on Indian TV, attracting more than twenty-five million viewers on an average morning, or five times the viewership of *Good Morning America*. In fact, Naik happily noted that the version of yoga Ramdev teaches "has become synonymous with yoga" in India. Ramdev, in turn, said the ministry's efforts will result in yoga and Ayurveda becoming the "national system of medicine" (Economic Times 2014).

Ramdev's ascent to the forefront of Indian consciousness has been closely tied to Modi's and the BJP's rise to power in 2014. He helped mainstream Hindutva under the guise of representing, qua his status as an authority on yoga, Indian culture. The guru served as a major source of support for Modi in his campaign for the position of prime minister, even hosting politically motivated and highly visible yoga demonstrations during the election campaign as tools of his "Vote for Modi" effort—the demonstrations were stymied by the Election Commission of India. Once elected, Modi met with Ramdev and discussed the guru's personal policy concerns. The Indian media widely covered the meeting, publishing images of the two lifting their clasped hands high, perfectly embodying the Modi-Ramdev spiritual-political complex. On March 23, 2014, Modi participated in Ramdev's Yoga Mahotsav in Delhi and described the guru as having within him a "fire of truth." Allying himself with Ramdev, he heaped praise on the guru for his political activism, saying he approves of Ramdev's choice of political issues on which to focus attention (Express News Service 2014). Ramdev's involvement with Modi has been so substantial it earned the guru protection under the central government. Since 2014, a large round-the-clock team of Central Reserve Police Force personnel have protected Ramdev. And in 2015, Central Industrial Security Force commandos began providing security to Ramdev's Patanjali Yogpeeth campus in Haridwar.

The Yoga Ritual as an Instrument of Authority and Power

The 2015 Yoga Day demonstration produced an effervescent social setting, a space in which ritual performance catalyzes a collective emotional charge that leaves participants feeling connected to something special or extraordinary (Durkheim 2001, 164). On the surface, it seems best analyzed through a social solidarity lens that sees ritual as promoting social integration and value consensus. Consider Modi's first speech to the United Nations General Assembly on September 27, 2014, in which he pled for the establishment of an International Day of Yoga.[15] The following excerpt from that speech opens the yoga protocol:

> Yoga is an invaluable gift of ancient Indian tradition. It embodies unity of mind and body; thought and action; restraint and fulfillment; harmony between man and nature and a holistic approach to health and well-being.

[15] Modi's speech was continuous with his larger effort to position yoga at the center of Indian culture and identity and reclaim it from foreigners. The effort to reclaim yoga is, in turn, a part of Modi's larger economic plan, energized by the slogan "Make in India."

> Yoga is not about exercise but to discover the sense of oneness with our-
> selves, the world and Nature. By changing our lifestyle and creating con-
> sciousness, it can help us deal with climate change. Let us work towards
> adopting an International Yoga Day. (Ministry of AYUSH 2017a, v)

On the one hand, Modi's rhetoric comes across as solidarity-seeking. It
frames yoga as beneficial to all, united by worldwide concerns, including
the present climate crisis. Modi's invocation of *unity, harmony,* and *one-
ness* implies a desire for cooperation and consensus. Unsurprisingly, nearly
two hundred countries, including the United States, Canada, and China,
supported Modi's request to establish an International Day of Yoga, and it
was approved. After all, what could possibly be wrong with yoga, that innocuous body of spiritual (but not religious) practice so many find beneficial to
their health and wellness?

In the months leading up to the inauguration of Yoga Day, Modi continued to instrumentalize yoga in order to project himself as a unifier.
During the moments immediately prior to the demonstration, for example,
he told the crowd: "I believe that from the twenty-first of June, through the
International Day of Yoga, it is not just the beginning of a day but the beginning of a new age through which we will achieve greater heights of peace,
good will and train the human spirit." In Modi's address, he focused on the
health benefits of yoga and how it promotes peace, uniting the "fraternity"
of a global family (NTV Teluga 2015). The stunning visuals of the tens of
thousands of bodies brought together, united by their common leader, also
conjure a sense of communion. In fact, the embodied performance of yoga
postures generally, as bodies are side by side and front to back, uniformly (or
near uniformly) clothed, and contorted into unordinary and sometimes extraordinary postures in sync, lends itself to a social solidarity interpretation.

An interpretation that emphasizes social solidarity might frame the demonstration as a solemn national ritual (the rules of which were laid out in
the Common Yoga Protocol) at a special place (the iconic India Gate monument) that cultivated an effervescent setting, and, therefore, as a paragon
of civil religion. This interpretation would presume the ritual served to integrate society by refreshing national pride and highlighting values, behaviors,
and commitments deemed to have a special place in national identity.
Drawing on Peter Gardella's analysis of civil religion, the observer might suggest the demonstration and surrounding rhetoric served as examples of the
many "monuments, texts, and images, along with the behaviors and values

associated with them [that] amount to a real religion" (2014, 2). Analyzing Yoga Day through Robert N. Bellah's lens on civil religion might lead one to suggest it constituted the "powerful symbols of national solidarity" and mobilized "deep levels of personal motivation for the attainment of national goals" (1968, 15). Through these models of ritual, the Yoga Day demonstration appears to have united India under the gift of yoga, a powerful symbol of Indian identity.

A social solidarity interpretation concluding that the event represented civil religion, however, would fall short by failing to take account of how the ritual reflects social conflict and inequitable power structures. An analysis that more adequately accounts for the discourses and content of the demonstration requires consideration of its relationship to larger social and political dynamics. In short, understanding the ritual necessitates attention to, not only the discourses and content, but also the context. Ritual models social structures, reflects social norms, and presents them for internalization. As Catherine Bell argues, ritualization "reproduces and manipulates its own contextual ground" (Bell 1992, 8).

Lukes argues that the psychosocial Durkheimian notion of social integration and value consensus brought about in scenarios in which there is a collective effervescence does not adequately address the complexity of political rituals, arguing instead that the approach must consider social context by wedding itself to a "class-structured, conflictual and pluralistic model of society" (1975, 301).[16] Such an approach would uncover the ways political ritual can represent the cognitive dimension of social control. The degree of value consensus in liberal democracies is empirically questionable, and social cohesion cannot be attributed to a high degree of shared values across populations, although it may require shared values among elites.[17]

India is a society lacking in value consensus. In addition to being the world's most populous democracy, India also has twenty-two official languages and over three hundred spoken languages, dramatic variations in culture and history across regions, and large-scale religious diversity (about 82 percent of the population are Hindus [and within Hinduism alone, there is incalculable variation in belief, ritual, values, social practices, etc.],

---

[16] Lukes critiques the social solidarity approach, particularly as represented in such famous studies as Shils and Young 1953; Warner 1959 on American rituals; Bellah 1968 on American civil religion; and Verba 1965 on the media events following John F. Kennedy's assassination.

[17] On the lack of value consensus in liberal democracies, Lukes cites Mann 1970 and McClosky 1964.

11 percent are Muslims, and there are large numbers of Parsis, Christians, Sikhs, Buddhists, and Jains). None of these religious groups is homogenous. There are also extreme inequalities between rich and poor, men, women, and LGBTQ people, urban and rural, higher and lower caste, and Hindu and Muslim. Based on that diversity and the coinciding inequities, Doniger and Nussbaum comment, "Although at times one hears phrases such as 'Indian values' and 'Indian culture,' anyone who talks that way, without immediate qualification, is either confessing ignorance or pushing a party line" (2015, 1). Modi betrayed the latter when he inaugurated Yoga Day with a public ritual in celebration of yoga as India's collective gift to the world.

According to Lukes, when social inequity, conflict, and plurality are considered, it becomes apparent that collective effervescences do not unite contemporary communities, but strengthen the socially dominant group through a *mobilization of bias*, basically, the manipulation of a political agenda in order to make it appear that community power is at play when in fact it was generated by and empowers a select few (305). The symbols of political rituals do not necessarily hold society together through perpetuating value integration, but can, in fact, be disintegrative. In other words, the ritual can generate a group consciousness based in a politics of domination and inequality.

The ritual works strategically, according to Lukes, to highlight shared activity and goals while covertly perpetuating certain modes of authority and inequality:

> [Ritual] helps to define as authoritative certain ways of seeing society: it serves to specify what in society is of special significance, it draws people's attention to certain forms of relationships and activity—and at the same time, therefore, it deflects their attention from other forms, since every way of seeing is also a way of not seeing. (301)

Ritual places participants in a performance of domination and subordination, but in a mode that is indirect or subtle. In this sense, it can be akin to *microaggression*, the casual denigration of those belonging to marginalized groups (on the concept of microaggression, see Sue 2010 and Rankine 2014).

Evaluated through this lens, it becomes readily apparent that the 2015 yoga demonstration served as one step in a larger, ongoing Hindu nationalist effort to mainstream Hindutva, demarcate out-groups, and consolidate power. More specifically, such an analysis illuminates the ways the demonstration extended the power of those already dominant while essentializing Indian citizenship as if it represents a homogenous group with shared values and a common religion.

Although the external yoga performance catalyzed an effervescent social setting and gestured toward social cohesion around values of peace and environmental sustainability, it represented a subtle replication and reification of authoritarian and exclusionary neoliberal and Hindutva ideologies, which were meant to be internalized by participants and observers. Even Modi's speech to the UN gestured toward exclusion. Modi assumed the authority to demarcate what yoga is and is not, excluding, for example, many of the women around the world who frame yoga primarily in terms of progressive spirituality, self-care, or exercise. He also excluded those theological and philosophical traditions (including many Hindu ones) grounded in the argument that reality is, in fact, *not* one. Instead, Modi echoed the ongoing Hindu nationalist inclination to conflate Hindu ontology with a modern interpretation of the nondualist philosophical schools of Advaita Vedanta or neo-Vedanta.

Modi's extravagant and public way of attributing special significance to yoga stirred discomfort among some Indian citizens opposed to Hindutva. As plans for Yoga Day were still in progress, a fierce debate arose over his politicization of yoga as an instrument of domination. Many voices contextualized yoga within the BJP's series of efforts to demarcate the boundaries of full citizenship in Hindu terms. The prominent Muslim scholar and public figure Zafarul Islam Khan, for example, suggested:

> The problem is to bring religion into it . . . attempts by the government to undermine diversity in the name of nationalism, including the ban on beef, the opposition to serving eggs to students in schools, and the introduction of Hindu religious texts are an insult to the country's cultural diversity. By Hindu-izing yoga the BJP is compelling Muslims to react. (quoted in Kumar 2015)

The multi-million-dollar, carefully orchestrated, and massive demonstration inaugurating Yoga Day implied that yoga is essential to national identity. That was a problem, not because of *yoga* per se, but because of the ways the BJP government, the divisive yoga guru (Ramdev) to whom Modi attributes yogic authority, and the Sangh Parivar historically couched yoga in multivocal Hindu symbols and associations, the ways they "Hindu-ized yoga." It was, in other words, Modi's yoga that was the problem or, as one headline described it, "Yoga, by R.S.S." (Simeon 2015).

Kamal Farooqui, a member of the Muslim Personal Law Board, also publicly condemned the government's plans for Yoga Day, arguing that it was an extension of the BJP's Hindu nationalism (BBC 2015). The All India Council of the Union of Muslims encouraged Muslims to perform namaz, or prayers, on Yoga Day in protest against what it considered the BJP's attempt "to promote its saffron agenda" (Deccan Chronicle 2015).

On the one hand, Minister of AYUSH Shipad Yesso Naik denied the protests had any ground to stand on and reassured the public, "There is no religion to [yoga]" (Kumar 2015). In an explicit attempt to incite more conflict, on the other hand, the BJP parliamentarian Yogi Adityanath said opponents of Yoga Day or those who think surya namaskar, the most widely practiced sequence of yoga postures around the world, should be excluded from the Common Yoga Protocol should "leave Hindustan" or "drown themselves in the sea or live in a dark room for the rest of their lives."[18]

Whether covertly or overtly, RSS government representatives enforce their particular version of national identity vis-à-vis yoga as an incendiary strategy. Public intellectual and historian Dilip Simeon (2015) described the debate as a "manufactured controversy" by BJP politicians trying to stir tensions in an effort to unite Hindus under Hindutva. Simeon correctly notes that yoga is not definitively Hindu, nor can any of its parts be reduced to its symbolic origins. Yet, he adds,

> Standardisation, uniformity and compulsion are the ideals that inform the Parivar's concept of India (an imperium); its view of the Ramayana, whose many versions it wishes to sanitise, as well as suryanamaskar, whose health benefits are of less significance than the expectation that Muslims might object to it. All the gestures of the R.S.S. are assertions that they alone represent Hindus, and designed to evoke adverse reactions. Such reactions can be used to tell their critics yet again to "go to Pakistan." The R.S.S. thrives on animosity. They would have been truly upset had Muslims not objected to compulsory yoga. (Simeon 2015)

---

[18] The sequence was initially included, but was later cut from the protocol. However, if one believes certain scholarship, the physical format of surya namaskar is not an ancient Hindu practice—it is a modern bodybuilding regimen, conceived of and practiced by early twentieth-century Indian bodybuilders, who were likely inspired by the European ironman Eugen Sandow (Singleton 2010).

One overt way in which the government incited reaction was by asking all government offices, embassies, and public schools to hold yoga sessions simultaneously with the demonstration. Although attendance at the main event in Delhi where Modi inaugurated Yoga Day was officially optional for senior government officials, they received a memorandum advising familiarity with yoga ahead of time, and there were reports that officials felt compelled to participate or risk their careers (Barry 2015). One official reported, "There is a stick hanging over all of us. When the prime minister comes, if officials do not show up, of course it is bad for their career. The attitude is, we have to beat them with a stick to get the job done" (Barry 2015). There were several points leading up to Yoga Day when bureaucrats were pressured to prepare. Since Modi's 2014 election as prime minister, Nagendra visited Delhi on numerous occasions to provide yoga *shalas*, or camps, for government officials. On the day before Yoga Day, Ramdev led a preparatory demonstration at the Jawahar Lal Nehru Stadium in Delhi, where thousands of people scheduled to participate in the main Yoga Day program rehearsed the protocol.

Mythologizing yoga by grounding it in ancient Hindu texts was also a useful way to mainstream a Hindutva worldview and set of values.[19] It is not evidence-based historical knowledge Modi seeks, but, as Kesavan (2015) describes it, the construction of a "glorious Hindu present" built on "a storied Hindu past." In Simeon's (2015) words, "It is not wisdom that interests them, but the compulsory unification of thought and culture." In an effort to unify yoga under a narrow conception of Hinduism, the government wrote a story by carefully selecting from yoga's complex textual tradition, cutting Jains, Buddhists, Muslims, and others (including many Hindus) from that narrative. The protocol formulated by Modi's government describes yoga in a universalizing tone, as an ancient Indian "spiritual discipline" that leads to health. Nevertheless, the "guidelines for yoga practice" begin with a prayer based on South Asian literature's earliest known text and a text widely cited as canonical for Hindus, the *Rig Veda Samhita* (Ministry of AYUSH 2017a, 9).[20] Other texts cited in the protocol include the Gheranda Samhita,

[19] According to Clifford Geertz (1973), myths function to represent a culture's sense of proper moral behavior and feeling as well as its sense of how the world works. In other words, myths provide models for moral behavior as well as models of reality.

[20] As Geoffrey Samuel's historical study of yoga suggests, "There is nothing [in the Rigveda or Atharvaveda] . . . to imply yogic practice, in the sense of a developed set of techniques for operating with the mind-body complex" (2008, 8). Rather, the term *yoga* (from the Sanskrit root *yuj*, meaning "to bind" or "to yoke") refers to the yoke used to bind an animal to a plow or chariot and also to an entire war chariot (White 2012a, 3). More broadly, yoga refers to wartime itself (White 2012a, 3). Vedic

the Hatha Yoga Pradipika, and the Yoga Sutras, which are widely thought of as Hindu texts. Yoga appears in these and many more texts going back hundreds and even thousands of years in South Asia, but the disciplines represented in those texts bear scant resemblance to the majority of what was performed—what scholars of modern yoga term *modern postural yoga*—on Delhi's main thoroughfare on June 21, 2015. Instead of historicizing yoga by uncovering the many forms it takes and those forms' relationships to varying social contexts, the carefully selected texts served to ground the demonstration in a static mythology of ancient Hindu origins.[21] In mythologizing yoga, Modi was not unlike other modern yoga advocates who perpetuate myths of ancient origins in order to ground modern postural yoga in a linear trajectory of transmission (Jain 2014a, 114–115). Premodern yoga as envisaged based on a reading of "classical texts" functions for many modern yoga advocates as the "touchstone of authenticity" (Singleton 2010, 14). The context of Modi's efforts, however, reveals another function of mythologization. Although yoga practitioners outside of India are usually unaware of the religious nuances of South Asia's textual traditions, Modi's audience of Indian citizens is far more cognizant of them, making the *Hindu-ness* underlying the mythology of yoga's origins (as the protocol paints them) far more blatant.

Perhaps in their most significant move toward defining yoga as religious (and not just about the universal aims of health, peace, or environmental sustainability), the protocol's authors define yoga as a practice that "leads to the union of individual consciousness with universal consciousness," resulting in "freedom, referred to as *mukti, nirvāna, kaivalya* or *moksha*" (Ministry of AYUSH 2017a, 5). Although these terms appear in Hindu and non-Hindu yogic traditions, including Jain and Buddhist ones, demarcating an explicitly religious aim of yoga, couching that aim in particular ontological terms, and

---

hymns also refer to the gods moving about heaven and earth on yogas as well as priests yoking themselves "to poetic inspiration and so journeying—if only with the mind's eye or cognitive apparatus—across the metaphorical distance that separated the world of the gods from the words of their hymns" (White 2012a, 4). Yoga's warrior connotation was prevalent in ancient India, as evidenced by the later text the Mahabharata (circa 200 B.C.E. to 400 C.E.), in which dying heroic warriors are described as *yoga-yukta*, "yoked to yoga," the chariot believed to deliver them to heaven (White 2009, 73). In the sense of a systematic set of techniques, Samuel and Johannes Bronkhorst both suggest that yoga developed in the context of a non-Vedic religious culture, the *shramana* culture of "Greater Magadha" (Bronkhorst 2007, 1–9), also known as the "Central Gangetic region" (Samuel 2008, 8). The *shramana* culture was primarily composed of Buddhist, Jain, and ajivika renouncers (circa the sixth and fifth centuries B.C.E.), those who rejected Brahmanical orthodoxy and whose axiological focus was salvation from the conventional and ordinary world, a goal that required ascetic practices. For a brief and concise map of these developments, see Jain 2014a, 1–19.

[21] On mythologizing modern postural yoga, see Jain 2014a, 114–115.

situating these alongside citations pointing to Hindu texts amount to a re-construction of history to reflect a unifying vision of yoga as Hindu.

As Victor Turner (1961) suggests, ritual symbols are *multivocal* or *polyse-mous;* that is, they stand for many things at once. Each has a "fan" or "spec-trum" of referents, which tend to be interlinked by association, its simplicity enabling it to interconnect a wide variety of *significate.* When embedded in ritual, symbols "condense many references, uniting them in a single cognitive and affective field" (Turner 1974, 55). This lens on symbols helps illuminate the ways authority was demarcated and exercised in the yoga demonstration.

Yoga symbolizes the neoliberal values of individual responsibility, worker productivity, and health, all of which Modi and his associates, including Naik and Ramdev, as well as the Common Yoga Protocol echo repeatedly. Yoga is promoted as a scientific, stress-reducing, life-extending therapeutic practice that increases worker productivity, prevents disease, and even bolsters the economy. Modi, Naik, Ramdev, and the Common Yoga Protocol also all cite key texts, especially the Yoga Sutras, and the mythic status of Patanjali as the "father of yoga" to sanction the body practices they prescribe, reifying a form of neoliberal subjectivity conducive to the BJP's neoliberal economic vision. As Christopher Miller argues, Modi's government uses yoga to reform and produce healthy bodies capable of supporting both bureaucratic and corpo-rate operations so that India might harness a similar share of the wealth and power existing within Western democracies (Miller forthcoming), thereby reflecting a novel form of national self-discipline (Kale and Novetzke 2016).

The symbolic reach of Yoga Day, however, extended far beyond neoliberal values. The demonstration was also rich in Hindutva symbolism. Consider the official Yoga Day logo, which adorned the protocol, T-shirts, and other accoutrements and advertising materials. The logo features a seated yoga practitioner, hands raised over the head into the air, and brought together palm to palm, in a gesture of obeisance. Behind the yoga practitioner lies a rising sun, which encircles a world map, with India cleverly placed squarely at the center of the yoga practitioner's head. Yoga, here, directs us toward sacred things, represented by the gesture of obeisance in the direction of the life-giving sun, and has its center in India, and therefore represents a gift from India to the world. Note that this symbol was chosen despite the fact that some Indian citizens vocally protested the threat Modi's yoga campaign posed to religious plurality, and, more specifically, many Muslims who op-posed government-sponsored yoga frequently targeted the performance of surya namaskar, a sequence of postures often construed as a gesture of obeisance to the sun (*surya*) and, therefore, in conflict with certain theological commitments.

Authority was clearly demarcated in the protocol by means of the texts cited therein, but also during the ritual performance itself. Modi became a symbol of yogic authority as he spread his mat at the head of the crowd. His placement at the head of the demonstration seated yogic authority in the prime minister and linked that authority to Modi's past and present, for example: his public boasting about his daily yoga performance and the ways it enhances his abilities as a politician; his political career rife with questions about complicity in communal violence against Muslims; a Hindutva agenda expanded and embellished through his associations with the RSS; and loyalty to Ramdev, a vocal and divisive, right-wing Hindu nationalist yoga guru whose social campaigns targeted LGBTQ Indians. Close attention to the demonstration's performance further highlights the authoritarian nature of Modi's role. At first he surprised audiences by taking a seat at the head of the demonstration and following the instructions for the protocol alongside all other participants. Yet just about seven minutes into the demonstration, Modi broke from the protocol and, in a way akin to yoga teachers and gurus around the world, walked around in an imposing manner, pausing at various participants, overlooking and appearing to inspect their postures. Although Modi got close to many participants, sometimes even stepping onto their mats, participants chosen for Modi's inspection remained focused on the protocol, following it meticulously and maintaining impressive composure even as the prime minister closely inspected them.

Throughout the program, yogic authority was also seated in Ramdev and Naik, as both sat on an elevated stage beside the crowd, also overlooking participants' performance, and only participating in those parts of the protocol that did not require them to stand up. Ramdev's role was particularly significant given the celebrity stature of his yogic authority. From guiding bureaucrats through yoga postures to holding hands with Modi for photo ops with the press, Ramdev contributed to the use of yoga as a ritual meant to give the appearance of unifying India, but in fact perpetuating a divisive vision of Indian identity. The power of Ramdev's celebrity combined with the symbolism of the yoga guru catapulted Modi's yoga campaign to international attention and established the tenor of its cultural politics. Modi's selection of Ramdev as one of his celebrity spokespersons guaranteed media coverage within India, and Ramdev's previous forays into political reform marked him as a symbol of Hindu nationalism who was courageous and patriotic.

Furthermore, the bearded Ramdev's saffron robes are a multivocal symbol of traditional Hindu monasticism and spiritual authority. Ramdev lent his well-established authority as a Hindu sannyasi (orthodox renunciate) to Modi in the time leading up to the 2015 demonstration (making several appearances with Modi and leading the formal preparation for Yoga Day), at the demonstration (seated on stage, overlooking the crowd), and immediately following it that same day (attending photo ops with the press in which Modi appeared with Ramdev by his side). Although in an unofficial role, in the days surrounding Yoga Day, Ramdev lent his authority to Modi in the same way he lends it to his "natural" foods and medicine corporation Patanjali Ayurved (discussed in more length in chapter 3), about which Ramdev once said, "People buy our products because they believe I will only sell them good things" (Anand 2016).

Conclusion

The Hindu right wing in India treats culture as a "means of political domination" (Simeon 2015). Modi's campaign to elevate yoga to a special part of Indian identity and all the nuances of that campaign are extensions of that right-wing strategy. The massive public ritual that inaugurated Yoga Day on June 21, 2015, was meant to mainstream, not only neoliberal values, but also Hindu nationalist ones, in other words, to Hinduize India's national identity and promote centralized uniformity in values and practices deemed necessary for economic growth and productivity as well as orthodox by the authoritarian movement Modi has been entrenched in for much of his life. The demonstration was an attempt to link a narrowly defined vision of yoga as a Hindu form of self-care to national pride as part of India's ancient legacy and future cultural and economic aspirations so that opposition or reluctance to participate could be easily written off as irresponsible and anti-Indian. In Indian journalist Sanjay Kumar's words, participation in Yoga Day became "the yardstick of one's patriotism" (2015, para. 5).

The state-sponsored Yoga Day demonstration reinforced and perpetuated dominant and official models of social structure. An RSS model of Hindu orthodoxy was represented as central to Indian identity by Modi himself, the leader of the demonstration, his associates and advisors on yoga—Ramdev, Naik, and Nagendra—and the Common Yoga Protocol. Modi's associations with Ramdev especially evoked a representation of the social and political order that reflects the values and interests of those in a position of privilege, that is, of heteropatriarchal—even openly and publicly homophobic—Hindu entrepreneurs. In Yoga Day, appropriate political activity included religious apologetics—here, yoga was not merely about the neoliberal pursuit of self-care and self-control, but also particular ontological commitments, symbolism connoting Hindu worship, the concentration of authority and neoliberal governmentality, a celebrity and right-wing Hindu entrepreneurial guru known for his associations with divisive political activity, rhetoric, and policies, and a mythology of ancient Hindu origins, all grounded in a predetermined set of premodern texts widely considered representative of "classical" Hinduism. In all of these ways, the 2015 Yoga Day demonstration was a political ritual that distinctly manifested the cognitive dimension of social control.

In sum, I suggest that yoga here is a ritual instrument for pushing a particular socioeconomic agenda and conservative party line, namely, mainstreaming both neoliberalism and Hindutva. Modi's approach to yoga represents a political, ahistorical, and essentializing strategy. His activities around yoga generally, particularly his alliance with Ramdev, and the Yoga Day demonstration serve to trap his audiences in myths of India's national identity and neoliberal aspirations as well as yoga's static Hindu essence and to perpetuate divisiveness in a society already rife with asymmetrical power relations and social conflict.

Modi would strongly differentiate the yoga he practiced alongside thousands of Indians that first Yoga Day in Delhi from that of the Western entrepreneurs appropriating and commodifying yoga and the white people who buy their products. Many of those entrepreneurs and their profit-making products were discussed in previous chapters. Here my aim was to illustrate some of the sameness across these neoliberal spiritual industries, pushing against not only Modi's argument that his yoga is the authentic brand but also the assumption underlying many of the conversations on neoliberal spirituality at large and cultural appropriation. Many of those studies cited in chapter 2, for example, assume that neoliberal yoga (and spirituality at large) is simply a Western phenomenon, but it is actually made up of far more decentralized, multifocal, and multidirectional industries that in many ways are related to the rise and success of conservative politics across a global neoliberal network.

AN INSIDE JOB

Concluding Remarks

Today, religion is largely about what a person buys. Hence, I have attempted to theorize global spirituality as a social, economic, cultural, religious, and political project, locating its disciplines, discourses, and institutions of self-care within a neoliberal capitalist network that sustains the dominant systems of oppression and environmental degradation around the world. Put differently, spiritual industries support neoliberal capitalism, in the pursuit of both surplus value and ideological control, that is, by reinforcing its structures, norms, and values and punishing deviations from them. Creating deviant out-groups by extending neoliberal governance and responsibilization, and claiming the members of such groups fail to choose the right spiritual interventions to cultivate self-improvement, serve these ends. In addition to the problems of cultural appropriation and racism, there are also gendered dimensions of neoliberal governance. In fact, gender is central (not peripheral) to its operations, especially insofar as heteropatriarchy shapes the ways authority is demarcated and exercised such that resolving the challenges of gender and sexual inequities is a burden placed on the shoulders of the oppressed, that is, women, queer people, and sexual minorities.

Of course, the argument that neoliberal capitalism molds cultures of self-care accords with the consensus academic position that the present moment's arrangement of the dominant culture and ideology shapes the ways people are capable of thinking, even when they seek to think beyond or against the dominant order. Whichever area of religion or culture one studies, be it the "spiritual but not religious," the religiously affiliated, or spiritual or religious commodities, one will uncover evidence that the needs of capital largely determine the priorities of the respective disciplines, discourses, and institutions, that they reproduce inequalities, perpetuate forces contributing to the climate change crisis, oppress the majority of the population, and produce surplus value for a privileged, primarily heteropatriarchal, minority.

Peace Love Yoga. Andrea R. Jain, Oxford University Press (2020). © Oxford University Press.
DOI: 10.1093/oso/9780190888626.001.0001

Most significantly, one will likely find that they individualize what are fundamentally social, environmental, and political issues in society. This is obviously cohesive with neoliberal capitalism. It follows an ideology that you need to work on yourself, rather than look to social resources for solutions to your (and the world's) greatest problems. I argue in the preceding chapters that this is why spiritual discourses have become all-encompassing (and I would add that they have also become hegemonic) over the last few decades; they are highly useful in depoliticizing the oppressive and ugly reality of life on this planet. The involvement of global spiritual discourses, disciplines, and institutions here is only one factor in the bigger problem, though, which is of course the way the neoliberal capitalist project destroys the social and the collective, not to mention the environment, all around the world.

I have argued that, when we speak of neoliberal spirituality's disciplines, which consumers often describe as empowering, transformative, or liberating, we are not talking about things that weaken dominant hierarchies, and certainly not the structural power of entrepreneurs or corporations, even when those same disciplines intersect with subversive discourses. Neither do they challenge the structures that uphold conservative leadership and social policies. The connections between spirituality and many other areas of public and private life are explicit insofar as much of neoliberal spirituality's products are rooted in concerns about deviancy, not only in the form of low productivity but also forms of social and sexual deviancy that, for example, challenge heteropatriarchy. The prescriptions for self-care or personal transformation have little or nothing to do with actual societal transformation, even though they often gesture toward the need for REVOLUTION; rather they denote the requirements for more productive, efficient, and conforming workers. In other words, as the demands on people to work and be productive have increased, so we have seen an increase in spiritual entrepreneurs, claiming they can enhance productivity and simultaneously conformity to a rigid moral standard, all while making the larger world a better place.

The material discussed in preceding chapters serves to make these points, yet I have also attempted to take seriously neoliberal spirituality's modes of valuation that sometimes result in discursive resistance to neoliberal capitalism (even if they do not do work to dismantle its social structures), suggesting that spirituality is not simply a numbing device; rather, spiritual entrepreneurs, corporations, and consumers often see the problems of neoliberal capitalism and confront them, though that confrontation is contained—it is limited—through *gestural subversions*. In other words,

rather than a mode through which consumers ignore the problems of neoliberal capitalism, neoliberal spiritual corporations, consumers, institutions,
and industries at times actually acknowledge those problems and, in fact,
subvert them. But they do so through subversions that largely function as
superficial points of resistance already contained within the totalizing framework of a neoliberal and conservative rationality.

Subversion, in short, is domesticated or colonized and, in the context
of neoliberal capitalism, it is often contained in commodities and their
discourses. Sometimes, even in the context of global consumer culture, those
discourses exist outside the realm of commodification. I endeavored to show
that there is a neoliberal spiritual subjectivity, one that is not simply commodified, always and endlessly merely reflecting the pursuit of profit. Rather,
it is religious, it is about axiology or valuation, which furthermore creates
meaning and community and demarcates authority above and beyond commodification and is narrated through story and embodied through ritual.

Following my earlier point, that spirituality has been put toward the
ends of neoliberal capitalism, that is, the goals of surplus value and ideological control, by reinforcing its structures, norms, and values and punishing deviations from them, I found that it intersects with much of what
characterizes modern incarceration. Of course, they are also very different,
since prisons physically confine problematic populations (primarily working
class and racially, religiously, and socially disenfranchised people). Yet, spirituality and incarceration in their contemporary forms are both products of
neoliberal capitalism and work toward socializing citizens into its structures,
norms, and values as the only "correct" way to be in, think in, and understand
the world.

Consider mass incarceration and the abusive forms of imprisonment that
prevail in the United States. American incarceration is a neoliberal "carceral state," which upholds a racialized regime of mass imprisonment; indeed, prisons are a "growth industry" (Thorpe 2015). According to Jeffrey
C. Isaac, mass incarceration in the United States, which is now the world's
largest penal population at 2.2 million, is "a serious normative blight on and
political dysfunction of American democracy" (2015, 610). According to
Amy E. Lerman and Vesla M. Weaver, mass incarceration arrests democratic
practice insofar as prisoners experience "civil death" (2014). In addition to
losing their basic rights as citizens, including the ability to vote, prisoners
experience "stark and pernicious gradations of citizenship" when they are
denied civil liberties, including decent employment and basic social benefits

(Gottschalk 2015, 561–563; see also Dilts 2014). Michelle Alexander explains how the war on drugs' large-scale criminalization of nonviolent offenses resulted in a racialized regime in which the "legal rules that structure the system guarantee discriminatory results" (2012, 17).

Neoliberal spirituality functions differently by covertly controlling populations, including some of the most privileged among us. Unlike the prison industrial complex, spiritual industries do not entail compulsory powers that confine and control people against their will, withdrawing the rights of full citizenship. Neoliberal society, in its weddedness to conservative values, cannot generally imprison the problematic among the privileged minority. Hence, spirituality, as opposed to imprisonment, becomes a mode through which to covertly control, contain, and correct problematic behaviors among society at large. How can we understand the intersections of these two complexes? As I demonstrate subsequently, we can do this by looking at how neoliberal spirituality, a hegemonic cultural complex, has entered the prison system itself through prison yoga and meditation programs.

Spiritual and prison industries have something in common; they both serve as containers of political and social dissent. Being a "criminal" and the social stigma of being spiritually inadequate, sick, or out of touch with oneself are all associated with failing or refusing to choose the right disciplines, discourses, and institutions, the ones that would maximize success and self-care, resulting in individual failures that break with the legal or moral status quo.

Prison Yoga

As I explained in the introduction, when I first came to this book project, I was in the preliminary stage of writing a book about "prison yoga," on the uses of yoga as an "alternative" mode of rehabilitation and transformation among prison populations in the United States, Africa, and India. I wanted to build on my work in *Selling Yoga* (2014a), which found that even though for many yoga proponents, the claim to possess knowledge of yoga is closely related to their quest for power, status, or money, there is much more to the contemporary yoga world than who profits. I found that the meaning of yoga is conveyed not only through what products and services consumers choose to purchase, but also through what they choose not to purchase. In other words, consumption usually requires the exchange of money and commodities; however, consumption can also lack such an exchange. Many contemporary yoga practitioners, in fact, opt out of the commodification of yoga by attending nonprofit yoga classes, in some cases while imprisoned (2014, 106–108).

Initially, in these prison yoga and meditation programs, I (perhaps naively) expected to find that yoga and meditation could serve as a political act of resistance, one that challenges the prison industrial complex by scrutinizing the inequities that lead to the torture and imprisonment of certain disenfranchised populations. I soon found, however, that rather than seek the abolition of the prison, such programs respond in other ways to the current era of mass incarceration. To start, the program leaders' focus is not on the immediate need to empty prisons; rather, their focus is most often on the need of prisoners to HEAL FROM THE INSIDE OUT, an approach that does not simply assume but *requires* prisoners to be imprisoned where they can undergo the transformative process.

As I explain in the introduction, the success of various right-wing movements, including the 2014 election of Narendra Modi to prime minister of India, the 2016 Brexit vote in the United Kingdom, the 2016 election of Donald Trump to president of the United States, and the subsequent grief in confrontation with the reality that things are not getting better—progress is an illusion—triggered my rethinking of prison yoga and mindfulness programs. The scope of my project broadened, and I looked at several areas of global spirituality, including yogaware, #MeToo, nationalist politics, and the other material strewn throughout this book and found that the discourses underlying their disciplines and institutions echo those of prison yoga and meditation programs. I kept returning to prison yoga, asking whether or not the practice of yoga by prisoners was an extension of their punishment, not a rebellion against it. Likewise, I considered whether global spirituality's concerns with correction, adjustment, and perfection, the training of expert teachers to observe and assess, technologies of physical, mental, and emotional labor, and individualized approaches to rehabilitation and transformation might be more akin to those corrective aims of modern punishment, enslaving problematic individuals to the dominant system by replacing violence with interventions meant to "improve" and "discipline" them. Could yoga or meditation as rehabilitative self-care simply reproduce forms of neoliberal governmentality, predicated on responsible, self-governing, manageable subjects? Are yoga and meditation programs extensions of the rehabilitative practices that claim to be alternative responses to incarceration, but ultimately function as supplements to rather than substitutes for it?

With their "trauma informed" approaches, prison yoga or meditation programs, which set out to reform the system—endeavoring to bring about "global well-being" by focusing on individuals, "one body at a time" (see, e.g., Africa Yoga Project 2019)—produce contradictory discourses: apolitical and disciplinary while critical and subversive. I do not want to suggest that the leaders of and participants in these programs are deaf to the horrific conditions of mass incarceration. But attention to the possibilities for the prisoner, by means of their good choices, to undergo healing and transforming while in prison far outweighs attention to the dire conditions of the millions of people currently incarcerated.

The Prison Yoga Project embodies some of these contradictions. In 2002 James Fox, yoga teacher and founder and director of the Prison Yoga Project, began teaching yoga to prisoners at the infamous San Quentin State Prison, a California prison for men. Since then Fox has expanded his project to other locations around the country, and the Prison Yoga Project has become the best-known program of its kind. The project clearly and forthrightly opposes mass incarceration in the name of social justice: "Punishing people through mass incarceration isn't making our communities safer, it's just making people suffer" (Prison Yoga Project 2019a). According to the Prison Yoga Project, most prisoners suffer from "original pain," pain caused by chronic trauma experienced early in life. The key to preventing offenders from reoffending is to help them resolve their own trauma, and yoga and mindfulness effectively do so. They provide a path toward "rehabilitation and transformation" (Prison Yoga Project 2019a).

In 2014, I attended a special session of a teacher training at the Yoga Moksha Center in Chicago. There Fox opened the special training with a talk about teaching yoga to prisoners in San Quentin. Several yoga teachers sat in attendance and appeared to eagerly soak in each word Fox spoke.[1] Fox described the inhumane conditions—the "human cages"—in which prisoners passed their time, suggesting the yoga class was sometimes the only habitable space for prisoners, a space where they could connect with themselves and others. Fox's imperative in teaching yoga in prisons was clearly to humanize life for the prisoners and facilitate healing.

---

[1] The workshop occurred on Friday, May 9, 2014.

Fox showed a slideshow of photos taken of his students and paused on one in which several men stood together and, arms around one another's shoulders, posed for the camera. Fox asked the teacher trainees in attendance if they noticed anything peculiar about the image. After a few people commented on the image's primary affect (most of the prisoners smiled) or the intimacy (the prisoners appeared emotionally close given their physical proximity to one another), Fox disclosed the answer he was looking for: in an environment where racial boundaries often impose limitations on who a prisoner might call his "friend," these men of different races were standing together, connected to one another through yoga. Here, a white man leading a teacher training for mostly white yoga practitioners illustrated through the image of mostly Black and Hispanic men how yoga apparently collapsed racial boundaries in American prisons.

Only it did not collapse racial injustice as it pertains to the prison system. After all, the racial and ethnic makeup of American prisons looks substantially different from the demographics of the country as a whole (statistics to date show that Blacks represent almost 38 percent of the prison population but only about 13 percent of the general population. Hispanics represent almost 32 percent of the prison population but only about 18 percent of the general population [Federal Bureau of Prisons 2020; U.S. Census Bureau 2018]).

There was a precedent for bringing yoga and meditation to American prison populations well before the Prison Yoga Project. By the 1960s, a secularized, rehabilitative penology included an individualized approach to treating prisoners, giving them more freedom in exchange for "good choices" in the forms of comprehensive therapy, including a twelve-step program. Yoga and meditation soon appeared as additional choices for American prisoners. Today, they are present in prisons in all fifty states, with over 185 organizations or projects and more than five thousand participants (Maull 2015).

In fact, this kind of work (introducing yoga and mindfulness to imprisoned populations) is taking place all around the world. When Fox started the Prison Yoga Project, he drew on the work of Joseph H. Pereira, an Iyengar Yoga teacher, Catholic priest, and founder and managing trustee of the Kripa Foundation in India (Kripa Foundation 2006–2007). Founded in 1981, the Kripa Foundation now operates over thirty recovery centers for people suffering from alcohol or drug addiction as well as support centers for people suffering from HIV and AIDS (Kripa Foundation 2006–2007). The Kripa

Foundation claims to provide a "supportive community living, empowering people to introspect and bring about a change in lifestyle" (Kripa Foundation 2006–2007).

In Nairobi, Kenya, Baptiste Yoga, another vigorous form of modern postural yoga, is used as a rehabilitative method and as an initiative to educate and empower impoverished people in the city of Nairobi and several locations throughout the informal settlements of Nairobi, especially through the Africa Yoga Project, a nonprofit organization that offers free yoga classes to impoverished, at-risk youth and incarcerated women and their children in and near Nairobi. American yoga teachers Paige Elenson and Baron Baptiste founded the Africa Yoga Project in 2007. Today the organization relies on Kenyan yoga teachers trained by the Africa Yoga Project to work among disadvantaged and imprisoned communities. Fox himself has conducted intensive training sessions with those teachers. Representatives of the Prison Yoga Project in collaboration with the Africa Yoga Project have called their work with incarcerated people in Kenya *seva*, a Sanskrit term meaning selfless service, performed without expectation of a result or award for the person doing it.

Prison yoga and meditation programs prescribe redemptive, transformative rehabilitation as the solution to mass incarceration. With their emphases on acceptance, nonjudgment, nonreaction, and the focus on individual choice, healing, and transformation (not the transformation of social or economic structures), they contain resistance to structurally determined political outcomes and systemic injustice. In other words, such programs serve to rehabilitate, that is, manage incarcerated populations without substantially challenging the fundamental validity of mass incarceration or the ways it targets certain populations. Yoga and meditation, in these contexts, is palatable to witnesses like those yoga teachers training with Fox in Chicago, because of the emphasis on individual responsibility over structural dismantalization. The imperative to humanize life for prisoners—to make conditions unconceivable to most yoga and meditation consumers palatable—avoids cultivating and sustaining a systemic critique of injustice on the part of the prison population itself as well as the teachers who bring yoga and meditation into the prisons.

These are strange spaces of the modern yoga and meditation worlds, where prisoners—people many would describe as "criminals"—move their bodies together or sit and meditate in ways akin to what we imagine when we envision spandex-clad suburbanites at a yoga studio or the mass yoga demonstrations, such as Modi's tens of thousands gathered in Yoga Day T-shirts. They also echo the discourses of other areas of spirituality, for example, the nonprofit benefiting from the annual "Monumental Yoga" event in my own city of Indianapolis. Its leaders describe the organization as empowering youth "to overcome challenges and lead mindful, purposeful and healthy lives through the development of life skills using yoga, mindfulness and other awareness practices" (Indy Yoga Movement 2019).

The logic of rehabilitation as personal transformation and healing serves as the most powerful justification for offering yoga and meditation to prisoners. The most frequently cited purpose for bringing meditation and yoga into prisons is rehabilitation and the prevention of recidivism, crime reduction, and successful reintegration into "law-abiding civil society" (Maull 2015, 8). These goals are repeated multiple times in conference papers, research reports, and teacher-training materials and on websites (Maull 2015). There is an emphasis on "the effort to reform our criminal justice institutions and processes," but with a moral undertone (Carlin 2015, 2). The work is characterized as "inseparable from our moral standards and dignity [as human beings]" and as offering to all "the opportunity for healing and transformation" (Maull 2015, 8). In other words, moral healing and transformation are uncritically conflated with "the efficient management of incarcerated individuals . . . [that] supports prisoners in developing healthy coping mechanisms and prosocial attitudes and behaviors" (Maull 2015, 8). The language of taking responsibility for one's actions is pervasive in these programs (see Maull 2015, 10 and Carlin 2015, 3, 17).

The Prison Yoga Project, for example, describes its mission in terms of the "transformational, rehabilitative value of yoga," designed to "address . . . behavioral issues" and "increase . . . empathy for others . . . and understand the harm [the incarcerated] have caused" (Prison Yoga Project 2019a). Most troubling are the words printed across Prison Yoga Project T-shirts: FREEING THE PRISONER INSIDE is printed beneath an OM encircled with barbed wire. Another "one-of-a-kind [design], created by a former San Quentin prisoner and dedicated yoga practitioner," a "soft v-neck tee," reads: PRISON YOGA PROJECT. AN INSIDE JOB (Prison Yoga Project Shop 2019). There are resonances in the Africa Yoga Project with its tagline: SHINE FROM THE INSIDE OUT. "The potential to change the world," according to the Africa Yoga Project, "lives in each of us." The project delivers "tools to bring wellbeing to the world, one body at a time" (Africa Yoga Project 2019).

The language here is apolitical, devoid of any mention of mass incarceration as a societal race or class problem. Incarceration, in this model, is an "inside" problem—a problem within the individual prisoner; therefore the burden of solving the problem of incarceration and what is ostensibly antisocial criminality rests on the shoulders of the individual prisoner, who is deeply in need of self-governance, a new mindset, and an emotional makeover. Although these prison yoga and meditation projects object to the dehumanization of incarceration, they do not target the structural factors contributing to mass incarceration, suggesting that the task is primarily one of reforming the prisoners themselves, the socially and morally defective.

Prison yoga and meditation, in these ways, extend the carceral system's turn toward rehabilitation in ways that valorize neoliberal self-governance. The carceral system at large produces the figure of the "responsible," "enterprising" prisoner, who is held accountable for managing their own risks (O'Malley 1992, 261). The offender is expected to make the right choices to ensure a self-sufficient future; personal responsibility is now construed as crucial to rehabilitation (see, e.g., Hannah-Moffat 2000 and Bosworth 2007).

Prison yoga and meditation represent another form of gestural subversion. The Prison Yoga Project acknowledges that the criminal justice system is deeply flawed and seeks to reform it. Reform is framed primarily in terms of making imprisonment more humane and making healing mechanisms accessible to prisoners, so they can take responsibility for their own transformation. Yoga and meditation are prescribed as the solutions. Prisoners are called upon to practice yoga and meditation in order to heal from the criminal impulses that landed them in prison, to learn to make better choices. A politically attuned understanding of an unjust carceral state and a call to restructure the criminal system are muted. The imperative to humanize life for prisoners stands in place of systemic critiques of the injustice—as opposed to "choices"—that led to incarceration to begin with.

Prison yoga and meditation uncritically reproduce the logic of neoliberal spirituality; effective self-management, healing, and rehabilitation are key to liberation and transformation, to solving the problem of mass incarceration. Basically, I fear prison yoga and meditation serve the purpose of "managing" incarcerated people without challenging the fundamental validity of mass incarceration. In other words, these programs' neoliberal discourses frame mass incarceration as a problem of self-governance. The solutions they offer are framed as "rehabilitating" and "transforming" traumatized prisoners, bolstering the neoliberal logic of the carceral state while undermining more radical critiques that point to the structurally unjust nature of mass incarceration.

Prison yoga and meditation contain resistance to the unjust structural problems that lead to mass incarceration within the framework of rehabilitative penology, sometimes called penal welfarism, an orientation toward punishment motivated by reformist goals of recidivism-reduction through therapeutic justice, therapy, and education (Garland 1990). Like the heteropatriarchal elements of spiritual commodities, the rehabilitative penology underlying prison yoga and meditation selectively deploys themes from the neoliberal toolkit, while also incorporating conservative, moralistic, and disciplinary ones.

Prison yoga and meditation extend modern punishment, which, according to Foucault, is corrective, meant to use various diagnostic, prognostic assessments and technical prescriptions to produce "normalized," improved individuals (1977, 19, 20–21, 251–255). This kind of penal system is noncorporeal in nature as it "no longer addresses itself to the body ... [but to] the soul," to "thoughts, will, inclinations," asking "what would be the best way of rehabilitating [the offender]?" (Foucault 1977, 16). The apparatus of violence is replaced with knowledge and routine intervention meant to "improve" problematic individuals.

Neoliberal forms of governance, from Bikram Yoga to prison yoga, are based on the presumption that a person's unfortunate circumstances are the outcome of their own poor choices, rather than of structural or systemic inequalities. In this way, correctional strategies govern "at a distance" (Hannah-Moffat 1999, 79), and prisoners manage themselves through their freedom, their own choices, preferably ones that make them less at risk of victimization, criminality, poverty, racism, classism, and unemployment. In interventions like prison yoga or meditation, a rehabilitative logic is conjoined to a voluntarist approach or what we might call "a good-choice approach" that functions as a new means of control meant to control and transform conduct; this approach addresses "manageable criminogenic problems" with individual behavioral changes, which the "good" criminal achieves with a positive attitude and willingness to embrace available interventions (Hannah-Moffatt 2005, 43).

The distinction these spiritual programs assume between rehabilitation and reform on the one hand and dehumanizing methods of control and imprisonment on the other is a false dichotomy: the rehabilitative and transformative practices of yoga and meditation are part and parcel of strategies of control, as rehabilitative strategies have been for a long time (see Garland 1990; also Harcourt 2010). The neoliberal forms they take today, with their emphases on acceptance, nonjudgment, and nonreaction and their focus on the individual and their healing through personal transformation stand in place of critical reflection on structurally determined political outcomes and systemic injustice.

All of this should seem familiar after one reads about the discourses of spiritual commodities, such as that of the Canadian yogaware corporation Lululemon in chapter 3. As a reminder, in 2011, Lululemon controversially printed on its retail bags the Ayn Rand quotation WHO IS JOHN GALT? as a message to customers that their class, careers, incomes, and even bodies are not the outcomes of forces beyond their control, of social structures, of systemic racism or sexism, or of any other form of oppression, but of personal effort and choice. In neoliberal spirituality, as in prison yoga and meditation, protests against injustice, harm, or suffering are contained within a neoliberal logic as adherents are called upon to HEAL FROM THE INSIDE.

The Question of Radical Self-Care

One might retort that introducing yoga and meditation programs in prisons can generate attention to social injustice and resistance to oppression. "Socially engaged" yoga and meditation, one might argue, can undermine the pacification imperative of a carceral state by assisting the imprisoned in basic self-preservation, simultaneously politicizing the question of incarceration.

Yet if self-care can be subversive in prison yoga and meditation programs, I have not uncovered where or when that seems to be the case. I have not uncovered, for example, where responsibility for incarceration and recovery is consistently placed, not on the shoulders of individuals, but on social and economic structures. Should we, nevertheless, consider whether the subversions of the spiritual discourses of self-care, in certain areas of culture (if not prisons), ever become more than mere gestures? Do they ever escape the bondage of neoliberal culture and ideology? I think only when created and led by activists who are among the disenfranchised and are those who refuse to cooperate with dominant powers, they can. In 1988, Black lesbian writer and activist Audre Lorde, after all, famously said, "Caring for myself is not self-indulgence, it is self-preservation, and that is an act of political warfare" (2017, 130). The call was to use self-care as a means to remaining ever alert to the threat of social inequality and the responsibility of radicals to sustain political commitment and to manifest social solidarity, which required that they insist to a violent and oppressive privileged minority that they were worthy of care. Since then, several prominent Black women activists have echoed Lorde's call, drawing connections between race, activism, and self-care. Speaking in 2014 at Pacific University, Angela Davis remarked, "Self-care has to be incorporated in all of our efforts. And this is something new. This holistic approach to organizing is, I think, what is going to eventually move us along the trajectory that may lead to some victories" (2014). LGBTQ people from across the world echoed this position following the 2016 mass shooting at a gay night club in Orlando, Florida, when people started posting selfies under the hashtag #queerselflove.

More recently, the most notable climate activist today, Greta Thunberg, has demanded action in the form of concrete policy changes to prevent catastrophic climate change. She addresses world leaders, attending UN climate summits around the world, and the general population. The sixteen-year-old climate activist is a leading figure in the climate justice movement, inspiring millions across the globe since she launched her school strike in 2018. Thunberg is also on the autism spectrum and has faced insults and criticisms in light of that. She has responded, using the hashtag #aspiepower, "When haters go after your looks and differences, it means they have nowhere left to go. And then you know you're winning!" While acknowledging that being on the autism spectrum has posed challenges, she also describes it as a "superpower."

These forms of self-care—when we love and uplift the deviant or divergent body, rather than burden it with the responsibility to recover or morally police it—are more than acts of mere self-preservation, they are also forms of embodied resistance.

Conclusion

Appropriation, commodification, and purchasing are a part of identity formation in contemporary consumer culture. Individuals build identities and gain a sense of belonging through participation in consumer groups. I have argued that neoliberal spiritual consumers fashion identities based on essentialized, exoticized, and sometimes orientalized images of other cultures and their ideas, practices, and symbols. Identity formation through their discourses, institutions, and disciplines facilitates the creation of spiritual communities, sometimes posing serious ethical problems when they elide contemporary and historical forms of oppression.

Some critics of spirituality have suggested that it can be reduced to market practices. A more nuanced approach, I have suggested, is necessary for understanding its dynamism, internal diversity, religious creativity, and connections to both neoliberal capitalism and conservative and nationalist politics. The fact is there is a wide range of cultural products and services that are both deeply religious or spiritual *and* commodified or exploitative. In other words, commodified spiritual products are not one thing—there are many varieties—and their religious or spiritual dimensions do not stand in opposition to economic or political activities. Neoliberal spirituality has not *replaced* religion; rather new religious complexes have emerged within areas of global spirituality.

Spiritual practices, discourses, and institutions appear everywhere, on the Spiritual Gangster website and other clothing retail outlets, health food outlets, from Whole Foods Market to Patanjali Ayurved, corporate training stress-reduction programs, and of course all varieties of yoga studios, but also in trade unions, immigrant rights movements, prisons, environmental justice organizations, civil rights projects, on college campuses, and elsewhere where there is also work to identify and sometimes undermine inequalities of all kinds. I have no doubt that many spiritual spaces facilitate sustained dissent against the dominant neoliberal and capitalist economic, political, and social structures. Those spaces of resistance, however, at best appear at the margins of spirituality. In other words, neoliberal spirituality represents just one strain of religious spaces increasingly described as "spiritual" or "the spiritual but not religious," but it is the most powerful and visible—indeed, it is increasingly hegemonic—so it should be of ultimate concern to us in our endeavors to theorize religion in contemporary society.

When we attend to the differentiated modes of spirituality, a lot changes about how we theorize it. For example, it is not always about the "unaffiliated." Furthermore, it appears that the rise of spirituality is not just a North Atlantic phenomenon nor is it predominantly so. The spiritual people are not always on the left or progressive end of the political spectrum in any sense of critically acknowledging and reflecting on the ways power is exercised through social structures and systemic forms of discrimination, such as racism, sexism, or homophobia, or on how capitalism led us to the climate crisis. They are certainly not necessarily egalitarian or antiauthoritarian.

In the academic study of spirituality and in popular yoga and other spiritual publications themselves, there is often a desire for a narrative of unity, as if there is an essence or core to spiritual industries and to the cultures they appropriate from that is somehow alternative to the reigning order. But the discomfort that comes with efforts to illuminate the differences, discrepancies, and contradictions, even and especially political ones, in spiritual industries is necessary. Ultimately, when we attend to these, acknowledging all of the moving parts of this phenomenon will strengthen the collective project to understand it.

Spirituality has been envisioned as a cohesive, primarily North American or Western movement that provides an *alternative* to mainstream religion and lifestyle, but the materials analyzed in this book suggest we should rethink spirituality and attend to the ways it is religious, politically disjointed, sometimes socially divisive, global, and, in many forms, quite mainstream.

I have examined the political logics that neoliberal spirituality bolsters, even in the carceral context, and ascertained that they serve as yet another modern mode of discipline that repackages self-care in a neoliberal guise, reinforcing the current system in order to make it more effective. Sold as a tool for individual transformation and personal growth, the products of neoliberal spirituality are disconnected from political resistance to social structures, instead sustaining neoliberal capitalism, including the prison industrial complex, in its current forms.

Is it possible to combine yoga, mindfulness, or other spiritual disciplines, discourses, or institutions, and their peaceful, loving, liberating gestures, with righteous anger and revolutionary, disruptive political action? If so, how could people sustain and broaden the rise of global spirituality as resistance, while rejecting the rationality underlying neoliberal capitalism? How could people build and maintain spiritual disciplines, discourses, and institutions that threaten the many forces that continue to oppress, exclude, and disenfranchise whole segments of society and destroy the environment? Such spiritual movements would need to demand revolutionary economic, social, and cultural transformations, thereby creating alternative visions as well as hope for the future. Because countless forms of neoliberal spirituality have already been rendered popular and desirable, an oppositional form might be able to gain widespread traction at this particular moment in history. In other words, the infrastructure for an oppositional spiritual groundswell might already be in place. Another way to put this is that, even though the discourses, institutions, and disciplines of what I have called *neoliberal spirituality* appear everywhere and nothing about them threatens the powers that be, one of its unintended effects may well constitute a threat. Precisely because neoliberal spiritual industries have facilitated the widespread visibility and global embrace of spirituality, they might have concurrently paved the way for socialist and feminist spiritual movements that encourage mass mobilization in order to challenge not only Trump's heterosexist and xenophobic policies and Modi's Islamophobia, but more broadly an increasingly dominant neoliberal agenda that, to borrow Noam Chomsky's words, puts "profit over people."

I have no doubt that yoga and meditation serve the critical purpose of assisting with survival amid everyday violence, oppression, and environmental destruction. The impulse to reduce people's suffering, or to give them mechanisms for coping with it, is understandable. Yet the efforts to improve people's quality of life in the context of neoliberal spirituality basically amount to making a destructive and oppressive system—and at its worst in the carceral context, a brutal disciplinary system—more palatable, and the most vulnerable more compliant. As with carceral systems, these do not usually offer institutions that function in society's or the environment's interests.

An example of protest that refuses to cooperate, and that therefore amounts to more than gestural subversion, is embodied by climate activist Greta Thunberg, with her demands for action in the form of concrete policy changes to prevent catastrophic climate change. Other examples of contemporary uncooperative political resistance include the efforts of groups like the antiwar Code Pink, which resorts to reason, empirical evidence, and visibility to challenge US development policies, and the Platform for the Movement for Black Lives, one of the most advanced and inclusive political visions ever articulated; the Fight for $15 movement that successfully campaigned to raise the minimum wage in many parts of the United States; and the Poor People's Campaign, which is building political power through the unity of the poor to center the ethical framework of the poor and dispossessed. Twenty-first-century Indian women's movements, which have used social media campaigns against the culture of sexual violence to launch a radically new kind of feminist politics, include numerous examples: the 2003 Blank Noise Project against eve-teasing, the 2009 Pink Chaddi (underwear) movement against moral policing, the 2011 SlutWalk protest against victim-blaming, the 2011 Why Loiter project on women's right to public spaces, the 2015 Pinjra Tod (Break the Cage) movement against sexist curfew rules in student halls, and the 2017 Bekhauf Azadi (Freedom without Fear) March.

The kind of spiritual protest that similarly refuses to cooperate with the dominant power structures and that is called for by thinkers in the Black feminist tradition of Lorde could serve as an important counter to the rise of gestural, that is, defanged and nonoppositional, invocations of spirituality. This kind of political subversion would require spiritual consumers to combine their individual privileges, skills, and knowledge with collective resistance even if it meant putting those toned, spandex-clad bodies in between oppressive governments and the most vulnerable populations—black bodies, brown bodies, queer bodies, the differently abled, divergent, and atypical, women, and people living in poverty. To be activists against social inequity and the destruction of the environment, in short, they would need to embody resistance through concrete action.

If spirituality avoided being depoliticizing or accommodationist, it could challenge the edifice of neoliberal capitalism by offering practices that develop greater awareness of systemic oppression and the climate crisis, along with skills to combine survival with active resistance. This would require a mode of education meant to be counterhegemonic and emancipatory, providing a critical lens for understanding the oppressive strategies of neoliberal capitalism and encouraging insurrectionist responses to power at every cultural site, from incarceration to education.

Within neoliberal spirituality alone, the diverse array of texts, discourses, and practices that industries, corporations, entrepreneurs, and consumers appropriate cannot be thought to align with either conservative or counterhegemonic political commitments in any inherent sense, though some have argued otherwise, for example, when Farah Godrej suggests yoga contains ample resources for challenging neoliberalism (2016). I would argue, rather, that spiritual communities need to access resources to counter hegemonic neoliberalism, not by turning to some resource from the past, but by turning to the socialist, civil rights, environmentalist, and feminist forms of activism in the present, those that embrace the political task of changing structures of inequity, policies contributing to climate change, and social practices that accommodate the status quo.

* * *

I have argued that neoliberal spiritual discourses, disciplines, and institutions—including their countless commodities, for example, T-shirts with PEACE LOVE YOGA printed across the front—often enact an orientalist fantasy of enlightenment-ethics that is especially seductive in a world of ever-expanding obligations and needs. A desire to subvert the violence of neoliberal capitalism is expressed and then contained. In and through its creative usage of neoliberal governance, for example, its capitalist-orientalist and feminist tropes, the text of spirituality provides a theoretical model and ideological justification for a neoliberal ethic.

Yet for all of the peace and love it offers through yoga, health foods, mindfulness, and countless other modes of self-governance, neoliberal spirituality plays a divisive and conservative game that thrives on nostalgia about lost cultural norms demarcating outsiders, as well as narratives about transformation and liberation and the value of purification and self-care.

I do not know the way forward for spiritual communities. This book does not offer a constructive vision for them to embrace. Our reality, as it stands, is a terrible one, and my work here was to provide a nuanced account of the ways neoliberal spiritual entrepreneurs, corporations, and consumers' pervasive gestural subversions signal that the products are characterized by values antagonistic to or at least in tension with the forces and relations of capitalist production. They provide the language for spiritual consumers' discontent. Yet they also contain their dissent, preventing efforts to dismantle the destructive social and economic structures upholding our current terrible reality. My hope is that such work in cultural diagnostics might help pave the way for something more constructive.

Acknowledgments

This book is an extended love letter to my dear friends. They carried me through the years I wrote it. When the subjects were troubling or the arguments unsettling, our connections sustained me. Whenever I looked up from the page, my friends were there, a sturdy and substantive presence. My work often feels lonely, but in the loneliest moments, I am never really alone. It is as if they uphold the surface on which I work; in this, they conjure the paper on which I write.

There are many people I want to acknowledge, but anyone who knows me will not be surprised when I start with Jeff Kripal. No one has done more to remind me that connections are everything. I lean on Jeff's steady love and support. For his unceasing habits of argument and creativity, for the intensity of his commitments and the energy of his doubts, and for his willingness to come with me when I drop off the edge of convention and into reinvention, my deepest gratitude.

There has been day-by-day friendship in Edward Curtis. I wrote most of this book just on the other side of the wall from him, and we often crossed over. Thank you to Edward for the solidarity, substance, playfulness, and comfort of those conversations.

Thank you to my friend, colleague, and editorial teammate on the *Journal of the American Academy of Religion,* Kevin Schilbrack. Our connection was often my safe retreat.

I have benefited from Adam Hayden's insurmountable capacity for friendship, intellectual and otherwise. Adam read an early version of the book manuscript and provided helpful feedback. More notably, however, Adam's own work, which pushes us toward a radical confrontation with our mortality, shaped my thoughts in significant and surprising ways. For being remarkably strong, kind, and generous with your insights, thank you, Adam.

Thank you also and always to my co-parent and friend, Tim Lyons.

There are many more friends whose intellectual camaraderie, humor, and affection sustained me. I am especially grateful for Bill Barnard, Paul Bramadat, Mark Chancey, David Craig, Chris Goto-Jones, Brett Grainger, and Adriel Trott.

Finally, I am grateful, with every cell of my body, for my children, Huxley and Everson. Nothing warms my heart like witnessing the love and friendship between them.

* * *

I am fortunate to have had the opportunity to present parts of this work at several events and institutions, including the following: the "Politics of Yoga" symposium at the Centre for Studies in Religion and Society, University of Victoria; the "Cultures of Sexual Assault" symposium at the College of Arts and Social Sciences, College of Asia and the Pacific, and the Gender Institute, Australian National University; the symposium "Yoga, Ethics, and Neoliberalism" at the Rock Ethics Institute, Penn State University; the "Being Spiritual But Not Religious: Past, Present, and Future(s)" conference at the Department of Religious Studies, Rice University; the Annual Conference on South Asia at the University of Wisconsin Madison; the "Spiritual but Not Religious: Past, Present, Future(s)" conference at the Center for the Study of World Religions, Harvard Divinity School; the "New Religions @ the GTU: Theories, Practices Peoples" conference, Graduate Theological Union; the Watson Institute and Center for Contemporary South Asia, Brown University; the Department of Liberal Arts and Sciences at Western Illinois University; the Department of Religious Studies at the University of Missouri; the Department of Religious Studies at the University of Pennsylvania; the SOAS Centre of Yoga Studies, University of London; the Department of Religion at Denison University; the School of Liberal Studies at Spalding University; and meetings of the American Academy of Religion.

As a part of the conversations that unfolded at these institutions and elsewhere, I benefited from the thoughtful and scrupulous feedback from many of the friends and colleagues I already named, as well as from Shameem Black, Jeffrey Brackett, Jeremy Engels, Anya Foxen, Amanda Lucia, Patrick McCartney, Chris Miller, Suzanne Newcombe, Karen O'Brien-Kop, Bill Parsons, Charlie Stang, and Chris White.

I also want to express my gratitude for the following institutions that generously supported various stages of my writing, travel, and research: the Department of Religious Studies, the Indiana University School of Liberal Arts, and the Arts and Humanities Institute at Indiana University–Purdue University Indianapolis; as well as the New Frontiers in the Arts and Humanities and the Consortium for the Study of Religion, Ethics, and Society at Indiana University.

I am grateful to my editor at Oxford University Press, Cynthia Read, for her patience and confidence while I completed this book. I am also grateful to the anonymous readers for Oxford University Press whose close readings of and feedback on the proposal and then first draft of the manuscript greatly enhanced the final product.

Some parts of this book have appeared in different incarnations elsewhere, including essays published in *Religion Dispatches* and *Tricycle*; "Namaste All Day: Containing Dissent in Commercial Spirituality," *Harvard Divinity Bulletin*; "Yogi Superman, Master Capitalist: Bikram Choudhury and the Religion of Commercial Spirituality," *Being Spiritual but not Religious: Past, Present, and Future(s)*, edited by William B. Parsons; "Neoliberal Yoga," *Routledge Handbook of Yoga and Meditation Studies*, edited by Suzanne Newcombe and Karen O'Brien-Kop; and "Pain, Stigma, and the Politics of Self-Management," *Pain Medicine*.

Andrea R. Jain,
Indianapolis
December 31, 2019

Bibliography

#metoo in yoga. n.d. "Sex, Intimacy, Ethics and Intuition: How Best to Safeguard Students and Prevent Abuses of Power in Yoga Teaching Environments." *Yoga Nidra Network.* Accessed July 1, 2017. https://www.yoganidranetwork.org/metooinyoga.

"4 Essential Oils to Inspire Mindfulness." 2016. *The Essential Life,* December 1, 2016. http://theessentiallife.com.au/theessentialblog/2016/essential-oils-to-inspire-mindfulness.

Abeysekara, Ananda. 2002. *Colors of the Robe: Religion, Identity, and Difference.* Columbia: University of South Carolina Press.

Academe Blog. 2015. "Faculty Statement on Narendra Modi Visit to Silicon Valley." August 27, 2015. https://academeblog.org/2015/08/27/faculty-statement-on-modi-visit-to-silicon-valley/.

Acker, Joan. 1990. "Hierarchies, Jobs, Bodies: A Theory of Gendered Organizations." *Gender & Society* 4 (2): 139–158.

Acker, Joan. 2006. "Inequality Regimes. Gender, Class, and Race in Organizations." *Gender & Society* 20 (4): 441–464.

Africa Yoga Project. 2019. https://www.africayogaproject.org.

Ahmad, Khurshid. "The Challenge of Global Capitalism: An Islamic Perspective." *Policy Perspectives* 1 (1) (April): 1–29.

Al Jazeera. 2015. "India's Hindu Fundamentalists." *Al Jazeera,* October 8, 2015. http://www.aljazeera.com/programmes/peopleandpower/2015/10/indias-hindu-fundamentalists-151008073418225.html.

Albanese, Catherine L. 2007. *A Republic of Mind and Spirit: A Cultural History of American Metaphysical Religion.* New Haven: Yale University Press.

Aldred, Lisa. 2000. "Plastic Shamans and Astroturf Sun Dances: New Age Commercialization of Native American Spirituality." *American Indian Quarterly* 24 (3): 329–352.

Alexander, Michelle. 2012. *The New Jim Crow: Mass Incarceration in the Age of Colorblindness.* New York: New Press.

Allen, Amy. 1999. *The Power of Feminist Theory: Domination, Resistance, Solidarity.* Boulder, CO: Westview Press.

Alter, Joseph S. 1994. "Celibacy, Sexuality, and the Transformation of Gender into Nationalism in North India." *Journal of Asian Studies* 53 (1): 45–66.

Alter, Joseph S. 2004. *The Body between Science and Philosophy: Yoga in Modern India.* Princeton, NJ: Princeton University Press.

Alvarez, Lisette. 2011. "Rebel Yoga." *New York Times,* January 23, 2011. https://www.nytimes.com/2011/01/23/nyregion/23st retch.html?pagewanted = all.

Anand, Geeta. 2016. "A Yoga Master, the King of 'Baba Cool,' Stretches Out an Empire." *The New York Times.* April 2, 2016. https://www.nytimes.com/2016/04/02/world/asia/a-yoga-master-the-king-of-baba-cool-stretches-out-an-empire.html.

Appadurai, Arjun. 1996. *Modernity at Large: Cultural Dimensions of Globalization.* Minneapolis: University of Minnesota Press.

Apple. 2020. "Use the Breathe App." https://support.apple.com/en-us/HT206999.

Arnold, Catherine. 2000. "Namaste." *Yoga Journal*, May–June 2000, 10.

Arvidsson, Adam. 2005. "Brands: A Critical Perspective." *Journal of Consumer Culture* 5 (2): 235–258.

Asad, Talal. 2009. "Free Speech, Blasphemy, and Secular Criticism." In *Is Critique Secular? Blasphemy, Injury, and Free Speech*. 2nd ed., edited by Talal Asad, Wendy Brown, Judith Butler, and Saba Mahmood, 14–57. New York: Fordham University Press.

Aschoff, Nicole. 2015. *The New Prophets of Capital*. London: Verso Books.

Askegaard, Søren, and Giana Eckhardt. 2012. "Glocal Yoga: Re-appropriation in the Indian Consumptionscape." *Marketing Theory* 12 (1): 45–60.

Aslan, Özlem, and Zeynep Gambetti. 2011. "Provincializing Fraser's History: Feminism and Neoliberalism Revisited." *History of the Present* 1 (1): 130–147.

Austen, Ian. 2011. "Lululemon Athletica Combines Ayn Rand and Yoga." *New York Times*, November 27, 2011. https://www.nytimes.com/2011/11/28/business/media/combines-ayn-rand-and-yoga.html.

Austen, Ian. 2012. "Lululemon Athletica's Founder Takes a Step Back." *New York Times*, January 6, 2012. http://www.nytimes.com/2012/01/07/business/lululemon-athleticas-founder-takes-a-step-back.html.

Bahr, Elen. 2015. "The 'Better Than' Epidemic." *Yoga for Every Body Blog*. http://everyyogi.com/2015/04/22/the-better-than-epidemic/.

Barry, Ellen. 2015. "Modi's Yoga Day Grips India, and 'Om' Meets 'Ouch!'" *New York Times*, June 15, 2015. https://www.nytimes.com/2015/06/16/world/asia/india-modi-yoga.html.

Baudrillard, Jean. 1983. *Simulations*. Translated by Paul Foss, Paul Patton, and Philip Beitchman. New York: Semiotext(e).

BBC. 2004. *This World: The Secret Swami*. Directed by Eamon Hardy. Television broadcast.

BBC. 2015. "Why Is Yoga Day Stressing India?" June 19, 2015. https://www.bbc.com/news/world-asia-india-33153506.

Bell, Catherine. 1988. "Ritualization of Texts and Textualization of Ritual in the Codification of Taoist Liturgy." *History of Religions* 27 (4): 366–392.

Bell, Catherine. 1992. *Ritual Theory, Ritual Practice*. New York: Oxford University Press.

Bell, Charlotte. 2012. "Living Gracefully with the Financial Challenges of Teaching Yoga." *Hugger Mugger Blog*, June 2012. http://www.huggermugger.com/blog/2012/teaching-yoga-financial/#comment-82551.

Bellah, Robert N. 1968. "Civil Religion in America." In *Religion in America*, edited by William G. McLoughlin and Robert N. Bellah, 3–23. Boston: Houghton Mifflin.

Bender, Courtney. 2010. *The New Metaphysicals: Spirituality and the American Religious Imagination*. Chicago: University of Chicago Press.

Benford, Robert D. 1993. "Frame Disputes within the Nuclear Disarmament Movement." *Social Forces* 71 (3): 677–701.

Bennett, Jane. 2010. *Vibrant Matter: A Political Ecology of Things*. Durham, NC: Duke University Press.

Berlant, Lauren. 2011. *Cruel Optimism*. Durham, NC: Duke University Press.

Beyer, Stephan. 1974. *The Buddhist Experience: Sources and Interpretations*. Encino, CA: Dickenson Publishing Company.

Bhasin, Kim. 2013. "Shunning Plus-Size Shoppers Is Key to Lululemon's Strategy, Insiders Say." *Huffington Post*, July 31, 2013. http://www.huffingtonpost.com/2013/07/31/lululemon-plus-size-n_3675605.html.

Bhikkhu, Thanissaro, trans. 2013. "Mahanama Sutta: To Mahanama (2)" (AN 11.13). *Access to Insight (BCBS Edition)*, November 30, 2013. Barre Center for Buddhist Studies. http://www.accesstoinsight.org/tipitaka/an/an11/an11.013.than.html.

Bianca. 2011. "Vanessa Lee and Ian Lopatin, Founders of Spiritual Gangster (Interview)." Trendhunter, December 23, 2011. https://www.trendhunter.com/trends/vanessa-lee.

Bikram Yoga. 2016a. "What Is Bikram Yoga?" https://www.bikramyoga.com/about/bikram-yoga/.

Bikram Yoga. 2016b. "Bikram Yoga Franchise." https://www.bikramyoga.com/franchise/.

Birch, Jason. 2018. "The Proliferation of Asana in Late-Medieval Yoga Texts." *Yoga in Transformation: Historical and Contemporary Perspectives* 16:101–180.

Birla, Ritu. 2009. *Stages of Capital: Law, Culture, and Market Governance in Late Colonial India*. Durham, NC: Duke University Press.

Block, Melissa. 2011. "Lululemon Customers Asked 'Who Is John Galt?'" *NPR's All Things Considered.* http://www.npr.org/2011/11/17/142472057/lululemon-customers-asked-who-is-john-galt.

Bode NYC. 2017. https://bodenyc.com.

Boltanski, Luc. 1999. *Distant Suffering: Politics, Morality and the Media*. Cambridge: Cambridge University Press.

Bornstein, Erica, and Peter Redfield. 2011. *Forces of Compassion: Humanitarianism between Ethics and Politics*. Santa Fe, NM: School for Advanced Research Press.

Bosworth, Mary. 2007. "Creating the Responsible Prisoner: Federal Admission and Orientation Packs." *Punishment and Society* 9 (1): 67–85.

Bourdieu, Pierre. 1977. *Outline of a Theory of Practice*. Translated by Richard Nice. Cambridge: Cambridge University Press.

Bourdieu, Pierre. 1984. *Distinction: A Social Critique of the Judgment of Taste*. Translated by Richard Nice. London: Routledge and Kegan.

Bourdieu, Pierre. 1985. "The Market of Symbolic Goods." *Poetics* 14:13–44.

Bourdieu, Pierre. 1990. *The Logic of Practice*. Translated by Richard Nice. Stanford, CA: Stanford University Press.

Bourdieu, Pierre. 1991. "Genesis and Structure of the Religious Field." *Comparative Social Research* 13 (1): 1–44.

Bourdieu, Pierre. 1992. *The Rules of Art: Genesis and Structure of the Literary Field*. Stanford, CA: Stanford University Press.

Bowler, Kate. 2013. *Blessed: A History of the American Prosperity Gospel*. New York: Oxford University Press.

"Boycott the Banks: Actor Shailene Woodley Calls for Action against Funders of Dakota Access Pipeline." 2017. Democracy Now!, January 25, 2017. https://www.democracynow.org/2017/1/25/boycott_the_banks_actor_shailene_woodley.

Bramadat, Paul. 2019. "A Bridge Too Far: Yoga, Spirituality, and Contested Space in the Pacific Northwest." *Religion, State, and Society* 7 (4–5): 491–507.

Brancatisano, Emma. 2016. "These 3 Mindfulness Exercises Take Less Than 10 Minutes." *Huffington Post*, October 19, 2016. https://www.huffingtonpost.com.au/2016/10/19/3-mindfulness-exercises-to-try-that-take-less-than-10-minutes_a_21586547/.

Braun, Erik. 2013. *The Birth of Insight: Meditation, Modernism, and the Burmese Monk Ledi Sayadaw.* Chicago: University of Chicago Press.

Brennan, Teresa. 2004. *The Transmission of Affect.* Ithaca, NY: Cornell University Press.

Broad, William J. 2012. "Yoga and Sex Scandals: No Surprise Here." *New York Times,* February 27, 2012. http://www.nytimes.com/2012/02/28/health/nutrition/yoga-fans- sexual-flames-and-predictably-plenty-of-scandal.html?pagewanted=all&_r=0.

Bronkhorst, Johannes. 2007. *Greater Magadha: Studies in the Culture of Early India.* Leiden: Brill.

Browder, Laura. 2000. *Slippery Characters: Ethnic Impersonators and American Identities.* Chapel Hill: The University of North Carolina Press.

Brower, Elena. 2015. "On Wearing White for Practice, for Peace." *MindBodyGreen,* August 2015.   https://www.mindbodygreen.com/0-21194/3-renowned-yoga-teachers-on-why-theyre-wearing-white-for-yoga.html.

Brown, Candy Gunther. 2011. *Global Pentecostalism and Charismatic Healing.* New York: Oxford University Press.

Brown, Candy Gunther. 2019. *Debating Yoga and Mindfulness in Public Schools: Reforming Secular Education or Reestablishing Religion.* Chapel Hill: University of North Carolina Press.

Brown, Coral. 2015. "Why Make a Yoga Pilgrimage to India?" *Yoga Journal,* March 31, 2015. https://www.yogajournal.com/lifestyle/make-yoga-pilgrimage-india.

Brown, Wendy. 1995. *States of Injury: Power and Freedom in Late Modernity.* Princeton, NJ: Princeton University Press.

Brown, Wendy. 2005. "Neo-liberalism and the End of Liberal Democracy." *Theory & Event* 7 (1): 37–59.

Brown, Wendy. 2013. "Introduction." In *Is Critique Secular? Blasphemy, Injury, and Free Speech,* 2nd ed., edited by Talal Asad, Wendy Brown, Judith Butler, and Saba Mahmood. New York: Fordham University Press.

Brown, Wendy. 2015. *Undoing the Demos: Neoliberalism's Stealth Revolution.* Cambridge, MA: MIT Press.

Bruce, Steve. 2018. *Secular Beats Spiritual: The Westernization of the Easternization of the West.* New York: Oxford University Press.

Buchanan, B. B. 2017. "White Supremacy Has Been Bolstered, and Not in the Way You Think." *Medium,* August 17, 2017. https://medium.com/@BlaQSociologist/white-supremacy-has-been-bolstered-4c4372341e3c.

Buddhaghosa. [1975] 1999. *The Path of Purification: Visuddhimagga.* Translated by Bhikku Ñāṇamoli. Seattle: Buddhist Publication Society.

Burchell, G., C. Gordon, and P. Miller, eds. 1991. *The Foucault Effect: Studies in Governmentality.* London: Harvester Wheatsheaf.

Burke, M. C., and M. Bernstein. 2014. "How the Right Usurped the Queer Agenda: Frame Co-optation in Political Discourse." *Sociological Forum* 29 (4): 830–850.

Buswell, Robert E., Jr. and Donald S. Lopez Jr. 2014. "Which Mindfulness?" *Tricycle,* May 8, 2014. https://tricycle.org/trikedaily/which-mindfulness/.

Butler, Jess. 2013. "For White Girls Only? Postmodernism and the Politics of Inclusion." *Feminist Formations* 25 (1): 35–58.

Butler, Judith. 1990. *Gender Trouble.* New York: Routledge.

Buyukokutan, Baris. 2011. "Toward a Theory of Cultural Appropriation: Buddhism, the Vietnam War, and the Field of U.S. Poetry." *American Sociological Review* 76 (4): 620–639.

Carlin, Dan. 2015. "Mindfulness and Criminal Justice: The State of the Field." Pre-conference working paper, "Mindful Justice: Creating a Criminal Justice System Grounded in Mindfulness, Compassion, and Human Dignity," Kalamazoo, MI, September 2015. http://media.wix.com/ugd/4581e8_3939c60c082e4f7ab9e7bf98be24df4c.pdf, 2.

Carmody, James. 2015. "Reconceptualizing Mindfulness: The Psychological Principles of Attending in Mindfulness Practice and Their Role in Well-Being." In *Handbook of Mindfulness: Theory, Research, and Practice*, edited by Kirk Warren Brown, J. David Creswell, and Richard M. Ryan, 62–78. New York: Guilford Press.

Carrette, Jeremy, and Richard King. 2005. *Selling Spirituality: The Silent Takeover of Religion*. New York: Routledge.

Carson, Rachel. [1962] 2018. *Silent Spring*. New York: Library of America.

Center for Study of Society and Secularism and Minority Rights Group International. 2017. *A Narrowing Space: Violence and Discrimination Against India's Religious Minorities*. London: Minority Rights Group International.

Chan, M. 2017. "It Started Raining the Moment Donald Trump Was Inaugurated President." *Time*, January 20, 2017. http://time.com/4641165/donald-trump-inauguration-rain/.

Chapple, Christopher Key. 2003. *Reconciling Yogas: Haribhadra's Collection of Views on Yoga, with a New Translation of Haribhadra's Yogadṛṣṭisamuccaya*. Albany: State University of New York Press.

Chapple, Christopher Key. 2011. "Recovering Jainism's Contribution to Yoga Traditions." In "Contextualizing the History of Yoga in Geoffrey Samuel's *The Origins of Yoga and Tantra*: A Review Symposium." *International Journal of Hindu Studies* 15 (3): 323–333.

Chhabra, Esha. 2018. "Why This Female Founder Is Investing in Organic Agriculture for Her Clothing Startup." Forbes, February 27, 2018. https://www.forbes.com/sites/eshachhabra/2018/02/27/why-this-female-founder-is-investing-in-organic-agriculture-for-her-clothing-startup/#59471e315a33.

Chomsky, Noam. 1999. *Profit over People: Neoliberalism and Global Order*. New York: Seven Stories Press.

Choudhury, Bikram. 2007. *Bikram Yoga: The Guru behind Hot Yoga Shows the Way to Radiant Health and Personal Fulfillment*. New York: HarperCollins.

Chowdhry, Geeta. 2000. "Communalism, Nationalism, and Gender: Bharatiya Janata Party (BJP) and the Hindu Right in India." In *Women, States, and Nationalism: At Home in the Nation?*, edited by Sita Ranchod-Nilsson and Mary Ann Tetreault. New York: Routledge.

CNN Staff. 2015. "Guru Convicted of Abusing Followers' Children Fled Justice." *The Hunt with John Walsh*, August 13, 2015. https://www.cnn.com/2015/08/06/us/guru-convicted-of-abusing-followers-children-fled-justice/index.html.

"CODEPINK." 2019. *CODEPINK*. https://www.codepink.org/.

Collard, Patrizia. 2014. *The Little Book of Mindfulness: 10 Minutes a Day to Less Stress, More Peace*. London: Octopus Books.

Connell, R. W. 1987. *Gender and Power: Society, the Person, and Sexual Politics*. Stanford, CA: Stanford University Press.

Cooperman, Alan. 2012. *The Guru in South Asia: New Interdisciplinary Perspectives*. London: Routledge.

Cooperman, Alan. 2016. "The Rise of the Religiously Unaffiliated: Why the 'Nones' Are Growing, and Why It Matters." A presentation to the Lake Institute on Faith & Giving, Indiana University–Purdue University Indianapolis, October 6, 2016.

Copeman, Jacob, and Aya Ikegame. 2012a. "Guru Logics." *HAU: Journal of Ethnographic Theory* 2 (1): 289–336.

CorePower Yoga. 2017. "CorePower Teacher Training." https://www.corepoweryoga.com/yoga-teacher-training.

Cox, Collette. 1992. "Mindfulness and Memory: The Scope of *Smṛti* from Early Buddhism to the Sarvāstivādin Abhidharma." In *In the Mirror of Memory: Reflections on Mindfulness and Remembrance in Indian and Tibetan Buddhism*, edited by Janet Gyatso, 67–108. Albany: State University of New York Press.

CRISIL. 2018. "Indian Economy: Rise of the Machines." CRISIL Insights, August 2018. https://www.crisil.com/content/dam/crisil/our-analysis/reports/gr-a/documents/2018/august/crisil-insights-indian-economy-rise-of-the-machines.pdf.

Crockett, Emily. 2016. "Melissa Harris-Perry: 'Since When' Has Racism or Sexism Disqualified an American President? *Vox*, December 14, 2016. https://www.vox.com/identities/2016/12/14/13938396/gender-presidential-election-atlantic-melissa-harris-perry-racism-prerequisite.

Croucher, Sheila. 2018. *Globalization and Belonging: The Politics of Identity in a Changing World*. London: Rowman & Littlefield.

Cruikshank, Barbara. 1996. "Revolutions within: Self-Government and Self-Esteem." *In Foucault and Political Reason*, edited by A. Barrry, T. Osborne, *and* N. Rose, 231–251. Chicago: University of Chicago Press.

Crutzen, Paul and Eugene F. Stoermer. 2000. "Have We Entered the 'Anthropocene'"? *IGBP Global Change* 41. Accessed January 10, 2017. http://www.igbp.net/news/opinion/opinion/haveweenteredtheanthropocene.5.d8b4c3c12bf3be638a8000578.html.

Damasio, Antonio. 2017. "Assessing the Value of Buddhism, for Individuals and for the World." *New York Times*, August 7, 2017. https://www.nytimes.com/2017/08/07/books/review/why-buddhism-is-true-science-meditation-robert-wright.html.

Dasa, Gadadhara Pandit. 2016. "What Is Mindfulness and Why We Need It." *Huffington Post*, October 2, 2016. https://www.huffingtonpost.com/gadadhara-pandit-dasa/what-is-mindfulness-and-why-we-need-it_b_12530946.html.

Davenport, Coral, and Campbell Robertson. 2016. "Resettling the First American 'Climate Refugees.'" *New York Times*, May 2, 2016.

Davidson, Ronald M. 2002. *Indian Esoteric Buddhism: A Social History of the Tantric Movement*. New York: Columbia University Press.

Davies, Will. 2017. *The Limits of Neoliberalism: Authority, Sovereignty, and the Logic of Competition*. Los Angeles: Sage.

Davis, Angela. 1981. *Women, Race and Class*. New York: Vintage Books.

Davis, Angela. 2003. *Are Prisons Obsolete?* New York: Seven Stories Press.

Davis, Angela. 2014. Talk delivered at Pacific University. https://vimeo.com/94879430.

Davis, Angela. 2017. Speech at the Women's March on Washington. January 23, 2017. Accessed January 23, 2017. https://www.youtube.com/watch?v=bSGPGNJpaE0.

de Michelis, Elizabeth. 2004. *A History of Modern Yoga: Patañjali and Western Esotericism*. New York: Continuum.

Dean, Mitchell. 1995. "Governing the Unemployed Self in an Active Society." *Economy and Society* 24 (4): 559–583.

Death, Carl. 2013. "Governmentality at the Limits of the International: African Politics and Foucauldian Theory." *Review of International Studies* 39 (3): 763–787.

Deccan Chronicle. 2015. "Yoga Day Row: AIMIM Appeals Muslims to Offer Namaz in Protest." *Deccan Chronicle*, June 10, 2015. http://www.deccanchronicle.com/150610/nation-current-affairs/article/yoga-day-row-aimim-appeals-muslims-offer-namaz-protest.

Dei, George J. Sefa. 2006. "Introduction: Mapping the Terrain—towards a New Politics of Resistance." In *Anti-colonialism and Education: The Politics of Resistance*, edited by George J. Sefa Dei and Arlo Kempf. Boston: Sense Publishers.

"Delhi High Court Judgement on Homosexuality and IPC 377." July 2, 2009. http://www.scribd.com/doc/17059723/Delhi-Highcourt-Judgement-on-Homosexuality-and-IPC-377#scribd.

Deloria, Philip Joseph. 1998. *Playing Indian*. New Haven: Yale University Press.

Despres, Loraine. 2000. "Yoga's Bad Boy: Bikram Choudhury." *Yoga Journal*, March–April 2000.

Dilts, Andrew. 2014. *Punishment and Inclusion: Race, Membership and Limits of American Liberalism*. Bronx, NY: Fordham University Press.

Dixon, Marc, Andrew W. Martin, and Michael Nau. 2016. "Social Protest and Corporate Change: Brand Visibility, Third-Party Influence, and the Responsiveness of Corporations to Activist Campaigns." *Mobilization* 21 (2): 65–82.

Dixon, Ronaldo. 2017. "The Job Description of Yoga Instructor." *LiveStrong*, September 11, 2017. https://www.livestrong.com/article/402751-the-job-description-of-a-yoga-instructor/.

Doniger, Wendy. 1980. *Women, Androgynes, and Other Mythical Beasts*. Chicago: University of Chicago Press.

Doniger, Wendy, and Martha C. Nussbaum. 2015. "Introduction." In *Pluralism and Democracy in India: Debating the Hindu Right*, edited by Wendy Doniger and Martha C. Nussbaum, 1–20. New York: Oxford University Press.

Doolin, Bill. "Enterprise Discourse, Professional Identity and the Organizational Control of Hospital Clinicians." *Organization Studies* 23 (3): 369–390.

Doran, Peter. 2017. *A Political Economy of Attention, Consumerism and Mindfulness: Reclaiming the Mindful Commons*. New York: Routledge.

Douglas, Mary. 1990. "Foreword." In *The Gift: The Form and Reason for Exchange in Archaic Societies*, by Marcel Mauss, ix–xxii. London: Routledge.

Dreyfus, Georges. 2011. "Is Mindfulness Present-Centred and Non-judgmental? A Discussion of the Cognitive Dimensions of Mindfulness." *Contemporary Buddhism* 12 (1): 41–54.

Dreyfus, H. L., and P. Rabinow. 1982. *Michel Foucault: Beyond Structuralism and Hermeneutics*. Brighton: Harvester Wheatsheaf.

du Gay, Paul. 1996. *Consumption and Identity at Work*. London: Sage Publications.

du Gay, Paul, Graeme Salaman, and Bronwen Rees. 1996. "The Conduct of Management and the Management of Conduct: Contemporary Managerial Discourse and the Constitution of the 'Competent' Manager." *Journal of Management Studies* 33 (3): 263–282.

Durkheim, Émile. [1912] 2001. *The Elementary Forms of Religious Life*. Translated by Carol Cosman. Oxford: Oxford University Press.

Dworkin, Shari L., and Michael A. Messner. 2002. "Just Do . . . What? Sport, Bodies, Gender." In *Gender and Sport: A Reader*, edited by Sheila Scraton and Anne Flintoff. New York: Routledge.

Economic Times. 2014. "Ramdev Popularizes Yoga, Ayurveda across the Globe: Shripad Naik." *Economic Times*, November 20, 2014. https://economictimes.indiatimes.com/news/politics-and-nation/ramdev-popularises-yoga-ayurveda-across-the-globe-shripad-naik/articleshow/45220615.cms.

Ehrenreich, Barbara. 2018. *Natural Causes: An Epidemic of Wellness, the Certainty of Dying, and Our Illusion of Control*. New York: Hachette Book Group.

Einstein, Mara. 2008. *Brands of Faith: Marketing Religion in a Commercial Age*. New York: Routledge.

Eisenstein, Zillah. 2013. "'Leaning in' in Iraq." http://www.aljazeera. com/indepth/opinion/2013/03/2013323141149557391.html.

Ellwood, Robert, and Harry Partin. 1988. *Religious and Spiritual Groups in Modern America*. New York: Routledge.

Express News Service. 2014. "Narendra Modi Heaps Praise on Ramdev at Yoga Mahotsav." *Indian Express*, March 23, 2014. https://indianexpress.com/article/india/india-others/narendra-modi-heaps-praise-on-ramdev/.

Express News Service. 2015. "Over Rs 32 Crore Spent on Yoga Day." *Indian Express*, July 24, 2015. https://indianexpress.com/article/india/india-others/over-rs-32-crore-spent-on-yoga-day/.

Featherstone, Mike. 1991. "The Body in Consumer Culture." In *The Body: Social Process and Cultural Theory*, edited by Mike Featherstone, Mike Hepworth, and Bryan S. Turner, 170–196. London: Sage.

Featherstone, Mike. 2007. *Consumer Culture and Postmodernism*. 2nd ed. London: Sage.

Ferner, Matt. 2012. "One Marijuana Arrest Occurs Every 42 Seconds in U.S.: FBI Report." *HuffPost*, October 29, 2012. https://www.huffpost.com/entry/one-marijuana-arrest-occu_n_2041236.

Fight for $15. n.d. Accessed August 1, 2019. https://fightfor15.org/?home.

Fish, Allison Elizabeth. 2006. "The Commodification and Exchange of Knowledge in the Case of Transnational Commercial Yoga." *International Journal of Cultural Property* 13:189–206.

Fish, Allison Elizabeth. 2010. "Laying Claim to Yoga: Intellectual Property, Cultural Rights, and the Digital Archive in India." Dissertation, University of California, Irvine.

Fisher, Mark. 2009. *Capitalist Realism: Is There No Alternative?* Hampshire, UK: Zero Books.

Flanagan, Caitlin. 2017. "Bill Clinton: A Reckoning." *The Atlantic*, November 13, 2017. https://www.theatlantic.com/entertainment/archive/2017/11/reckoning-with-bill-clintons-sex-crimes/545729/.

Foster, John Bellamy, Hannah Holleman, and Brett Clark. 2019. "Imperialism in the Anthropocene." *Monthly Review*, July 1, 2019. https://monthlyreview.org/2019/07/01/imperialism-in-the-anthropocene/?fbclid = IwAR2zj_2J2frw8eVQB9_hiZXWbhbPpO1OqwSYYzYxNDQ54gNgeBPv3P2n2BU#en2.

Foucault, Michel. [1977] 1991. *Discipline and Punish: The Birth of the Prison*. Translated by Alan Sheridan. London: Penguin.

Foucault, Michel. 1978. *The History of Sexuality*. Vol. 1: The Will to Knowledge. London: Penguin.

Foxen, Anya P. 2017a. *Biography of a Yogi: Paramahansa Yogananda and the Origins of Modern Yoga*. New York: Oxford University Press.

Foxen, Anya P. 2017b. "Yogi Calisthenics: What the 'Non-yoga' Yogic Practice of Paramahansa Yogananda Can Tell Us about Religion." *Journal of the American Academy of Religion* 85 (2): 494–526.

Foxen, Anya P. 2020. *Inhaling Spirit: Harmonialism, Orientalism, and the Western Roots of Modern Yoga.* New York: Oxford University Press.

Fraser, Nancy. 1997. *Justice Interruptus: Critical Reflections On the "Postsocialist" Condition.* New York: Routledge.

Fraser, Nancy. 2013. *Fortunes of Feminism: From State-Managed Capitalism to Neoliberal Crisis.* New York: Verso.

Friedan, Betty. 1963. *The Feminine Mystique.* New York: Norton.

Fronsdal, Gil. [2001] 2008. *The Issue at Hand: Essays on Buddhist Mindfulness Practice.* Redwood City, CA: Insight Meditation Center.

Fuller, C. J., and John Harriss. 2005. "Globalizing Hinduism: A 'Traditional' Guru and Modern Businessmen in Chennai." In *Globalizing India: Perspectives from Below.* edited by Jackie Assayag and C. J. Fuller, 211–236. London: Anthem Press.

Gallagher, B. J. 2013. "Mindfulness at Work: Eastern Wisdom for Western Business." *Huffington Post*, March 7, 2013. https://www.huffingtonpost.com/bj-gallagher/mindfulness-at-work_b_2802870.html.

Gardella, Peter. 2014. *American Civil Religion: What Americans Hold Sacred.* New York: Oxford University Press.

Garfield, L. 2017. "An Anti-Trump Movement Is Calling for the Boycott of These 36 DAPL-Linked Banks." *Business Insider*, March 25, 2017. https://www.businessinsider.com/trump-boycott-dapl-banks-standing-rock-2017-3.

Garland, David. 1990. *Punishment in Modern Society: A Study in Social Theory.* Chicago: The University of Chicago Press.

Garland, David. 2012. *Punishment and Modern Society: A Study in Social Theory.* Chicago: University of Chicago Press.

Geertz, Clifford. 1973. "Religion as a Cultural System." In *The Interpretation of Cultures.* New York: Basic Books.

Gettleman, Jeffrey, Kai Schultz, and Raj Suhasini. 2018. "India Gay Sex Ban Is Struck Down. 'Indefensible,' Court Says." *New York Times*, September 6, 2018. https://nyti.ms/2CnBJQR.

Global Wellness Institute. 2018. *Global Wellness Economy Monitor.* October 2018. Miami: Global Wellness Institute.

Goldberg, Philip. 2010. *American Veda: From Emerson and the Beatles to Yoga and Meditation, How Indian Spirituality Changed the West.* New York: Three Rivers Press.

Goodchild, Philip. 2002. *Capitalism and Religion: The Price of Piety.* New York: Routledge.

Gordon, C. 1994. "Governmental Rationality: An Introduction." In *The Foucault Effect: Studies in Governmentality,* edited by G. Burchell, C. Gordon, and P. Miller, 1–51 (eds.) Chicago: University of Chicago Press.

Gottschalk, Marie. 2015. "Bring It On: The Future of Penal Reform, the Carceral State, and American Politics." *Ohio State Journal of Criminal Law* 12: 559–603.

Green, Rayna. 1988. "The Tribe Called Wannabee: Playing Indian in America and Europe." *Folklore* 99 (1): 30–55.

Griffiths, Paul J. 1993. "Indian Buddhist Meditation." In *Buddhist Spirituality: Indian, Southeast Asian, Tibetan, and Early Chinese,* edited by Takeuchi Yoshinori. New York: Crossroad Publishing Company.

Gunaratana, Venerable Henepola. 1991. *Mindfulness in Plain English*. Somerville, MA: Wisdom Publications.

Hall, Donald E. 1994. *Muscular Christianity: Embodying the Victorian Age*. New York: Cambridge University Press.

Hall, Stuart [1981] 2002. "Notes on Deconstructing 'the Popular.'" In *Cultural Resistance Reader*, edited by Stephen Duncombe, 185–192. London: Verso.

Hamann, T. H. 2009. "Neoliberalism, Governmentality, and Ethics." *Foucault Studies* 6: 37–59.

Hamner, Gail. 2014. "Filming Reconciliation: Affect and Nostalgia in *The Tree of Life*." *Journal of Religion and Film* 18 (1): 1–40.

Hamner, Gail. 2019. "Theorizing Religion and the Public Sphere: Affect, Technology, Valuation." *Journal of the American Academy of Religion* 87 (4): 1008–1049.

Hanegraaff, Wouter J. 1998. *New Age Religion and Western Culture: Esotericism in the Mirror of Secular Thought*. Albany: State University of New York Press.

Hannah-Moffat, Kelly. 1999. "Moral Agent or Actuarial Subject: Risk and Canadian Women's Imprisonment." *Theoretical Criminology* 3 (1): 71–94.

Hannah-Moffat, Kelly. 2000. "Prisons That Empower: Neo-liberal Governance in Canadian Women's Prisons." *British Journal of Criminology* 40 (3): 510–531.

Hannah-Moffat, Kelly. 2005. "Criminogenic Needs and the Transformative Risk Subject." *Punishment and Society* 7 (1): 29–51.

Haraway, Donna. 1991. *Simians, Cyborgs and Women: The Reinvention of Nature*. London: Free Association Books.

Harcourt, B. E. 2010. "Neoliberal Penalty: A Brief Genealogy." *Theoretical Criminology* 14 (1): 74–92.

Harris, Gardiner. 2013. "India's Supreme Court Restores an 1861 Law Banning Gay Sex." *New York Times*, December 11, 2013. http://www.nytimes.com/2013/12/12/world/asia/court-restores-indias-ban-on-gay-sex.html?_r=0.

Harvey, David. 2005. *A Brief History of Neoliberalism*. New York: Oxford University Press.

HBO. 2016. "Bikram Choudhury Sexual Misconduct Allegations: Real Sports Trailer (HBO)." YouTube video, 1:17. Posted October 21, 2016. https://youtu.be/NZ4BF0WdY1s.

Heelas, Paul, ed. 2012. *Spirituality in the Modern World*. 4 vols. New York: Routledge.

Heuman, Linda. 2013. "Context Matters: An Interview with Buddhist Scholar David McMahan." *Tricycle* 23 (2): 42–45, 101–102.

Huffer, Lynne. 2013. "It's the Economy Sister." http://www.aljazeera. com/indepth/opinion/2013/03/201331885644977848.html.

Human Rights Watch. 2002. "'We Have No Orders to Save You': State Participation and Complicity in Communal Violence in Gujarat." *Human Rights Watch* 14 (3): 1–68.

Huntington, C. W., Jr. 2015. "The Triumph of Narcissism: Theravāda Buddhist Meditation in the Marketplace." *Journal of the American Academy of Religion* 83 (3): 624–648.

Husgafvel, Ville. 2016. "On the Buddhist Roots of Contemporary Non-religious Mindfulness Practice: Moving beyond Sectarian and Essentialist Approaches." *Temenos* 52 (1): 87–126.

Hussain, Sajjad. 2015. "Not Only Is BJP Refusing to Scrap Section 377, It's Back to Saying Gays Have a 'Genetic Disorder.'" *Scroll.in*, June 30, 2015. https://scroll.in/article/737871/not-only-is-bjp-not-scrapping-section-377-its-back-to-saying-gays-have-a-genetic-disorder.

Huxley, Aldous. [1931] 2006. *Brave New World*. New York: Harper.

India Today. 2017. "Baba Ramdev Exclusive on Spirituality, Sexual Desire, Fake Babas & More | On the Couch with Koel." YouTube video 24:05. Posted September 21, 2017. https://youtu.be/3wvo1H7GlOE.

Indy Yoga Movement. 2019. https://www.indyyoga.org/about/.

Isaac, Jeffrey. 2015. "The American Politics of Policing and Incarceration." *Perspectives on Politics* 13 (3): 609–616.

Jaffrelot, Christophe. 2003. "Communal Riots in Gujarat: The State at Risk?" *Heidelberg Papers in South Asian and Comparative Politics* 17, July 2003.

Jaffrelot, Christophe. 2013. "Gujarat Elections: The Sub-text of Modi's 'Hattrick'—High Tech Populism and the 'Neo-Middle Class.'" *Studies in Indian Politics* 1 (1): 79–95.

Jain, Andrea R. 2014a. *Selling Yoga: From Counterculture to Pop Culture.* Oxford: Oxford University Press.

Jain, Andrea R. 2014b. "Claiming Yoga for India." *Religion Dispatches,* December 15, 2014. http://religiondispatches.org/claiming-yoga-for-india/.

Jain, Andrea R. 2014c. "Who Is to Say Modern Yoga Practitioners Have It All Wrong? On Hindu Origins and Yogaphobia." *Journal of the American Academy of Religion* 82 (2): 427–471.

Jain, Andrea R. 2016. "Being a Superman Who Can't Be F*$#d With: Bikram Choudhury, the Yoga Industry, and Neoliberal Religion." Conference presentation at "Being Spiritual but Not Religious: Past, Present, and Future(s)," Rice University.

Jain, Andrea R. 2017. "The Case of Bikram Yoga: Can 'Pop Spiritualities' Be Truly Transformative." *Tricycle,* Spring 2017.

Jain, Andrea R. 2018. "Yogi Superman, Master Capitalist: Bikram Choudhury and the Religion of Commercial Spirituality." In *Being Spiritual but Not Religious: Past, Present, and Future(s),* edited by William B. Parsons. New York: Routledge.

Jain, Andrea R. 2020. "Pain, Stigma, and the Politics of Self-Management." *Pain Medicine,* May 3, 2020. https://doi.org/10.1093/pm/pnaa064.

Jain, Andrea R., and Michael Schulson. 2016. "The World's Most Influential Yoga Teacher Is a Homophobic Right-Wing Activist." *Religion Dispatches,* October 4, 2016. http://religiondispatches.org/baba-ramdev/.

Jameson, Frederic. 1981. *The Political Unconscious: Narrative as a Socially Symbolic Act.* Ithaca, NY: Cornell University Press.

Jameson, Frederic. 1991. *Postmodernism: Or, the Cultural Logic of Late Capitalism.* Durham, NC: Duke University Press.

Jenkins, Philip. 2011. *The Next Christendom: The Coming of Global Christianity.* New York: Oxford University Press.

Jilani, Zaid. 2016. "Indians Staged One of the Largest Strikes in History, but No One on U.S. Cable News Covered It." *The Intercept,* September 6, 2016. https://theintercept.com/2016/09/06/indians-staged-one-of-the-largest-strikes-in-history-but-no-one-on-u-s-cable-news-covered-it/.

Jivamukti Yoga. 2017. "Teacher Training." October 5, 2017. YouTube. https://www.youtube.com/watch?time_continue=204&v=H3jINMzPG_M.

Jivamukti Yoga. 2019. https://jivamuktiyoga.com.

Joiner, Thomas. 2017. *Mindlessness: The Corruption of Mindfulness in a Culture of Narcissism.* New York: Oxford University Press.

Juergensmeyer, Mark. 2003. *Terror in the Mind of God: The Global Rise of Religious Violence.* Berkeley: University of California Press.

Juergensmeyer, Mark. 2008. *Global Rebellion: Religious Challenges to the Secular State, from Christian Militias to al Qaeda*. Berkeley: University of California Press.

Kabat-Zinn, Jon. 1994. *Wherever You Go, There You Are: Mindfulness Meditation in Everyday Life*. New York: Hyperion Books.

Kabat-Zinn, Jon. 2013. *Full Catastrophe Living: Using the Wisdom of Your Body and Mind to Face Stress, Pain, and Illness*. Rev. ed. New York: Bantam Books.

Kale, Sunila S. and Christian Lee Novetzke. 2016. "Some Reflections on Yoga as Political Theology." *The Wire*. January 28, 2016. https://thewire.in/culture/some-reflections-on-yoga-as-political-theology.

Kalra, Aditya. 2014. "India Gets Minister for Yoga and Traditional Medicine." *Reuters News*, November 11, 2014. https://www.reuters.com/article/us-india-health-yoga/india-gets-minister-for-yoga-and-traditional-medicine-idUSKCN0IV13M20141111.

Kantor, Jodi. 2013. "A Titan's How-To on Breaking the Glass Ceiling." *New York Times*, February 21, 2013. http://www.nytimes.com/2013/02/22/us/sheryl-sandberg-lean-in-author-hopes-to-spur-movement.html?pagewanted=all&_r=0.

Kantor, Jodi, and Megan Twohey. 2017. "Harvey Weinstein Paid Off Sexual Harassment Accusers for Decades." *New York Times*, October 5, 2017.

Kapstein, Matthew. 2000. *The Tibetan Assimilation of Buddhism: Conversion, Contestation, and Memory*. New York: Oxford University Press.

Karma Keepers. 2018. https://karmakeepers.net/.

Karnik, Madhura. 2017. "Three Years of Modi: Big-Bang Experiments, Great GDP Numbers, and Uneven Growth." *Quartz India*, May 26, 2017. https://qz.com/india/991501/three-years-of-narendra-modi-big-bang-experiments-great-gdp-numbers-and-an-uneven-growth/.

Keegan, Paul. 2002. "Yogis Behaving Badly." *Business 2.0*, September 2002.

Kesavan, Mukul. 2011. "Three Hundred Ramayanas—Delhi University and the Purging of Ramanujan." *The Telegraph*, October 27, 2011. https://www.telegraphindia.com/opinion/three-hundred-ramayanas-delhi-university-and-the-purging-of-ramanujan/cid/340912.

Kesavan, Mukul. 2015. "Hindus and Others: The Republic's Commons Sense." *The Telegraph*, September 21, 2015. https://www.telegraphindia.com/opinion/hindus-and-others/cid/1443767.

Kingston, Jeff. 2017. "The Politics of Religious Hatemongering in India." *Japan Times*, June 24, 2017. http://www.japantimes.co.jp/opinion/2017/06/24/commentary/politics-religious-hatemongering-india/#.WXePEXeZONY.

Kingston, Lindsey. 2015. "The Destruction of Identity: Cultural Genocide and Indigenous Peoples." *Journal of Human Rights* 14 (1): 63–83.

Kino Yoga. n.d.a. "Shop." Kino MacGregor. Accessed October 8, 2018. https://www.kinoyoga.com/shop/.

Kino Yoga. n.d.b. "A Spiritual Journey." Kino MacGregor. Accessed October 8, 2018. https://www.kinoyoga.com/about/kino-macgregor.

Klein, Naomi. 2014. *This Changes Everything: Capitalism vs. the Climate*. New York: Simon and Schuster.

Kornfield, Jack. 2017. *No Time Like the Present: Finding Freedom, Love, and Joy Right Where You Are*. New York: Atria Books.

Kosmin, Barry A., and Ariela Keysar, with Ryan Cragun and Juhem Navarro-Rivera. 2009. "American Nones: The Profile of the No Religion Population, a Report Based on the American Religious Identification Survey 2008." Hartford: Trinity College. http://commons.trincoll.edu/aris/files/2011/08/NONES_08.pdf.

Kotsko, Adam. 2018. *Neoliberalism's Demons: On the Political Theology of Late Capital.* Stanford, CA: Stanford University Press.

Kramer, Joel, and Diana Alstad. 1993. *The Guru Papers: Masks of Authoritarian Power.* Berkeley, CA: North Atlantic Books.

Kripa Foundation. 2006–2007. *Kripa Foundation.* http://www.kripafoundation.org.

Kumar, Sanjay. 2015. "International Yoga Day Sparks Controversy in India." *The Diplomat,* June 20, 2015. https://thediplomat.com/2015/06/international-yoga-day-sparks-controversy-in-india/.

Kurian, Alka. 2017. "Decolonizing the Body: Theoretical Imaginings on the Fourth Wave Feminism in India." In *New Feminisms in South Asian Social Media, Film, and Literature,* edited by Sonora Jha and Alka Kurian, 15–41. New York: Routledge.

Larner, Wendy. 2000. "Neo-liberalism: Policy, Ideology, Governmentality." *Studies in Political Economy* 63: 5–25.

Larson, Gerald J. 2012. "Pātañjala Yoga in Practice." In *Yoga in Practice,* edited by David Gordon White, 73–96. Princeton, NJ: Princeton University Press.

Lau, Kimberley J. 2000. *New Age Capitalism: Making Money East of Eden.* Philadelphia: University of Pennsylvania Press.

Lechner, Frank, and John Boli, eds. 2011. *The Globalization Reader.* Malden, MA: Wiley-Blackwell.

Lemke, T. 2001. "'The Birth of Bio-Politics': Michel Foucault's Lecture at the Collège de France on Neo-liberal Governmentality." *Economy and Society* 30 (2): 190–207.

Leopold, Aldo. [1949] 1986. *A Sand County Almanac.* New York: Ballentine Books.

Lerman, Amy, and Vesla Weaver. 2014. *Arresting Citizenship: The Democratic Consequences of American Crime Control.* Chicago: University of Chicago Press.

Li, Tania Murray. 2007. "Governmentality." *Anthropologica* 49:275–294.

"Like Body, Like Mind." 2018. *Mindful* [Foundation for a Mindful Society] 6 (2): 6.

Lincoln, Bruce. 2006. *Holy Terrors: Thinking about Religion after September 11.* Chicago: University of Chicago Press.

Linden, Ian. 2009. *Global Catholicism: Diversity and Change since Vatican II.* New York: Columbia University Press.

Lofton, Kathryn. 2011. *Oprah: The Gospel of an Icon.* Berkeley: University of California Press.

Lofton, Kathryn. 2017. *Consuming Religion.* Chicago: University of Chicago Press.

Lolë. 2018. https://www.lolelife.com/pages/about. Accessed March 8, 2018.

Lopez, Donald S. 2012. *The Scientific Buddha: His Short and Happy Life.* New Haven: Yale University Press.

Lorde, Audre. 2017. *A Burst of Light and Other Essays.* Mineola, NY: Ixia Press.

Lorr, Benjamin. 2012. *Hell-Bent: Obsession, Pain, and the Search for Something Like Transcendence in Bikram Yoga.* London: Bloomsbury, 2012.

Lucia, Amanda. 2014. *Reflections of Amma: Devotees in a Global Embrace.* Berkeley: University of California Press.

Lucia, Amanda. 2018. "Guru Sex: Charisma, Proxemic Desire, and the Haptic Logics of the Guru-Disciple Relationship." *Journal of the American Academy of Religion* 86 (4): 953–988.

Lukes, Stephen. 1975. "Political Ritual and Social Integration." *Sociology: Journal of the British Sociological Association* 9 (2): 289–308.

Lululemon. n.d. "Yoga Clothes Running Gear | Lululemon Athletica." Accessed October 7, 2018. https://shop.lululemon.com/.

Magdoff, Fred and John Bellamy Foster. 2011. *What Every Environmentalist Needs to Know About Capitalism*. New York: Monthly Review Press.

MacGregor, Hilary E. 2002. "Had Your McYoga Today? A Stretch of Success." *Los Angeles Times*, July 7, 2002. http://articles.latimes.com/2002/jul/07/news/lv-bikram7.

MacGregor, Kino. 2015. "Kino MacGregor: India Is a Yoga Teacher." *Yoga Journal*, March 26, 2015. https://www.yogajournal.com/lifestyle/kino-macgregor-surrendering-india-teacher.

Macherey, Pierre, and Terry Eagleton. 2006. *Theory of Literary Production*. 2nd ed. New York: Routledge.

Mackey, John, and Rajendra Sisodia. 2014. *Conscious Capitalism, with a New Preface by the Authors: Liberating the Heroic Spirit of Business*. Boston: Harvard Business Review Press.

MacKinnon, Catherine A. 1987. "Women, Self-Possession, and Sport (1982)." In *Feminism Unmodified: Discourses on Life and Law*, 117–124. Cambridge, MA: Harvard University Press.

Mallinson, James, and Mark Singleton. 2017. *Roots of Yoga*. New York: Penguin Classics.

Mann, Michael. 1970. "The Social Cohesion of Liberal Democracy." *American Sociological Review* 35 (3): 423–439.

Marcuse, Herbert. 1955. *Eros and Civilization: A Philosophical Inquiry into Freud*. Boston: Beacon Press.

Marino, Andy. 2015. *Narendra Modi: A Political Biography*. Delhi: HarperCollins.

Martin, Clancy. 2011. "The Overheated, Oversexed Cult of Bikram Choudhury." *GQ*, February 1, 2011.

Marx, Karl, and Friedrich Engels. 1957. *On Religion*. Moscow: Foreign Languages Publishing House.

Matthes, Erich Hatala. 2016. "Cultural Appropriation without Cultural Essentialism?" *Social Theory and Practice* 42 (2): 343–366.

Maull, Fleet. 2015. "The Prison Meditation Movement & the Current State of Mindfulness-Based Programming for Prisoners." http://mindfuljustice.org/wpcontent/uploads/2015/11/PrisonMeditationMaull.pdf.

McClosky, Herbert. 1964. "Consensus and Ideology in American Politics." *American Political Science Review* 58 (2): 361–382.

McIntyre, R. 1992. "Consumption in Contemporary Capitalism: Beyond Marx and Veblen." *Review of Social Economy* 50 (Spring): 50–57.

McKean, Lisa. 1996. *Divine Enterprise: Gurus and the Hindu Nationalist Movement*. Chicago: University of Chicago Press.

McMahan, D. 2008. *The Making of Buddhist Modernism*. New York: Oxford University Press.

McMahan, David L. 2012. "Buddhist Modernism." In *Buddhism in the Modern World*, edited by David L. McMahan, 159–176. New York: Routledge.

McNay, L. 2009. "Self as Enterprise: Dilemmas of Control and Resistance in Foucault's *The Birth of Biopolitics*." *Theory, Culture & Society* 26 (6): 55–77.

McNeill, J.R. 2016. *The Great Acceleration: An Environmental History of the Anthropocene since 1945*. Cambridge, MA: Harvard University Press.

Mercadante, Linda. 2014. *Belief beyond Borders*. New York: Oxford University Press.

Miller, Christopher Patrick. Forthcoming. "Modi-fying Patañjali: Biopolitics and the 'Hostile Takeover of Bodies' in an Aspiring Neoliberal Nation State." *Contemporary Yoga and Sacred Texts*, edited by Susanne Scholz and Caroline Vander Stichele. New York: Routledge.

Miller, Donald. 2007. *Global Pentecostalism: The New Face of Christian Social Engagement.* Berkeley: University of California Press.

Miller, Donald, Kimon H. Sargeant, and Richard Flory, eds. 2004. *Spirit and Power: The Growth and Global Impact of Pentecostalism.* New York: Oxford University Press.

Ministry of AYUSH. 2017a. 21st of June International Day of Yoga: Common Yoga Protocol. 3rd ed. May 2017. New Delhi: Morarji Desai National Institute of Yoga. http://www.ayush.gov.in/sites/default/files/Common%20Yoga%20Protocol%20English_0.pdf.

Ministry of AYUSH. 2017b. "Yoga." May 23, 2017. http://ayush.gov.in/about-the-systems/yoga.

Ministry of Tourism, Government of India. 2018. "Swadesh Darshan." Ministry of Tourism Government of India. http://swadeshdarshan.gov.in/.

Moi, Toril. 1995. *Sexual/Textual Politics: Feminist Literary Theory.* 2nd ed. New York: Routledge.

Møllgaard, Eske. 2008. "Slavoj Žižek's Critique of Western Buddhism." *Contemporary Buddhism* 9 (2): 167–180.

Moreton, Bethany. 2010. *To Serve God and Wal-Mart: The Making of Christian Free Enterprise.* Cambridge, MA: Harvard University Press.

Mudimbe, V. Y. 1988. *The Invention of Africa: Gnosis, Philosophy, and the Order of Knowledge.* Bloomington: Indiana University Press.

Najar, Suhasini Raj, and Nida. 2018. "State in India Plans to Help Gay Youth 'Get over Same-Sex Feelings.'" *New York Times*, January 10, 2018. https://nyti.ms/1xXAH3q.

Nanda, Meera. 2011. *The God Market: How Globalization Is Making India More Hindu.* New York: Monthly Review Press.

NDTV. 2013. "Is Homosexuality Conflicting with Cultural Values of India?" YouTube video, 17:37. Posted December 12, 2013. https://youtu.be/9ppftcSAHA4.

Nelson, Dean. 2009. "Hindu Guru Claims Homosexuality Can Be 'Cured' by Yoga." *The Telegraph*, July 8, 2009. http://www.telegraph.co.uk/news/worldnews/asia/india/5780028/Hindu-guru-claims-homosexuality-can-be-cured-by-yoga.html.

Nhat Hanh, Thich. [1975] 1987a. *The Miracle of Mindfulness: An Introduction to the Practice of Mindfulness.* Boston: Beacon Press.

Nhat Hanh, Thich. 1987b. *Interbeing: Commentaries on the Tiep Hien Precepts.* Berkeley, CA: Parallax Press.

Nhat Hanh, Thich. 2003. *Buddha Mind, Buddha Body: Walking toward Enlightenment.* Berkeley, CA: Parallax Press.

Nhat Hanh, Thich. 2009a. *The Heart of Understanding: Commentaries on the Prajnaparamita Heart Sutra.* Rev. ed. Edited by Peter Levitt. Berkeley, CA: Parallax Press.

Nhat Hanh, Thich. 2009b. *Peaceful Action, Open Heart: Lessons from the Lotus Sutra.* Berkeley, CA: Parallax Press.

Nhat Hanh, Thich. [1975] 2016. *The Miracle of Mindfulness: A Manual on Meditation.* Boston: Beacon Press.

Nhat Hanh, Thich, and Lilian Cheung. 2010. *Savor: Mindful Eating, Mindful Life.* New York: HarperCollins.

Nicholson, Andrew. 2010. *Unifying Hinduism: Philosophy and Identity in Indian Intellectual History*. New York: Columbia University Press.

Kale, Sunila S. and Christian Lee Novetzke. 2016. "Some Reflections on Yoga as Political Theology." *The Wire*. January 28, 2016. https://thewire.in/culture/some-reflections-on-yoga-as-political-theology.

NTV Teluga. 2015. "PM Narendra Modi Speech on International Yoga Day at Rajpath | NTV." YouTube video. 9:41. Posted on June 20, 2015. https://youtu.be/XYUjncdxiT4.

Nussbaum, Martha C. 2007. *The Clash Within: Democracy, Religious Violence, and India's Future*. Boston: Harvard University Press.

Nye, Malory. 2000. "Religion, Post-religionism, and Religioning: Religious Studies and Contemporary Cultural Debates." *Method & Theory in the Study of Religion* 12 (1): 447–476.

Office of the Federal Register. 2012. "Registration of Claims to Copyright." *Federal Register: The Daily Journal of the United States Government*, June 22, 2012. www.federalregister.gov/articles/2012/06/22/2012-15235/registration-of-claims-to-copyright.

Ojakangas, M. 2005. "Impossible Dialogue on Bio-Power: Agamben and Foucault." *Foucault Studies* 2:5–28.

Olssen, Mark and Michael A. Peters. "Neoliberalism, Higher Education and the Knowledge Economy: From the Free Market to Knowledge Capitalism." *Journal of Education Policy* 20 (30): 313–345.

O'Malley, Pat. 1992, "Risk, Power, and Crime Prevention." *Economy and Society* 21 (3): 252–275.

O'Reilly, Camille Caprioglio. 2006. "From Drifter to Gap Year Tourist: Mainstreaming Backpacker Travel." *Annals of tourism Research* 33 (4): 998–1017.

, 2002()():

Palmié, Stephan. 2013. *The Cooking of History: How Not to Study Afro-Cuban Religion*. Chicago: University of Chicago Press.

Payne, Richard K. 2014. "Mindfulness 1.0." *Critical Reflections on Buddhist Thought: Contemporary and Classical*, August 26, 2014. https://rkpayne.wordpress.com/2014/08/26/mindfulness-1-0/.

Pew Research Center. 2012. "Nones on the Rise." www.pewforum.org/2012/10/09/nones-on-the-rise/.

"Platform." n.d. *The Movement for Black Lives*. Accessed July 15, 2019. https://policy.m4bl.org/platform/.

Pocock, John G. A. 1962. "The Origins of Study of the Past: A Comparative Approach." *Comparative Studies in Society and History* 4 (2): 209–246.

Porterfield, Amanda. 2018. *Corporate Spirit: Religion and the Rise of the Modern Corporation*. New York: Oxford University Press.

Price, L. 2012. *How to Do Things with Books in Victorian Britain*. Princeton, NJ: Princeton University Press.

Prison Yoga Project. 2019a. https://prisonyoga.org.

Prison Yoga Project. 2019b. Shop. https://shop.prisonyoga.org.

Purser, Ronald E. 2017. "The Branding of Mindfulness." *Huffington Post*, December 18, 2017. https://www.huffingtonpost.com/entry/the-branding-of-mindfulness_us_5a35a283e4b02bd1c8c60750.

Purser, Ronald E. 2019. *McMindfulness: How Mindfulness Became the New Capitalist Spirituality*. London: Repeater Books.

Purser, Ronald E., and David Forbes. 2017. "How to Be Mindful of McMindfulness." *Alternet*, May 30, 2017. https://www.alternet.org/culture/hollow-mindful-overkill-david-gelles#.WS3dfuDzBnk.facebook.

Purser, Ronald E., David Forbes, and Adam Burke, eds. 2016. *Handbook of Mindfulness: Culture, Context, and Social Engagement*. Cham, Switzerland: Springer International Publishing.

Purser, Ronald E., and David Loy. 2013. "Beyond McMindfulness." *Huffington Post*, July 31, 2013. https://www.huffingtonpost.com/ron-purser/beyond-mcmindfulness_b_3519289.html.

Pyysiäinen, Jarkko, Darren Halpin, and Andrew Guilfoyle. 2017. "Neoliberal Governance and 'Responsibilization' of Agents: Reassessing the Mechanisms of Responsibility-Shift in Neoliberal Discursive Environments." *Distinktion: Journal of Social Theory* 18 (2): 215–235.

Rabbitt, Meghan. 2018. "The Mindful Diet." *Yoga Journal: The Power of Mindfulness* (Special Edition): 42–51.

Rabinow, Paul, and Nikolas Rose. 2006. "Biopower Today." *BioSocieties* 1: 195–217.

Rahula, Walpola. 1959. *What the Buddha Taught*. New York: Grove Press.

Ramachandran, Tanisha. 2015. "A Call to Multiple Arms! Protesting the Commoditization of Hindu Imagery in Western Society." Material Religion 10 (1): 54–75.

Ramdev, Baba. 2008. *Jeevan Darshan (Complete Guidance to Yog-Discipline, Self-Righteousness & Nationalism)*. Haridwar, India: Divya Prakashan.

Ramdev, Baba. 2014. "Brand Patanjali New AD." YouTube video, 0:30. Posted February 21, 2014. https://youtu.be/EdbgxXzPml8.

Rankine, Claudia. 2014. *Citizen: An American Lyric*. Minneapolis: Graywolf Press.

Remski, Matthew. 2018. "Yoga's Culture of Sexual Abuse: Nine Women Tell Their Stories." *The Walrus*, July–August 2018. https://thewalrus.ca/yogas-culture-of-sexual-abuse-nine-women-tell-their-stories/.

Remski, Matthew. 2019. *Practice and All Is Coming: Abuse, Cult Dynamics, and Healing in Yoga and Beyond*. Embodied Wisdom Publishing.

Repetti, Rick. 2016. "Meditation Matters: Replies to the Anti-McMindfulness Bandwagon!" In *Handbook of Mindfulness: Culture, Context, and Social Engagement*, edited by Ronald E. Purser, David Forbes, and Adam Burke. Cham, Switzerland: Springer International Publishing.

Reuters. 2017. "Economic Survey Highlights: India's Economy Forecast to Grow 6.75 to 7.5 percent in 2017/18." *Reuters*, January 31, 2017. https://in.reuters.com/article/india-budget-survey/economic-survey-highlights-indias-economy-forecast-to-grow-6-75-to-7-5-percent-in-2017-18-idINKBN15F0OV.

Rogers, Richard A. 2006. "From Cultural Exchange to Transculturation: A Review and Reconceptualization of Cultural Appropriation." *Communication Theory* 16 (4): 474–503.

Roof, Wade Clark. 1999. *Spiritual Marketplace: Baby Boomers and the Remaking of American Religion*. Princeton, NJ: Princeton University Press.

Rosaldo, Renato. 1993. *Culture & Truth: The Remaking of Social Analysis. With a New Introduction*. Boston: Beacon Press.

Rose, Nikolas. 1996. "Governing 'Advanced' Liberal Democracies." *Foucault and Political Reason: Liberalism, Neo-liberalism, and Rationalities of Government*, edited by Andrew Barry, Thomas Osborne, and Nikolas Rose, 37–64. Chicago: The University of Chicago Press.

Rose, Nikolas, Pat O'Malley and Mariana Valverde. 2006. "Governmentality." *Annual Review of Law and Social Science* 2:83–104.

Rottenberg, Catherine. 2013. "The Rise of Neoliberal Feminism." *Cultural Studies* 28 (3): 418–437.

Rottenberg, Catherine. 2018. *The Rise of Neoliberal Feminism*. New York: Oxford University Press.

Rottenberg, Catherine. Forthcoming. "Containing the Liberal Imagination: How Superwoman Became Balanced." *Feminist Studies*.

Rowell, John. 1995. "The Politics of Cultural Appropriation." *Journal of Value Inquiry* 29 (1995): 137–142.

Rudnyckyj, Daromir. 2018. "Exorcising Leverage: Sleight of Hand and the Invisible Hand in Islamic Finance." *Magical Capitalism: Enchantment, Spells, and Occult Practices in Contemporary Economies*, edited by Brian Moeran and Timothy de Waal Malefyt, 65–78. London: Palgrave Macmillan.

Said, Edward W. 1978. *Orientalism*. New York: Pantheon.

Samuel, Geoffrey. 2008. *The Origins of Yoga and Tantra: Indic Religions to the Thirteenth Century*. Cambridge: Cambridge University Press.

Sanghvi, Vir. 2017. "Ramdev Is a Symbol or Symptom of Today's India." Vir Sanghvi. August 29, 2017. http://www.virsanghvi.com/Article-Details.aspx?key=1357.

Satva. 2018a. "Our Story." https://satvaliving.com/pages/about-us.

Satva. 2018b. "Sports Clothing & Organic Clothing, Yoga Wear, Sports Wear." https://satvaliving.com/.

Schaeffer, K. 2015. "Introduction: The Story of the Buddha. A Narrative for Human Development." In *The Life of the Buddha*, by Tenzin Chogyel, translated by Kurtis R. Schaeffer. New York: Penguin.

Schlanger, Z. 2017. "Rogue Scientists Race to Save Climate Data from Trump." *Wired*, January 19, 2017. https://www.wired.com/2017/01/rogue-scientists-race-save-climate-data-trump/.

Schopen, Gregory. 1997. "Filial Piety and the Monk in the Practice of Indian Buddhism." In *Bones, Stones, and Buddhist Monks: Collected Papers on Archaeology, Epigraphy, and Texts of Monastic Buddhism in India*, 56–71. Honolulu: University of Hawaii Press.

Schulson, Michael. 2017. "Trickle-Down Metaphysics and the Dawn of a Trumpian New Age." *Religion Dispatches*, January 9, 2017. http://religiondispatches.org/trickle-down-metaphysics-and-the-dawn-of-a-trumpian-new-age/.

Scott, David. 1991. "That Event, This Memory: Notes on the Anthropology of African Diasporas in the New World." *Diasporas* 1 (3): 261–284.

Scott, David. 1999. *Refashioning Futures: Criticism after Postcoloniality*. Princeton, NJ: Princeton University Press.

Scott, Melissa. 2017. *White Girl in Yoga Pants: Stories of Yoga, Feminism, Inner Strength*. CreateSpace Independent Publishing Platform.

Scott, S. J., and Barrie Davenport. 2017. *10-Minute Mindfulness: 71 Simple Habits for Living in the Present Moment*. Cranbury, NJ: Oldtown Publishing.

Scroll Staff. 2017. "Patanjali's Turnover for Financial Year 2016–2017 Is Rs 10,561 Crore, Says Ramdev." *Scroll.in*, May 4, 2017. https://scroll.in/latest/836561/patanjalis-turnover-for-financial-year-2016-2017-is-rs-10561-crore-says-ramdev.

Sen, Amartya. 2013. "As an Indian Citizen, I Don't Want Modi as My PM." *Times of India*, July 22, 2013. http://timesofindia.indiatimes.com/india/Amartya-Sen-As-an-Indian-citizen-I-dont-want-Modi-as-my-PM/articleshow/21241669.cms.

Shamir, R. 2008. "The Age of Responsibilization: On Market-Embedded Morality." *Economy and Society* 37 (1): 1–19.

Sharf, Robert. 1995. "Buddhist Modernism and the Rhetoric of Meditative Experience." *Numen* 42 (3): 228–283.

Sharf, Robert. 2016. "Epilogue: Is Mindfulness Buddhist? (and Why It Matters)." *Transcultural Psychology* 52 (4): 470–484.

Sharma, Kapil. 2017. "Destabilizing Section 377: An Indological Approach to Gender and Sexuality. *Postcolonial Interventions* 2 (1). postcolonialinterventions.files.wordpress.com.

Shils, Edward, and Michael Young. 1953. "The Meaning of the Coronation." *Sociological Review* 1 (2): 63–81.

Shores, Monica. 2010. "Yoga's Feminist Awakening." *Ms. Magazine Blog*, September 8, 2010. http://msmagazine.com/blog/2010/09/08/yogas-feminist-awakening/.

Sian, S. 2011. "Operationalising Closure in a Colonial Context: The Association of Accountants in East Africa, 1949–1963." *Accounting, Organizations and Society* 26:363–381.

Siddiquee, Imran. 2017. "We've Been Killing South Asians for as Long as They've Been Arriving to the U.S." *The Establishment*, April 12, 2017. https://theestablishment.co/weve-been-killing-south-asians-for-as-long-as-they-ve-been-arriving-to-the-u-s-3160fc80d25.

Simeon, Dilip. 2015. "Yoga, by RSS: It Would Have Been Upset Had Muslims Not Objected to Compulsory Yoga." *Indian Express*, June 16, 2015. https://indianexpress.com/article/opinion/columns/yoga-by-rssit-would-have-been-upset-had-muslims-not-objected-to-compulsory-yoga/.

Singleton, Mark. 2007. "Yoga, Eugenics, and Spiritual Darwinism in the Early Twentieth Century." *International Journal of Hindu Studies* 11 (2): 125–246.

Singleton, Mark. 2010. *Yoga Body: The Origins of Modern Posture Practice.* New York: Oxford University Press.

Singleton, Mark, and Jean Byrne, eds. 2008. *Yoga in the Modern World: Contemporary Perspectives.* New York: Routledge.

Sinha, Kounteya. 2011. "India Pulls the Plug on Yoga as Business." *Times of India*, February 6, 2011. http://articles.timesofindia.indiatimes.com/2011-02-06/india/2835560 2_1_hot-yoga-patanjali-tkdl.

Sinha, Mrinalini. 1999. "Giving Masculinity a History: Some Contributions from the Historiography of Colonial India." *Gender & History* 11 (3): 445–460.

Sium, Aman, Chandi Desai, and Eric Ritskes. 2012. "Towards the 'Tangible Unknown': Decolonization and the Indigenous Future." *Decolonization: Indigeneity, Education & Society* 1 (1): i–xiii.

Sjoman, N. E. 1996. *The Yoga Tradition of the Mysore Palace.* New Delhi: Abhinav Publications.

Smith, Andrea. 2012. "Indigeneity, Settler Colonialism, White Supremacy." In *Racial Formation in the Twenty-First Century*, edited by Daniel Martinez HoSang, Oneka LaBennett, and Laura Pulido, 66–90. Berkeley: University of California Press.

Smith, Tom W. 2007. "Counting Religious Nones and Other Religious Measurement Issues: A Comparison of the Baylor Religion Survey and General Social Survey." GSS Methodological Report No. 110.

Smookler, Elaine. 2018. "Look on the Bright Side . . . ?" *Mindful* [Foundation for a Mindful Society] 6 (2): 63–73.

Spiritual Gangster. 2018a. "DIY Sage Smudge Sticks with @CatherineRising."

Spiritual Gangster. 2018b. "Giving Back." https://spiritualgangster.com/pages/giving.

Spiritual Gangster. 2019. "Yoga Inspired Clothing, Swimwear & Activewear." https://spiritualgangster.com/.

Sri Swami Satchidananda. 1967. *Integral Yoga Hatha.* Satchidananda Ashram—Yogaville.

Srinivas, Smriti. 2008. *In the Presence of Sai Baba: Body, City, and Memory in a Global Religious Movement.* Leiden: Brill.

Srinivas, Tulasi. 2010. *Winged Faith: Rethinking Globalization and Religious Pluralism through the Sathya Sai Movement.* New York: Columbia University Press.

Staggenborg, Suzanne, and Verta Taylor. 2005. "Whatever Happened to the Women's Movement?" *Mobilization* 10 (1): 37–52.

Staskus, Ed. 2012. "The Torture Chamber." *Elephant Journal,* May 4, 2012. https://www.elephantjournal.com/2012/05/the-torture-chamber-ed-staskus/.

Steingass, Matthias. 2014. "The Zombification of Speculative Non-Buddhism." *Speculative Non-Buddhism: Ruins of the Buddhist Real,* November 25, 2014. https://thenonbuddhist.com/2014/11/25/the-zombification-of-speculative-non-buddhism/.

Sue, Derald Wing. 2010. *Microaggressions in Everyday Life: Race, Gender, and Sexual Orientation.* Hoboken, NJ: John Wiley & Sons.

Swartz, Mimi. 2010. "The Yoga Mogul." *New York Times Magazine,* July 21, 2010. http://www.nytimes.com/2010/07/25/magazine/25Yoga-t.html.

Syman, Stefanie. 2010. *The Subtle Body: The Story of Yoga in America.* New York: Farrar, Straus, and Giroux.

Theocharis, Yannis, Will Lowe, Jan W. van Deth, and Gema Garcia-Albacete. 2015. "Using Twitter to Mobilize Protest Action: Online Mobilization Patterns and Action Repertoires in the Occupy Wall Street, Indignados, and Aganaktismenoi Movements." *Information, Communication & Society* 18 (2): 202–220.

Thera, Nyanasatta, trans. 2013. "Satipatthana Sutta: The Foundations of Mindfulness." (MN 10) *Access to Insight (BCBS Edition),* December 1. Barre Center for Buddhist Studies. http://www.accesstoinsight.org/tipitaka/mn/mn.010.nysa.html.

Therberge, Nancy. 1981. "A Critique of Critiques: Radical and Feminist Writings on Sport." *Social Forces* 60 (2): 341–353.

Thomas, P. N. 2012. "Whither Televangelism: Opportunities, Trends, Challenges." In *Global and Local Televangelism,* edited by Pradip Ninan Thomas and Philip Lee, 234–246. London: Palgrave Macmillan.

Thomas, Scott M. 2005. *The Global Resurgence of Religion and the Transformation of International Relations: The Struggle for the Soul of the Twenty-First Century.* New York: Palgrave Macmillan.

Thorpe, Rebecca. 2015. "Perverse Politics: The Persistence of Mass Imprisonment in the Twenty First Century." *Perspectives on Politics* 13 (3): 618–637.

Thursby, Gene. 1995. *Hindu Movements since Mid-Century: America's Alternative Religions.* Albany: State University of New York.

Timmons, Heather, and Hari Kumar. 2009. "Indian Court Overturns Gay Sex Ban." *New York Times,* July 3, 2009. http://www.nytimes.com.2009/07/03/world/asia/03india.html.

Tinker, George E. 1993. *Missionary Conquest: The Gospel and Native American Cultural Genocide.* Minneapolis: Fortress Press.

Trigg, Andrew B. 2001. "Veblen, Bourdieu, and Conspicuous Consumption." *Journal of Economic Issues* 35 (1): 99–115.

Trump, Donald J. (@realdonaldtrump). 2014. Twitter post. August 1, 2014, 9:22pm EST. https://twitter.com/realdonaldtrump/status/495379061972410369.

Turner, Bryan S. 1997. "The Body in Western Society: Social Theory and Its Perspectives." In *Religion and the Body*, edited by Sarah Coakley, 15–41. New York: Cambridge University Press.

Turner, Victor. 1961. "Ritual Symbolism, Morality and Social Structure among the Ndembu." *Rhodes-Livingstone Journal* 30:1–10.

Turner, Victor. 1974. *Dramas, Fields, and Metaphors: Symbolic Action in Human Society.* Ithaca, NY: Cornell University Press.

Ulmer, Alexandra. "Indian Guru's Tips to Ward Off Coronavirus Anger Health Professionals." *Reuters.* Accessed March 18, 2020. https://www.reuters.com/article/us-health-coronavirus-india-ayurveda/indian-gurus-tips-to-ward-off-coronavirus-anger-health-professionals-idUSKBN21515M.

Upadhya, Carol. 2008. "Rewriting the Code: Software Professionals and the Reconstitution of Indian Middle Class Identity." In *Patterns of Middle Class Consumption in India and China*, edited by Christophe Jaffrelot and Pter Van der Veer, 55–87. New Delhi: Sage.

Urban, Hugh. 2000. "The Cult of Ecstasy: Tantrism, the New Age, and the Spiritual Logic of Late Capitalism." *History of Religions* 39 (3): 268–304.

Urban, Hugh. 2003. *Tantra: Sex, Secrecy, Politics, and Power in the Study of Religion.* Berkeley: University of California Press.

Urban, Hugh. 2015. *Zorba the Buddha: Sex, Spirituality, and Capitalism in the Global Osho Movement.* Berkeley: University of California Press.

Vaca, Daniel. 2019. *Evangelicals Incorporated: Books and the Business of Religion in America.* Cambridge, MA: Harvard University Press.

Vajpeyi, Ananya. 2014. "The Triumph of the Hindu Right." *Foreign Affairs* 93 (5): 150–156.

Vajpeyi, Ananya. 2016. "Of Statesmen and Strongmen." *The Hindu*, November 29, 2016. https://www.thehindu.com/todays-paper/tp-opinion/Of-statesmen-and-strongmen/article16718256.ece.

Van der Veer, Peter. 2001. *Imperial Encounters: Religion and Modernity in India and Britain.* Princeton, NJ: Princeton University Press.

Veblen, Thorstein. [1899] 1994. *The Theory of the Leisure Class.* In *The Collected Works of Thorstein Veblen*, vol. 1. London: Routledge.

Verba, Sidney. 1965. "The Kennedy Assassination and the Nature of Political Commitment." In *The Kennedy Assassination and the American Public: Social Communication in Crisis*, edited by Bradley Greenberg and Edwin Parker, 348–360. Stanford, CA: Stanford University Press.

Viswanathan, Gauri. 2000. "The Ordinary Business of Occultism." *Critical Inquiry* 27 (1): 1–20.

Vivekananda, Swami. 1894. "Letters Written Between January and July 1894." Accessed July 1, 2019. https://www.vivekananda.net/KnownLetters/1894Jan_July.html.

Wallace, Vesna. 2011. "Mahayana Insights into the Origins of Yoga and Tantra." In "Contextualizing the History of Yoga in Geoffrey Samuel's The Origins of Yoga and Tantra: A Review Symposium." *International Journal of Hindu Studies* 15 (3): 333–337.

Wallis, Christopher. 2016. "Remake/Remodel: Four Points on the Reinvention of the Guru-Disciple Relationship in the West." *Christopher Wallis Blog*, August 16, 2016. https://tantrikstudies.squarespace.com/blog/2016/8/16/remakeremodel-four-points-on-the-reinvention-of-the-guru-disciple-relationship-in-the-west.

Wallis, Glenn, Tom Pepper, and Matthias Steingass. 2013. *Cruel Theory–Sublime Practice: Toward a Reevaluation of Buddhism*. Roskilde, Denmark: Eyecorner Press.

Warner, W. Lloyd. 1959. *The Living and the Dead: A Study of the Symbolic Life of Americans*. New Haven: Yale University Press.

Weber, Max. 1992. *The Protestant Ethic and the Spirit of Capitalism*. Translated by Talcott Parsons. New York: Routledge.

Wehr, Kevin, and Elyshia Aseltine. 2013. *Beyond the Prison Industrial Complex: Crime and Incarceration in the 21st Century*. New York: Routledge.

Wessinger, Catherine. 1995. "Hinduism Arrives in America: The Vedanta Movement and the Self-Realization Fellowship." In *America's Alternative Religions*, edited by Timothy Miller. Albany: State University of New York Press.

"What Is Mindful." 2015. *Mindful*, July 7, 2015. Foundation for a Mindful Society. https://www.mindful.org/about-mindful/.

White, David Gordon. 1996. *The Alchemical Body: Siddha Traditions in Medieval India*. Chicago: University of Chicago Press.

White, David Gordon. 2009. *Sinister Yogis*. Chicago: University of Chicago Press.

White, David Gordon. 2012a. "Introduction." In *Yoga in Practice*, edited by David Gordon White, 1–23. Princeton, NJ: Princeton University Press.

White, David Gordon. 2012b. *Yoga in Practice*. Princeton, NJ: Princeton University Press.

Whitson, David. 2002. "The Embodiment of Gender: Discipline, Domination, and Empowerment." In *Gender and Sport: A Reader*, edited by Sheila Scraton and Anne Flintoff. New York: Routledge.

Williams, Raymond. 1981. *The Sociology of Culture*. Chicago: University of Chicago Press.

Williams, Timothy. 2016. "Marijuana Arrests Outnumber Those for Violent Crimes, Study Finds." *New York Times*, October 12, 2016. www.nytimes.com/2016/10/13/us/marijuana-arrests.html.

Williamson, Oliver E. 1975. *Markets and Hierarchies, Analysis and Antitrust Implications: A Study of the Economics of Internal Organization*. New York: Free Press.

Wilson, Jeff. 2014. *Mindful America: The Mutual Transformation of Buddhist Meditation and American Culture*. New York: Oxford University Press.

Wilson, Jeff. 2015. "Mindfulness Studies." *Professor Jeff Wilson*, January 13, 2015. https://professorjeffwilson.wordpress.com/mindfulness-research/.

Wilson, Jeff. 2016. "Selling Mindfulness: Commodity Lineages and the Marketing of Mindful Products." In *Handbook of Mindfulness: Culture, Context, and Social Engagement*, edited by Ronald E. Purser, David Forbes, and Adam Burke, 109–119. Cham, Switzerland: Springer International Publishing.

Wilson, Yolanda. 2018. "Why Black Women's Experiences of #MeToo Are Different." *The Conversation*, June 14, 2018. https://theconversation.com/why-black-womens-experiences-of-metoo-are-different-96091.

Wingert, Pat. 2010. "Priests Commit No More Abuse Than Other Males." *Newsweek*, April 7, 2010. https://www.newsweek.com/priests-commit-no-more-abuse-other-males-70625.

Wise, Tim. 2010. *Colorblind: The Rise of Post-racial Politics and the Retreat from Racial Equity*. San Francisco: City Lights Books Open Media Series.

Wittier, Nancy. 1995. *Feminist Generations: The Persistence of the Radical Women's Movement*. Philadelphia: Temple University Press.

Witz, Anne. 1992. *Professions and Patriarchy*. New York: Routledge.

Wolf, Naomi. 1990. *The Beauty Myth: How Images of Beauty Are Used against Women*. London: Chatto & Windus.

Wright, Robert. 2017. *Why Buddhism Is True: The Science and Philosophy of Meditation and Enlightenment*. New York: Simon & Schuster.

Wright, Stephen C. 2001. "Restricted Intergroup Boundaries: Tokenism, Ambiguity, and the Tolerance of Injustice." In *The Psychology of Legitimacy: Emerging Perspectives on Ideology, Justice, and Intergroup Relations*, edited by J. T. Jost and B. Major, 223–254. New York: Cambridge University Press.

Wright, Stephen C., and Donald M. Taylor. 1999. "Success under Tokenism: Co-optation of the Newcomer and the Prevention of Collective Protest." *British Journal of Social Psychology* 38: 369–396.

Yakketyyak, Yolanda. 2017. "Alo Yoga CEO Danny Harris Stretches Out $30 Million in Holmby Hills." *Yolanda's Little Black Book Blog*, February 20, 2017. http://www. yolandaslittleblackbook.com/blog-1/2017/02/20/alo-yoga-danny-harris-house-holmby-hills/.

Yinger, J. Milton. 1977. "Presidential Address: Countercultures and Social Change." *American Sociological Review* 42 (6): 833–853.

Yinger, J. Milton. 1982. *Countercultures: The Promise and Peril of a World Turned Upside Down*. New York: Free Press.

Yoder, Janice D. 1991. "Rethinking Tokenism: Looking beyond Numbers." *Gender & Society* 5 (2): 178–192.

YogaGirl. 2019. https://www.yogagirl.com.

Yoga in America Study. 2016. "Yoga in America Study Executive Summary: Conducted by Yoga Journal and Yoga Alliance." https://www.yogaalliance.org/2016yogainamericastudy.

Yoga Journal. 2019. Media Kit. https://s3.amazonaws.com/static-yogajournal/pdfs/YJ-MK2019.pdf?utm_campaign=YOG%20-%20IP%20-%20Media%20Kit&utm_source=hs_automation&utm_medium=email&utm_content=72764344&_hsenc=p2ANqtz--WTJaIBAiW4RcUp_pjVKWc4CDbARMXxb-QW9fu-2A8CI1-25Esrrnk0wqmSv3hHhAtQ_yVkdpxQMjSMaljgc3WpO8U3g&_hsmi=72764344.

Yoga Journal and Yoga Alliance. 2016. "Yoga in America Study." http://www.yogajournal.com/page/yogainamericastudy.

Yoga Journal Editors. 2015. "By the Numbers: Yoga Stats That May Surprise You." *Yoga Journal*, July 22, 2015. https://www.yogajournal.com/yoga-101/yoga-numbers-yoga-statistics.

Yoga Journal Staff. 2018. "#TimesUp: Ending Sexual Abuse in the Yoga Community." *Yoga Journal*, February 12, 2018. https://www.yogajournal.com/lifestyle/timesup-metoo-ending-sexual-abuse-in-the-yoga-community.

Young, Kevin, Philip White, and William McTeer. 1994. "Body Talk: Male Athletes Reflect on Sport, Injury, and Pain." *Kinesiology and Physical Education Faculty Publications* 11: 175–194.

Young, James O., and Conrad G. Brunk, eds. 2012. *The Ethics of Cultural Appropriation*. Oxford: Blackwell.

Zauberman, Gal. 2003. "The Intertemporal Dynamics of Consumer Lock-In." *Journal of Consumer Research* 30 (3): 405–419.

Zeidan, Fadel. 2015. "The Neurobiology of Mindfulness Meditation." In *Handbook of Mindfulness: Theory, Research, and Practice*, edited by Kirk Warren Brown, J. David Creswell, and Richard M. Ryan, 171–189. New York: Guilford Press.

Zeilser, Andi. 2016. *We Were Feminists Once: From Riot Grrrl to Covergirl®, the Buying and Selling of a Social Movement*. New York: Public Affairs.

Zerubavel, Eviatar. 1996. "Lumping and Splitting: Notes on Social Classification." *Sociological Forum* 11 (30): 421–433.

Zhao, Xiaogian, and Edward Park. 2013. *Asian Americans: An Encyclopedia of Social, Cultural, Economic, and Political History*. Westport, CT: *Greenwood Press*.

Ziff, Bruce, and Pratima V. Rao. 1997. "Introduction to Cultural Appropriation: A Framework for Analysis." In *Borrowed Power: Essays on Cultural Appropriation*, edited by Bruce Ziff and Pratima V. Rao, 1–3. New Brunswick, NJ: Rutgers University Press.

Zinnbauer, B., and K. Pargament. 1997. "Religion and Spirituality: Unfuzzing the Fuzzy." *Journal for the Scientific Study of Religion* 36 (4): 549–564.

Žižek, Slavoj. 1989. *The Sublime Object of Ideology*. New York: Verso.

Žižek, Slavoj. 2001a. "From Western Marxism to Western Buddhism." Cabinet 2. http://www.cabinetmagazine.org/issues/2/western.php.

Žižek, Slavoj. 2001b. *On Belief*. New York: Routledge.

Žižek, Slavoj. 2005. "Revenge of Global Finance." *In These Times*, May 21, 2005. These Times and The Institute for Public Affairs. http://inthesetimes.com/article/2122/revenge_of_global_finance.

Žižek, Slavoj. 2013. *The Pervert's Guide to Ideology*. Directed by Sophie Fiennes. Zeitgeist Films.

Zucker, L. G. 1977. "The Role of Institutionalization in Cultural Persistence." *American Sociological Review* 42:726–743.

Zulberg, David. 2015. "How to Change Your Attitude When You Cannot Change Your Situation." https://www.mindbodygreen.com/0-17106/how-to-change-your-attitude-when-you-cant-change-your-situation.html.

Index

For the benefit of digital users, indexed terms that span two pages (e.g., 52–53) may, on occasion, appear on only one of those pages.